AF710290

SF-36® Physical & Mental Health Summary Scales:
A Manual for Users of Version 1, Second Edition

John E. Ware, Jr., Ph.D.
Mark Kosinski, M.A.

QualityMetric Incorporated
Lincoln, Rhode Island

Eighth Printing
December 2005

ISBN: 1-891810-09-X

Licensing & Registration

The Medical Outcomes Trust (MOT), Health Assessment Lab (HAL), and QualityMetric Incorporated – the holders of copyrights and trademarks of all versions and translations of the SF-36® Health Survey – have merged and simplified their licensing and user registration programs. Any organization or individual wishing to reproduce the survey and/or any associated intellectual property (e.g., trademarks, scoring algorithms, interpretation guidelines, and normative data as documented or referred to in this manual) for any purpose must register or obtain a license. This can be done online by accessing the website http://www.qualitymetric.com, selecting "Marketplace", then selecting "Licensing and User Registration", and completing a License Application Form.

Permission to reproduce the SF-36® surveys and/or use the associated trademark(s) documented in this manual is routinely granted royalty-free to individuals and organizations that collect their own data for purposes of scholarly research.

All other uses, including commercial use and funded data collection efforts may require payment of an annual license fee. Completion of the License Application Form on the Internet will result in the quotation of any user fees, and upon request, the issuance of a license.

Disclaimer of Warranty

We make no warranties, express or implied, that the algorithms contained in this volume are free of error, or are consistent with any particular standard of merchantability, or that they will meet your requirements for any particular application. They should not be relied on for solving a problem whose incorrect solution could result in injury to a person or loss of property. If you do use the algorithms in such a manner, it is at your own risk. The authors and publisher disclaim all liability for direct or consequential damages resulting from your use of the algorithms.

Suggested Citation

Ware, J.E., Jr. and Kosinski M. *SF-36® Physical & Mental Health Summary Scales: A Manual For Users of Version 1.* Second Edition, Lincoln, RI: QualityMetric Incorporated, 2001.

Table of Contents

Acknowledgements

Development and validation of the SF-36 Health Survey was supported by a grant (#89-6515) from the Henry J. Kaiser Family Foundation, Menlo Park, California, to The Health Institute at New England Medical Center Hospitals (J.E. Ware, Jr., Ph.D., Principal Investigator).

Development of the physical (PCS) and mental (MCS) component summary health measures for the SF-36 was supported by unrestricted research grants for the International Quality of Life Assessment (IQOLA) Project from Glaxo Research Institute, Research Triangle Park, North Carolina, and Schering-Plough Corporation, Kenilworth, New Jersey, and by The Health Institute at New England Medical Center Hospitals (NEMCH) from its own research funds.

The national norming of the SF-36 Health Survey in the US population in 1998 was supported, in part, by the Musculoskeletal Education and Research Institute of the American Academy of Orthopedic Surgeons and by QualityMetric Incorporated, Lincoln, RI, from its own research funds. The 1990 national norming of the SF-36 in the US population, also documented here, was sponsored by the Functional Outcomes Program of the Henry J. Kaiser Family Foundation, The Health Institute, NEMCH, Boston, MA.

Several publications documenting the SF-36 were very useful in preparing the second edition of this manual. Most useful was the first edition entitled, *SF-36® Physical and Mental Health Summary Scales: A User's Manual* (Ware, Kosinski and Keller, 1994). We gratefully acknowledge the contributions of Susan D. Keller, PhD, our co-author, for her many contributions to that manual. Other useful documents include: *How To Score the MOS 36-Item Short-Form Health Survey (SF-36)* (Ware, 1988; Medical Outcomes Trust, 1991); *Scoring Exercise for the SF-36® Health Survey* (Medical Outcomes Trust, 1994); and *SF-36® Health Survey Manual and Interpretation Guide* (Ware, Snow, Kosinski, et al., 1993).

We also gratefully acknowledge our IQOLA Project collaborators in 10 countries for the very informative studies of the PCS and MCS, as summarized here, including: the Director of the IQOLA Project (Barbara Gandek, MS), and other collaborators from Denmark (Jakob Bjorner, MD, PhD), France (Alan Leplege, MD, PhD), Germany (Monika Bullinger, PhD), Italy (Giovanni Apolone, MD), The Netherlands (Neil K Aaronson, PhD), Norway (Stein Kaasa, Md, PhD), Spain (Jordi Alonso, MD, PhD), Sweden (Marianne Sullivan, PhD), and the United Kingdom (John Brazier, PhD). In addition to sharing their results, which are also published elsewhere (Gandek and Ware, 1998), our IQOLA Project collaborators provided valuable comments regarding the scoring and interpretation of the PCS and MCS summary health measures from the SF-36.

We gratefully acknowledge: William H. Rogers, PhD for his invaluable assistance with our analyses of mortality data from the Medical Outcomes Study (MOS) and for providing statistical consultation throughout the development of the SF-36 and other tools in the "SF" family of measures; Colleen A. McHorney, PhD, for her contribution to initial studies of the factor structure of the SF-36 in the U.S.; Martha Bayliss, MSc for her efforts during the first analyses of the PCS and MCS in the MOS; and both Marie Perrone and Rosamaria Amoros-Cherry for their assistance in preparing the second edition of this manual.

Finally, we acknowledge and thank our many colleagues in the US and around the world who have applied and evaluated the SF-36 PCS and MCS summary measures in population studies, clinical trials, and in clinical practice and who have provided very constructive and useful feedback regarding the strengths and weaknesses of these summary measures. We also thank those among them who granted permission to reanalyze their data and present their results for purposes of the examples discussed here.

Preface

Second Edition

This manual was written as a companion to the *SF-36® Health Survey Manual and Interpretation Guide*, which documents the development, psychometric evaluation and norming of the eight scales in the SF-36 Health Survey, Version 1 (v1). This manual provides comparable information for the physical (PCS) and mental (MCS) component summary measures from the standard (4-week recall) and acute (1-week recall) forms of the SF-36 (v1).

This manual also documents more up-to-date norms for SF-36 scales and summary measures based on 1998 surveys of the general US population and introduces norm-based scoring (NBS) for the eight SF-36 scales and two summary measures scored from the SF-36 (v1). Results from the original psychometric evaluations of the PCS and MCS summary measures are reproduced here. Results from more recent psychometric evaluations (e.g., reliability estimates from 1998 studies) are also documented and those evaluations have been expanded (e.g., replications of studies of the factor structure of the SF-36 in 10 countries) in this manual. This manual also documents, for the first time, the scoring of PCS and MCS summary measures based on the acute (1-week recall) version of the SF-36 (v1). More than 40 studies about the PCS and MCS summary measures, published after the first edition of this manual have been added to the reference list.

Because health status and outcomes monitoring efforts underway are using means and variances from the original 1990 SF-36 norming study, we have reproduced here (from the first edition of this manual) the entire chapter documenting 1990 scoring algorithms (see Appendix C) and the entire chapter documenting 1990 norms (see Appendix D). These appendices also serve the purpose of documenting the methods and results cited in published studies based on the original 1990 scoring and norm-based interpretation guidelines for the SF-36 (v1) Health Survey.

Although this manual was written to "stand alone," it does not contain complete background information about the development of the SF-36 or explanations of the psychometric methods used in evaluating assumptions underlying the construction and scoring of the eight SF-36 scales that are used to estimate the PCS and MCS summary scores. Those topics are more completely covered in the original *SF-36® Health Survey Manual and Interpretation Guide* (Ware, Snow, Kosinski and Gandek, 1993). The most up-to-date summary of the history of the development and usage of the SF-36 is published in Ware JE "SF-36® Health Survey Update," *Spine,* 2000, 25 (4), 3130-3139.

Health status and outcomes scores based on the two SF-36 summary measures are compared with scores based on the eight-scale profile in "Comparison of Methods for the Scoring and Statistical Analysis of the SF-36® Health Profile and Summary Measures: Summary of Results from the Medical Outcomes Study," *Medical Care*, 1995, 33 (Suppl 4), AS264-A5279 by JE Ware, M Kosinski, M Bayliss et al.

Because of the complexity of the algorithms required to estimate the SF-36 PCS and MCS summary measures, which are linear composites of standardized scale scores weighted using factor score coefficients, this manual includes a test data set and documented results for use in checking the accuracy of computations. We strongly recommend the use of this test data (also available at sfinfo@qualitymetric.com) to verify the accuracy of scores before they are interpreted or compared with results published in this manual.

First Edition

This manual was written as a companion to the *SF-36® Health Survey Manual and Interpretation Guide*, which documents the development of the SF-36 Health Survey and summarizes information about the eight SF-36 scales, including assumptions underlying their construction and scoring; reliability, precision, and data quality; and validation and interpretation guidelines based on content-, criterion-, and norm-based strategies.

This second manual provides the same information for the SF-36 physical and mental health summary measures, which were developed subsequently, and extends the normative data and other interpretation guidelines substantially. Although this manual was written to "stand alone," it does not contain complete background information about the development of the SF-36 or explanations of psychometric methods used in evaluating scaling assumptions, reliability, or validity. Those topics are more completely explained in the original *SF-36® Health Survey Manual*.

Results for the two summary measures are compared with previous results for the eight-scale profile in "Comparison of Methods for the Scoring and Statistical Analysis of the SF-36® Health Profile and Summary Measures: Summary of Results from the Medical Outcomes Study" by Ware, Kosinski, Bayliss, and others, which was published in *Medical Care* in 1995.

Because of the complexity of the algorithms required to estimate the SF-36 Physical and Mental Component Summary measures, which are linear composites aggregated using norm-based scoring methods, this manual includes a computer diskette with the code for scoring algorithms and also a test data set for checking the accuracy of computations.

As with the original SF-36 manual, we invite suggestions for improvements in our documentation of the SF-36. Many were received in response to the first manual, resulting in numerous additions to the content of this manual, including norms for change scores in the MOS, and expanded empirical tests of validity and interpretation guidelines. The result is a lengthier manual than we had originally intended. We have tried to organize it in a way that makes desired information easy to find and use.

Chapter 1: How To Use This Manual

This chapter offers suggestions on how to use this manual and how to find information quickly.

Licensing and Permission to Use

Steps in getting royalty-free permission to reproduce the SF-36 for scholarly research and for commercial licensing are explained on the Copyright page and on the Internet at http://www.qualitymetric.com.

Introduction

Chapter 2 provides an introductory explanation of how the discovery of the two-dimensional factor structure underlying the eight SF-36 scales led to the construction of physical and mental health summary measures.

Construction Of Summary Measures

Chapter 3 presents the SF-36 measurement model and reviews the psychometric methods used in the development of the SF-36 Physical (PCS) and Mental (MCS) Component Summary scales. The generalizability of results across populations is demonstrated and important methodological issues are discussed, including how the PCS and MCS led to construction of a new 12-item survey (SF-12).

Norm-Based Scoring

Chapter 4 provides an explanation of norm-based scoring methods and illustrates their advantages in interpreting data.

Scoring of Scales

Chapter 5 explains how to score SF-36 scales using norm-based scoring for both standard and acute forms.

Scoring of Summaries

Chapter 6 explains how to score the physical and mental summary scales using norm-based scoring for both standard and acute forms.

Reliability And Statistical Power

Chapter 7 presents numerous reliability estimates for the SF-36 summary scales, explains the internal-consistency and test-retest methods used in estimating reliability, provides estimates of sample sizes required to achieve statistical power for various study designs, and of confidence intervals for interpreting individual patient scores.

Empirical Validity

Chapter 8 summarizes results from the first two rounds of empirical tests of the validity of the PCS and MCS summary scales and compares results with those using the eight-scale SF-36 profile in the same tests. Correlations with specific symptoms and with numerous other MOS health scales are presented.

Content And Criterion-Based Interpretation

Chapter 9 explains the meaning of very high and low PCS and MCS scores and presents 19 tables of content-based and criterion-based interpretation guidelines and explains their use. Effect sizes from numerous cross-sectional and longitudinal analyses are ordered from largest to smallest.

Norms

Chapter 10 presents 42 tables of norms for a representative sample of the 1998 general U.S. population for both standard and acute forms by age, gender, and chronic conditions.

Applications: Outcomes Research

Chapter 11 illustrates the use of norms and content- and criterion-based interpretation guidelines in interpreting the summary measures in outcomes research and compares results with those using SF-36 profiles published by others.

Applications: Clinical Practice

Chapter 12 presents examples of how SF-36 summary measures can be used in monitoring individual patients over time, in screening patients, and illustrates different display formats.

References And Bibliography

Complete citations for more than 125 referenced publications, including more than 87 publications about the SF-36, are included.

Scoring Algorithms

Appendix D documents the algorithms for aggregating the eight SF-36 scales to score the PCS and MCS summary scales. Using 1990 norm-based scoring methods.

Norm-Based Interpretation

Appendix E presents 50 tables of norms for a representative sample of the 1990 general U.S. population (for seven age groups, men and women), as well as for MOS patients, including norms for one-year change scores. This chapter also describes sampling methods and sample characteristics.

Chapter 2: Introduction

The cycle of measurement development involves a model of health status components and the search for the most valid operational definitions of those components. The cycle must grapple with both uncertainty about the underlying conceptual framework of health and the validity of assessment methods. Out of necessity, the process is circular and tests of hypotheses about the structure of health are vulnerable to the limits of the measures used in hypothesis testing. Advances in understanding of the structure of health can lead to breakthroughs in measurement strategies.

Physical And Mental Health

Discovery of the physical and mental components of health has substantial implications for the construct validation of health measures and a new strategy for creating more useful summary measures of the information they contain. The observation that the eight SF-36 scales define distinct physical and mental health clusters in factor analytic studies of both patients participating in the Medical Outcomes Study (MOS) (McHorney, Ware, Raczek, et al., 1993; Ware, Gandek, & the IQOLA Project Group, 1994) and in the general U.S. population (Ware, Snow, Kosinski, et al., 1993) constitutes considerable support for the construct validity of the SF-36. The generalizability of these findings is underscored by results showing that the factor content of each SF-36 scale -- the extent to which each scale measures a physical and/or mental health component -- is also very similar across populations (Ware, Snow, Kosinski, et al., 1993; Ware, Kosinski, Bayliss, et al., 1995). These results have proven very useful in establishing interpretation guidelines for each of the SF-36 scales, as documented in the original *SF-36® Health Survey Manual and Interpretation Guide* (Ware, Snow, Kosinski, et al., 1993).

The discovery that from 80 to 85 percent of the reliable variance in the eight SF-36 scales is accounted for by physical and mental components of health opens the door for a breakthrough in scoring and interpretation. Specifically, this result suggests that psychometrically-based summary measures have the potential to reduce the number of statistical comparisons required in analyzing SF-36 data from eight to two without substantial loss of information. Preliminary tests of their potential have yielded promising results (Ware, Kosinski, Bayliss, et al., 1995).

Psychometric-Based Summary Measures

In support of aggregating highly related health measures using psychometric methods, initial results from the MOS suggested that scales with the same factor content are much more likely to lead to the same conclusions about health outcomes than scales with different factor content (McHorney, Ware, & Raczek, 1993). Thus, measures having the same factor content are good candidates for aggregation, because less information is likely to be lost. Factor analytic methods are likely to prove useful in deriving the weights used in aggregation. Although factor analytic methods have been used in construct validation (Ware, 1976; Goldberg & Hillier, 1979; Ware, Brook, Davies-Avery, et al., 1980; Veit & Ware, 1983; Derogatis, 1986; Wiklund, Lindvall, Swedberg, et al., 1987; Mason, Anderson, & Meenan, 1988; Hall, Epstein, & McNeil, 1989; Hays & Stewart 1990; Schag, Heinrich, Aadland, et al., 1990), the scoring of higher-order factors to achieve summary measures of health status has been pursued rarely (Davies & Ware, 1981; Veit & Ware, 1983). As a result, little is known about the tradeoffs between the simplicity of fewer statistical comparisons with aggregate summary measures versus the greater sensitivity of a scale to effects concentrated in a particular dimension of health (Ware, 1984). In theory, to the extent that results are the same across conceptually related scales, a summary measure that aggregates them should be *more* useful than any one of them in detecting a difference in health status at a point in time or a change in health over time. To the extent that differences are concentrated in a particular subscale, a summary measure is *less* likely to capture that difference or change (Ware, Kosinski, Bayliss, et al., 1995).

Standardized Scoring

Following several years of evaluating the factor structure of the SF-36 among those with various chronic conditions and among the "well" in general populations in the U.S. and in other countries, it is clear that physical and mental factors account for the great majority of the variance in SF-36 scales across populations. It follows that the standardized scoring of measures of physical and mental factors will add a useful option for the scoring of SF-36 data with advantages in interpreting and presenting results.

This user's manual summarizes the empirical work leading to the development of the SF-36 Physical Component Summary (PCS) and Mental Component Summary (MCS) scales and provides the documentation necessary to score and interpret those measures.

Chapter 3: Construction Of Summary Measures

This chapter documents the factor analytic methods used to evaluate the construct validity of the SF-36 in relation to a two-factor -- physical and mental -- model of health across populations. The construction of the PCS and MCS summary measures of physical and mental health based on those methods and some of the more important methodological issues are also explained. The PCS and MCS summary measures are referred to as "component" measures (Ware, Kosinski, Bayliss, et al., 1995) because they were derived and scored using a factor analytic method called principal *components* analysis (Harman, 1976).

Factor analyses of correlations among the eight SF-36 scales have consistently identified two factors, as documented below. On the strength of the pattern of their correlations with the eight scales, they have been interpreted as "physical" and "mental" dimensions of health status. These physical and mental components accounted for 81.5% of the reliable variance in SF-36 scales in the general U.S. population (Ware, Kosinski, Bayliss, et al., 1995), and 82.4% in the MOS (McHorney, Ware, Raczek, 1993). Similar physical and mental components have been observed for other comprehensive surveys, including the Health Insurance Experiment Medical History Questionnaire (Ware, Brook, Davies-Avery, et al., 1980), the MOS Functioning and Well-Being Profile (Hays & Stewart, 1990), and the Sickness Impact Profile (Bergner, Bobbitt, Carter, et al., 1981). In further support of the generalizability of this two-dimensional model of health, we would expect factor analytic studies of other comprehensive surveys to yield recognizably similar physical and mental components.

The psychometric approach to summarizing health measures illustrated here is in contrast to a utility index, in which measures are aggregated without regard to their inter-relationships. A utility index achieves a single summary score at the expense of sensitivity and specificity to physical versus mental components of health status. A strength of the PCS and MCS summary scales described here is their value in distinguishing a physical from a mental health outcome.

SF-36 Measurement Model

Figure 3.1 illustrates the measurement model underlying the construction of SF-36 multi-item scales and summary measures. This model has three levels: (1) items, (2) scales that aggregate items, and (3) summary measures that aggregate scales. All but one of the 36 items (self-reported health transition) are used to score the eight SF-36 scales.

FIGURE 3.1 SF-36 MEASUREMENT MODEL

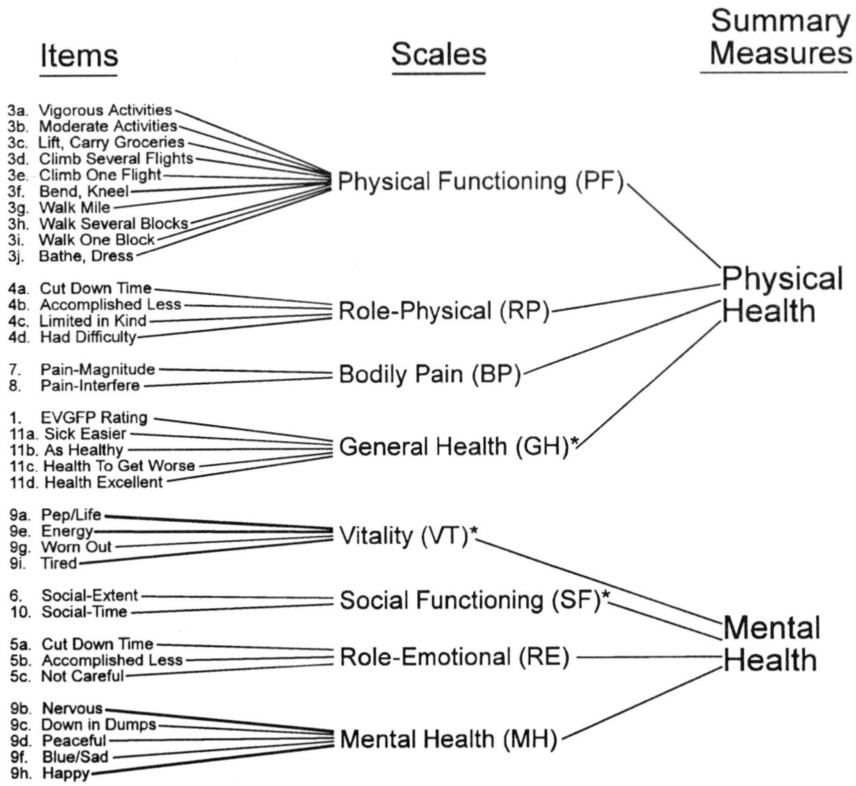

* Significant correlation with other summary measure.

As shown in the figure, each item is used in scoring only one scale. Tests of assumptions underlying the algorithms used in scoring the eight scales have been strongly supported in the U.S. (Ware, Snow, Kosinski, et al., 1993; McHorney, Ware, Lu, et al., 1994) and in other countries (Ware, Keller, Gandek, et al., 1998). The eight scales also form two distinct higher-ordered clusters. Three scales (Physical Functioning, Role-Physical, and Bodily Pain) correlate most highly with the physical component and contribute most to scoring of the PCS measure of that component. The mental component correlates most highly with the Mental Health, Role-Emotional, and Social Functioning scales, which contribute most to the scoring of the MCS measure of that component. Three of the scales have noteworthy correlations with both components: the Vitality scale correlates substantially with both; General Health correlates with both but higher with the physical component; and Social Functioning correlates much higher with the mental component. Reasons for these patterns of factor loadings are discussed elsewhere (Ware, Snow, Kosinski, et al., 1993).

Criteria And Hypotheses

Criteria commonly used to evaluate factor analyses using the principal components method were routinely applied (Harman, 1976) using SAS software (SAS Institute, 1989). First, we examined whether eigenvalues for the first two components were both greater than unity, as required for rotation. Other criteria, previously used, including the screen test, five percent rule, and common factor test, were also satisfied (Ware, Davies-Avery, & Brook, 1980). Second, we evaluated the pattern of correlations between the two rotated components and eight SF-36 scales to determine the basis for their interpretations as physical and mental components.

We hypothesized that the PF scale would have the highest and a very strong loading ($r > .80$) on the "physical" component followed by the RP and BP scales. The MH scale was hypothesized to have the strongest loading ($r > .80$) on the "mental" component, followed by the RE and SF scales. Because they are general measures, the GH and VT scales were hypothesized to correlate with both components. Lastly, we evaluated the adequacy of the two components in explaining the variation in each SF-36 scale. We hypothesized that a large proportion of the reliable variance in each scale (three-fourths) would be explained by the two components.

To evaluate the generalizability of the two-dimensional SF-36 model of health across different patient groups, we conducted principal component analyses in 23 subgroups of MOS patients differing in demographic characteristics and medical conditions. These are the same subgroups analyzed in tests of scaling assumptions for the eight SF-36 scales, as described elsewhere (McHorney, Ware, Lu, et al., 1994). These tests are extended here to include 12 subgroups differing in demographic characteristics from the general U.S. population, as well as general population samples from ten countries participating in the International Quality of Life Assessment (IQOLA) Project. In all analyses, we used the same method to extract two principal components from the correlations among the SF-36 scales and rotated them to orthogonal simple structure to facilitate interpretation.

Results

Tables 3.1 through 3.3 present results for the principal component analyses of SF-36 scales for the total 1998 general U.S. population standard (4-week recall) and acute (1-week recall) forms; the total patient sample from the MOS (McHorney, Ware, & Raczek, 1993); the total 1990 general U.S. population; and general populations in Denmark, France, Germany, Italy, Netherlands, Norway, Spain, Sweden, and the United Kingdom (Ware, Kosinski, Gandek, et al., 1998). Results for the 12 subgroups from the general U.S. population are summarized in Table 3.4. Results for the 23 patient subgroups from the MOS are summarized in Table 3.5. Results for age and gender subgroups in 9 countries are summarized in Table 3.6.

TABLE 3.1 CORRELATIONS BETWEEN SF-36 SCALES AND ROTATED PRINCIPAL COMPONENTS IN THE 1998 GENERAL U.S. POPULATION, STANDARD (N=1,982) AND ACUTE RECALL (N=1,646) FORMS

	Standard Form (4-Week Recall)			Acute Form (1-week Recall)		
Scales	**PCS**	**MCS**	**h^2/r_{tt}**	**PCS**	**MCS**	**h^2/r_{tt}**
Physical Function	.87	.13	.82	.87	.16	.83
Role Physical	.83	.28	.88	.82	.30	.88
Bodily Pain	.77	.31	.74	.79	.29	.84
General Health	.61	.50	.76	.64	.47	.75
Vitality	.43	.70	.76	.43	.69	.75
Social Function	.55	.65	.84	.55	.66	.86
Role Emotion	.25	.70	.70	.30	.73	.75
Mental Health	.10	.91	.98	.11	.90	.99
Reliable Variance[1]	81.3%			82.9%		

h^2/r_{tt} Variance in each SF-36® scale explained by the two principal components (h^2) divided by the reliability of each SF-36® scale (r_{tt}).

1 Percent of the total reliable variance in SF-36® scales explained by the two principal components.

As hypothesized, eigenvalues for the first two components were both greater than unity in all analyses, strongly supporting the two-dimensional model of health.

TABLE 3.2 CORRELATIONS BETWEEN SF-36 SCALES AND ROTATED PRINCIPAL COMPONENTS IN THE MEDICAL OUTCOMES STUDY (MOS) AND THE GENERAL U.S. POPULATION

	MOS (N = 3,445)			U.S. POPULATION (N = 2,474)		
SF-36 SCALES	**PCS**	**MCS**	**h^2/r_{tt}**	**PCS**	**MCS**	**h^2/r_{tt}**
Physical Functioning (PF)	.88	.04	.84	.85	.12	.78
Role Physical (RP)	.78	.30	.83	.81	.27	.82
Bodily Pain (BP)	.77	.24	.79	.76	.28	.72
General Health (GH)	.68	.32	.72	.69	.37	.78
Vitality (VT)	.59	.57	.77	.47	.64	.75
Social Functioning (SF)	.44	.71	.82	.42	.67	.92
Role Emotional (RE)	.19	.81	.83	.17	.78	.78
Mental Health (MH)	.12	.90	.91	.17	.87	.92
Reliable Variance[1]			82.4%			81.5%

h^2/r_{tt} Variance in each SF-36 scale explained by the two principal components (h^2) divided by the reliability of each SF-36® scale (r_{tt}).

1 Percent of the total reliable variance in SF-36® scales explained by the two principal components.

The pattern of correlations between SF-36 scales and the two rotated components in Tables 3.1 and 3.2 strongly support the physical and mental health interpretation of the two components. In each analysis, the PF scale loaded strongest on the "physical" component and weakest on the "mental" component. Also, the RP and BP scales both had stronger loadings on the "physical" component than the "mental" component. The MH scale had the highest loading and the RE and SF scales had stronger loadings on the "mental" component than the "physical" component. The GH and VT scales had noteworthy loadings ($r > .30$) on both physical and mental components, as expected for general measures.

TABLE 3.3 CORRELATIONS BETWEEN SF-36 SCALES AND ROTATED PRINCIPAL COMPONENTS IN 9 COUNTRIES

	Denmark		France		Germany		Italy		Netherlands		Norway		Spain		Sweden		United Kingdom	
Scales	**PC**	**MC**	**PC**	**MC**	**PC**	**MC**	**PC**	**MC**	**PC**	**MC**	**PC**	**MC**	**PC**	**MC**	**PC**	**MC**	**PC**	**MC**
PF	0.86	0.10	0.85	0.12	0.85	0.16	0.86	0.13	0.86	0.16	0.83	0.15	0.81	0.19	0.84	0.15	0.84	0.20
RP	0.78	0.30	0.78	0.29	0.79	0.28	0.64	0.42	0.69	0.44	0.82	0.26	0.76	0.24	0.78	0.30	0.80	0.27
BP	0.69	0.32	0.78	0.32	0.82	0.24	0.73	0.37	0.80	0.20	0.80	0.25	0.74	0.26	0.76	0.28	0.80	0.19
GH	0.70	0.41	0.60	0.49	0.72	0.38	0.75	0.34	0.75	0.31	0.74	0.39	0.73	0.34	0.66	0.50	0.73	0.39
VT	0.39	0.75	0.41	0.73	0.52	0.64	0.44	0.70	0.52	0.66	0.40	0.71	0.51	0.61	0.43	0.74	0.54	0.64
SF	0.33	0.72	0.37	0.78	0.33	0.75	0.27	0.81	0.49	0.68	0.33	0.78	0.50	0.62	0.32	0.78	0.55	0.62
RE	0.27	0.70	0.28	0.71	0.20	0.71	0.23	0.76	0.13	0.84	0.21	0.78	0.18	0.78	0.25	0.71	0.20	0.78
MH	0.11	0.89	0.09	0.91	0.16	0.87	0.25	0.81	0.25	0.86	0.14	0.90	0.22	0.84	0.15	0.90	0.18	0.87
Reliable Variance[1]	81.3		84.7		82.9		84.0		82.1		83.8		76.3		82.6		82.0	

Abbreviations: PC = Physical Component; MC = Mental Component; PF = Physical Functioning; RP = Role Physical; BP = Bodily Pain; GH = General Health; VT = Vitality; SF = Social Functioning; RE = Role Emotional; MH = Mental Health.

Source: Ware JE, Kosinski M, Gandek BG, et al.; 1998.

Table 3.4 summarizes the range of factor loadings observed in 12 analyses of subgroups of the general U.S. population differing in age, gender, race, and education. The two components explained from 77% to 87% (median = 81%) of the reliable variance in the eight scales, and the range of correlations observed for each scale and each component is strikingly similar to that observed in Table 3.1 for the general U.S. population.

Table 3.5 summarizes results for analyses of 23 subgroups of MOS patients differing in socio-demographic characteristics, diagnosis, and other clinical variables defined elsewhere (McHorney, Ware, Lu, et al., 1994). From 75% to 83% (median = 80%) of the reliable variance in the eight scales was explained. Again, the amount of reliable variance explained and the pattern of correlations between scales and the two components replicates other results to date.

Table 3.6 presents the range of correlations between SF-36 scales and rotated principal components for five subgroups differing in age (three groups) and gender (two groups) within each of the nine countries. The pattern of correlations observed are consistent with the patterns observed for the total populations in each country (see Table 3.3). Only in Italy are departures observed, particularly among the 65 and older group.

The results presented in Tables 3.1-3.6 also demonstrate the adequacy of the two components in explaining the reliable variance in each SF-36 scale. In all but four of the 40 factor analyses, the total reliable variance in SF-36 scales explained by the two components exceeded 81%. As hypothesized, the two components explained at least three-fourths of the reliable variance in each SF-36 scale, with few exceptions.

TABLE 3.4 RANGE OF CORRELATIONS BETWEEN SF-36 SCALES AND ROTATED PRINCIPAL COMPONENTS, 12 SUBGROUPS OF THE GENERAL U.S. POPULATION[1] (N = 2,474)

SF-36 SCALES	PCS	MCS
Physical Functioning (PF)	.77 - .88	.05 - .30
Role Physical (RP)	.67 - .82	.16 - .43
Bodily Pain (BP)	.70 - .84	.17 - .46
General Health (GH)	.53 - .76	.29 - .69
Vitality (VT)	.31 - .73	.44 - .82
Social Functioning (SF)	.34 - .62	.46 - .73
Role Emotional (RE)	.06 - .48	.57 - .83
Mental Health (MH)	.11 - .27	.84 - .90

1 Results above come from analyses of 12 subgroups in the general U.S. population: 3 age, 2 gender, 3 race, and 4 education groups.

TABLE 3.5 RANGE OF CORRELATIONS BETWEEN SF-36 SCALES AND ROTATED PRINCIPAL COMPONENTS, 23 MOS SUBGROUPS[1] (N = 3,445)

SF-36 SCALES	PCS	MCS
Physical Functioning (PF)	.83 - .90	.01 - .16
Role Physical (RP)	.69 - .81	.20 - .41
Bodily Pain (BP)	.65 - .83	.12 - .42
General Health (GH)	.56 - .76	.17 - .51
Vitality (VT)	.43 - .79	.27 - .66
Social Functioning (SF)	.30 - .72	.37 - .82
Role Emotional (RE)	.11 - .38	.66 - .88
Mental Health (MH)	.01 - .34	.75 - .92

1 Results above come from principal components analyses of 23 subgroups in the MOS: 3 age, 2 gender, 3 race, 4 education, 2 poverty status, 6 diagnoses, and 3 clinical groups.

TABLE 3.6 RANGE OF CORRELATIONS BETWEEN SF-36 SCALES AND ROTATED PRINCIPAL COMPONENTS ACROSS AGE AND GENDER GROUPS IN 9 COUNTRIES

	Denmark		France		Germany		Italy		Netherlands	
Scale	Physical	Mental	Physical	Mental	Physical	Mental	Physical	Mental	Physical	Mental
PF	.79-.86	.04-.16	.82-.86	.06-.19	.81-.86	.10-.24	.81-.86	.04-.20	.81-.86	.09-.20
RP	.72-.80	.25-.39	.68-.78	.25-.41	.73-.81	.26-.31	.60-.83	.29-.42	.60-.75	.30-.47
BP	.68-.79	.23-.37	.73-.81	.27-.34	.76-.86	.17-.32	.43-.77	.31-.63	.76-.85	.18-.26
GH	.58-.78	.33-.56	.56-.65	.44-.48	.62-.75	.33-.46	.53-.77	.33-.57	.58-.77	.22-.49
VT	.29-.56	.64-.79	.32-.51	.69-.76	.34-.69	.46-.76	.30-.48	.66-.82	.37-.70	.46-.74
SF	.22-.39	.69-.75	.33-.47	.71-.80	.27-.38	.70-.78	.26-.29	.76-.81	.38-.58	.56-.75
RE	.13-.44	.55-.79	.15-.41	.63-.76	.14-.24	.68-.73	.19-.61	.40-.79	.09-.24	.73-.91
MH	.06-.16	.86-.91	.07-.17	.90-.92	.12-.25	.82-.89	.18-.27	.80-.86	.11-.19	.70-.89

	Norway		Spain		Sweden		United Kingdom	
Scale	Physical	Mental	Physical	Mental	Physical	Mental	Physical	Mental
PF	.77-.85	.12-.22	.69-.81	.07-.23	.81-.85	.08-.29	.76-.86	.15-.26
RP	.76-.83	.21-.35	.62-.80	.14-.40	.75-.78	.26-.33	.76-.81	.21-.33
BP	.79-.83	.19-.27	.67-.77	.19-.35	.74-.80	.26-.30	.78-.81	.14-.27
GH	.66-.79	.36-.41	.49-.83	.19-.42	.61-.69	.47-.54	.57-.78	.35-46
VT	.37-.52	.66-.72	.19-.53	.59-.76	.42-.62	.64-.74	.37-.59	.59-.70
SF	.29-.46	.65-.80	.43-.53	.55-.66	.28-.35	.77-.79	.43-.56	.61-.74
RE	.10-.28	.75-.84	.13-.19	.66-.90	.11-.45	.64-.77	.10-.27	.76-.81
MH	.12-.20	.86-.91	.03-.36	.70-.86	.13-.19	.88-.91	.11-.29	.82-.89

Methodological Issues

Factor analysis has proven to be very useful in testing hypotheses about the structure of health and in evaluating the construct validity of the SF-36 and other health surveys (Ware, 1976; Goldberg & Hillier, 1979; Ware, Brook, & Davies-Avery, 1980; Veit & Ware, 1983; Derogatis, 1986; Hall, Epstein, & McNeil, 1989; Wiklund, Lindvall, Swedberg, et al., 1987; Mason, Anderson, & Meenan, 1988; Schag, Heinrich, Aadland, et al., 1990; Hays & Stewart, 1990; McHorney, Ware, & Raczek, 1993). We have given considerable attention to the implications of different methods of factor extraction and rotation. In many cases, conclusions do not vary across methods. When they do, the choice among methods depends on the purpose(s) of the factor analysis (Nunnally & Bernstein, 1994).

The choice of method for the SF-36 studies follows from the first author's earlier work and considerations of work published by others (Ware, Miller, & Snyder, 1973; Snyder & Ware, 1974; Ware & Snyder, 1975; Ware, Davies-Avery, & Brook, 1980). Consistent with guidelines suggested by Harris & Harris (1971), conclusions about the factor structure of the SF-36 were not of great consequence in choosing a method. That structure is robust across methods and populations. In fact, a good test of a structural model is its robustness across factor analytic methods (Harris & Harris, 1971). For example, comparisons across methods for the same matrices were often employed during the development of the Health Perceptions Questionnaire (Ware, Miller, & Snyder, 1973; Ware, 1976; Ware & Karmos, 1976), from which items were selected for the SF-36 GH Scale. Those studies also demonstrated the advantages of homogeneous, short, multi-item scales over single-item measures as the unit of analysis in factor analytic studies. These advantages are also well-documented in empirical studies of personality variables (Comrey, 1973).

The two-dimensional factor structure of the eight SF-36 scales has also been shown to satisfy criteria for "simple structure" (Nunnally & Bernstein, 1994) across patient and general population samples in the U.S. and across other countries (as summarized above). To facilitate re-analyses by others, the matrices of correlations for the SF-36 in general and patient populations are reproduced at the end of this section (see Tables 3.5 and 3.6).

Principal Components

As noted above, the interpretation of the first two factors as dimensions of physical and mental health has been straightforward and robust across methods. Thus, the choice of factor analytic method was not governed by considerations in interpreting the factors. The choice of the principal components method was based on other considerations, including the ease of estimation of factor scores for the two summary measures, estimation of the factor content of the eight SF-36® scales in relation to physical and mental health status, the explanatory power of the factors, and their validity in discriminating between physical and mental dimensions of health status. These considerations are discussed briefly below.

The advantages of components analysis over principal factor analysis are noteworthy for the purposes of achieving: (1) a simple additive model of factor content facilitating the interpretation of each scale; (2) summary measures that explain as much of the variance in the eight scales as possible; (3) summary scales that are easy to estimate statistically; and (4) summary scores that are interpretable as physical and mental dimensions of health. The goal in constructing the PCS and MCS scores was to explain as much of the variance in the eight SF-36 variables as possible with only two summary measures (Ware, Kosinski, Bayliss, et al., 1995). Components analysis attempts to explain as much of the variance as possible, in contrast to principal factors, which attempt to reproduce the original correlation matrix (Harman, 1976). Second, as explained in Chapter 4, the computation of scores for each principal component is a straightforward estimation using scores for the observed variables (i.e., the eight SF-36 scale scores) in contrast to approximations involved in estimating scores for principal factors. These differences and the advantages of components analysis are discussed in numerous texts on factor analysis and psychometric methods (e.g., Harman, 1976; Nunnally & Bernstein, 1994).

There are good theoretical arguments for both orthogonal and oblique factor rotations (Harman, 1976; Nunnally & Bernstein, 1994). As argued in numerous texts, orthogonal components are ideal for our purposes. Our initial objective in factor analyzing the correlations among SF-36 scales was to test the construct validity of the SF-36 and to establish guidelines for interpreting each scale, on the basis of its physical and mental health factor content (McHorney, Ware, & Raczek, 1993; Ware, Snow, Kosinski, et al., 1993; Ware, Kosinski, Bayliss, et al., 1995). For this purpose, orthogonal components, which are not correlated, have clear advantages. For example, "factor loadings," which are product moment correlations between scales and factors, can be squared and summed across factors to estimate the amount of variance in each scale accounted for by each factor and the amount of variance in each scale that is explained by all factors (i.e., the communality). As a result, factor content and implications for the interpretation of each scale are more straightforward (Ware, Snow, Kosinski, et al., 1993).

Orthogonal Components

To provide a visual image of the contribution of the eight SF-36 scales to the physical and mental components, their factor loadings are plotted in Figure 3.2 for the general U.S. population. This plot reveals a progression from the upper left corner, with the MH scale correlating most highly with the mental component (MCS) and least with the physical component (PCS), to the lower right corner, where the highest correlation with the PCS is observed for the PF scale, which also correlates the least with the MCS. In between is a progression of loadings from the lower right (PF) to the upper left (MH). This ordering of scales from PF in the lower right to MH in the upper left corresponds to their ordering in the SF-36 profile.

FIGURE 3.2 PLOT OF SF-36 SCALE FACTOR LOADINGS ON ORTHOGONAL PHYSICAL AND MENTAL COMPONENTS, GENERAL U.S. POPULATION (N=2,474)

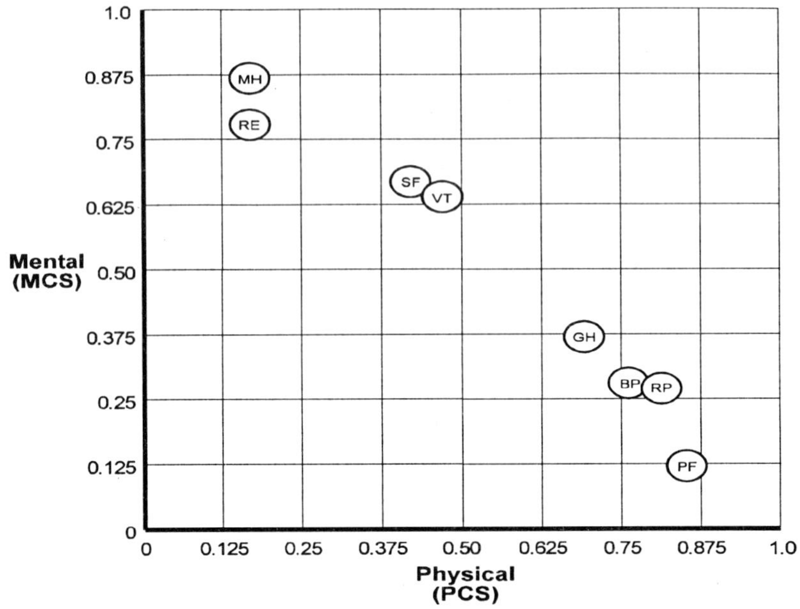

It is also apparent that the eight SF-36 scales form two distinct clusters with four scales (MH, RE, SF, VT) correlating highest with the MCS and lowest with the PCS, and a second cluster (PF, RP, BP, GH) correlating highest with the PCS and lowest with the MCS. As shown in Chapter 4, the factor score coefficients used to score the PCS and MCS correspond to these two clusters. Specifically, the highest positive coefficients (0.42 to 0.25) are used to weight the four best physical scales in scoring the PCS, and the highest positive coefficients (0.49 to 0.24) are used to weight the four best mental scales in scoring the MCS. Because the factor score coefficients take into account the correlations *among* the eight scales, they differ from the factor loadings; some are negative. Negative factor score coefficients were also observed in oblique principal factor solutions and are not unique to the principal components method (data not reported). Oblique solutions, which can allow substantial correlations between health dimensions (factors), can facilitate the identification of factors but they complicate understanding of the factor content of scales because loadings are not additive in an oblique solution. Correlations among factors and factor loadings must both be taken into account in interpreting an oblique solution, complicating the interpretation of each scale.

If the PF and MH scales had proven to be substantially correlated, or if the PCS and MCS were substantially correlated on cross-validation, there would be good reason to favor an oblique solution. However, it is clear that physical and mental health are only weakly positively correlated. Correlations between the PF and MH scales, the best physical and mental health measures among the eight SF-36 scales, are low, with medians ranging from only 0.22 to 0.30 in 39 patient and general population studies in the U.S., Germany, Sweden, and the U.K. Cross validation of the orthogonal two-dimensional model (using U.S. factor score coefficients) in these samples has demonstrated very low empirical correlations between the PCS and MCS scores (medians of -0.01 to 0.07 across 39 estimates in studies to date). These correlations would be much larger upon cross-validation if the orthogonal solution and scoring were a gross distortion.

Additional convincing empirical evidence favoring the scoring of orthogonal principal components in summarizing SF-36 information about physical and mental health is their superiority in discriminating between physical and mental health outcomes in empirical tests. Comparisons of alternative scoring strategies revealed that much of the advantage in interpretation gained with the SF-36 PCS and MCS is lost when the physical and mental components are scored with an oblique solution (data not shown).

TABLE 3.7 PRODUCT MOMENT CORRELATIONS AND RELIABILITY COEFFICIENTS (IN PARENTHESES), SF-36 SCALES (4-WEEK RECALL) FOR THE 1998 GENERAL U.S. POPULATION

	PF	RP	BP	GH	VT	SF	RE	MH
PF	(.94)							
RP	.66	(.88)					N=1,982	
BP	.57	.65	(.85)					
GH	.57	.54	.57	(.84)				
VT	.44	.52	.54	.63	(.88)			
SF	.54	.64	.59	.56	.60	(.86)		
RE	.35	.46	.38	.39	.42	.58	(.82)	
MH	.26	.34	.38	.51	.63	.59	.51	(.85)

TABLE 3.8 PRODUCT MOMENT CORRELATIONS AND RELIABILITY COEFFICIENTS (IN PARENTHESES), SF-36 SCALES (1-WEEK RECALL) FOR THE 1998 GENERAL U.S. POPULATION

	PF	RP	BP	GH	VT	SF	RE	MH
PF	(.94)							
RP	.69	(.88)						
BP	.62	.66	(.86)				N=1,646	
GH	.58	.57	.60	(.84)				
VT	.46	.54	.53	.61	(.88)			
SF	.55	.66	.59	.58	.60	(.86)		
RE	.42	.52	.41	.43	.48	.64	(.83)	
MH	.29	.35	.39	.50	.61	.59	.55	(.83)

TABLE 3.9 PRODUCT MOMENT CORRELATIONS AND RELIABILITY COEFFICIENTS (IN PARENTHESES), SF-36 SCALES FOR THE 1990 GENERAL U.S. POPULATION

	PF	RP	BP	GH	VT	SF	RE	MH
PF	(.93)							
RP	.65	(.89)					N=2,474	
BP	.52	.61	(.90)					
GH	.55	.55	.56	(.81)				
VT	.44	.50	.52	.58	(.86)			
SF	.45	.52	.49	.47	.51	(.68)		
RE	.30	.42	.32	.35	.44	.53	(.82)	
MH	.28	.35	.39	.46	.63	.56	.54	(.84)

TABLE 3.10 PRODUCT MOMENT CORRELATIONS AND RELIABILITY COEFFICIENTS (IN PARENTHESES), SF-36 SCALES FOR THE MOS (N = 3,445)

	PF	RP	BP	GH	VT	SF	RE	MH
PF	(.93)							
RP	.60	(.84)						
BP	.56	.62	(.82)					
GH	.53	.48	.50	(.78)				
VT	.49	.57	.50	.57	(.87)			
SF	.45	.52	.53	.47	.57	(.85)		
RE	.29	.48	.34	.37	.51	.55	(.83)	
MH	.20	.34	.38	.41	.58	.66	.60	(.90)

SF-12 Health Survey

The construction of the PCS and MCS and evidence to date supporting their usefulness in cross-sectional and longitudinal tests provides the foundation for the construction of a health survey that is much shorter than the SF-36. The number of items in a survey is, at least in part, a function of the number of health dimensions for which separate scores are to be estimated with precision. If two summary scores are useful for most purposes, as suggested by results reported here and elsewhere (Ware, Kosinski, Bayliss, et al., 1995), it is likely that the two summary scores can be estimated with fewer items well enough for some purposes.

Following discovery of the PCS and MCS summary scales, we began evaluating how well these scales could be reproduced using much shorter questionnaires. Those studies identified ten items from six of the eight SF-36 scales that reproduced at least 90% of the variance in both the PCS and MCS, as defined using the SF-36 scales. Addition of two more items created a 12-item short-form yielding satisfactory estimates of the PCS and MCS, as well as scores for the two additional concepts necessary to represent the profile of eight SF-36 concepts. We refer to this new short form as the SF-12. Four of the eight concepts (physical functioning, role-physical, role-emotional, and mental health) are estimated using two items each. The remaining scales (bodily pain, general health, vitality, and social functioning) are measured using one item each. The eight-concept profile based on SF-12 items (calibrated to reproduce the original eight SF-36 scales) appears to be very similar, on average, to the original SF-36 profile, although each score is estimated with less precision. This disadvantage of single-item scales and very short multi-item scales has been demonstrated in previous studies (McHorney, Ware, Rogers, et al., 1992).

Results from preliminary tests of empirical validity, like those described in Chapter 6 for the SF-36 PCS and MCS summary scales, suggest that 12-item versions of the PCS and MCS will correlate with the SF-36 versions in the 0.93 to 0.97 range, upon cross-validation. However, the SF-12-based PCS and MCS define fewer levels and should be expected to yield less reliable assignments of individuals to those levels. For large group studies these differences in measurement reliability are not as important, because confidence intervals for group averages are more determined by sample size. Given that the SF-12 can be self-administered in about two to three minutes, the trade-off may be worthwhile for many purposes.

We have prepared documentation of items and scoring algorithms for the SF-12 (Ware, Kosinski, & Keller, 1995), and results of the preliminary evaluation of empirical validity for the SF-12 have been published (Ware, Kosinski & Keller, 1995). The SF-12 should be most useful for purposes of large group and population monitoring of health status and changes in health over time. Because SF-12 items are a subset of the original SF-36, complete comparability can be maintained across data sets using SF-12 scoring algorithms and data for either short-form survey.

Chapter 4: Norm-Based Scoring And Interpretation

The interpretation of results has been made much easier with the norm-based scoring of SF-36 scales and summary measures. Specifically, norm-based scoring has proven to be very useful when interpreting differences across scales in the SF-36 profile and the physical and mental summary measures. As originally documented in the first edition of this manual (Ware et al, 1994), linear transformations were performed to transform scores to a mean of 50 and standard deviations of 10, in the general US population for both the SF-36 physical and mental health summary measures. This same transformation can be applied to all eight SF-36 scales to simplify the interpretation of scores on each scale.

We use 1998 norms to introduce norm-based scoring (NBS) for the eight-dimension profiles because these norms are much more up-to-date and reflect substantial differences in most "physical health" scales, in comparison with 1990 norms. These differences from 1990 to 1998 should be taken into account when drawing conclusions about population health, disease burden and treatment benefits. 1998 norms and associated scoring algorithms for SF-36, SF-12 and SF-8 also make it possible to estimate scores for the eight dimensions of health, which they all have in common, and for their two summary measures using either SF-36, SF-12 or SF-8. Finally, the 1998 norms and NBS scoring algorithms provide the long awaited linkage necessary to compare results across studies relying on the eight-scale profile or two summary measures based on any of these three forms.

Advantages Of Norm-Based Scoring

The advantage of norm-based scoring can be illustrated by comparing the SF-36 profile scored using the original 0 – 100 algorithms with the profile based on the norm-based scoring algorithms for the same sample. For purposes of this comparison, we scored SF-36 profiles both ways for a sample of asthmatic patients who participated in a clinical trial (Okamoto et al, 1996). The original SF-36 0-100 scoring produced the profile shown in Figure 4.1. The shape of this profile – the peaks and valleys due to higher and lower scores across scales – reflect both the impact of asthma on SF-36 health concepts, as well as arbitrary differences in the ceilings and floors of the SF-36 scales. Three scales, namely General Health (GH), Vitality (VT), and Mental Health (MH), measure relatively wide score ranges and set the ceiling relatively high by measuring very favorable levels of those health concepts (Ware et al, 1993). Other scales, such as Physical Functioning (PF), and Role-Physical (RP), assess a narrower range based on a lower ceiling. For these scales the most favorable levels (scored 100 using the original SF-36 algorithms) represent the absence of limitations and do not extend the range into well-being. Thus, the average score for each scale differs substantially across the profile for reasons that have nothing to do with asthma, using the original SF-36 0 – 100 scoring (see "norm" in Figure 4.1). Ignoring these norms, a reasonable inference from the profile in Figure 4.1,is that asthma has a greater impact on Physical Functioning than on Vitality, this inference is incorrect. (See the two shaded scales).

General population norms provide a basis for meaningful comparisons across scales (see Figure 4.1). For example, the PF scale averages between 80 and 90 while the VT average score is below 60 (on the 100-point score range) in the general population. In relation to these norms, the impact of asthma is actually, much larger on the Physical Functioning Scale than on the Vitality Scale, although both are statistically significant. Using the original 0 – 100 scoring, these differences in norms must be kept in mind when interpreting a profile. Differences in standard deviations, which are also substantial across some scales, must also be considered for purposes of comparing results across scales.

0 – 100 SCORING

Figure 4.1 SF-36 ® Health Profile: Adults with Asthma Compared with U.S. Norm

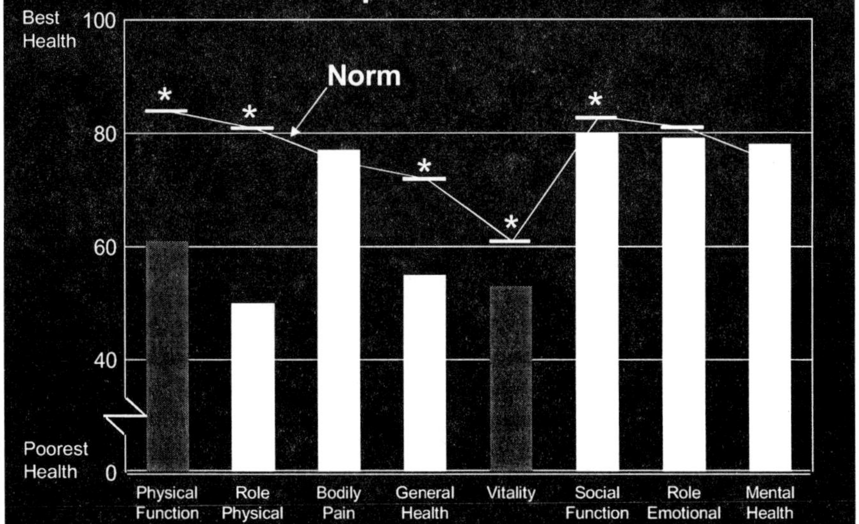

Source: Okamoto, 1996. * Norm significantly higher

In norm-based scoring, each scale is scored to have the same average (50) and the same standard deviation (10 points). Without referring to tables of norms, it is clear with this method that anytime a scale score is below 50, health status is below average, and each point is one-tenth of a standard deviation. As shown in Figure 4.2, with norm-based scoring, differences in scale scores much more clearly reflect the impact of the disease, in this example the impact of asthma. Clinicians can more quickly and appropriately interpret the effect of asthma on a SF-36 health profile.

Norm-Based Scoring

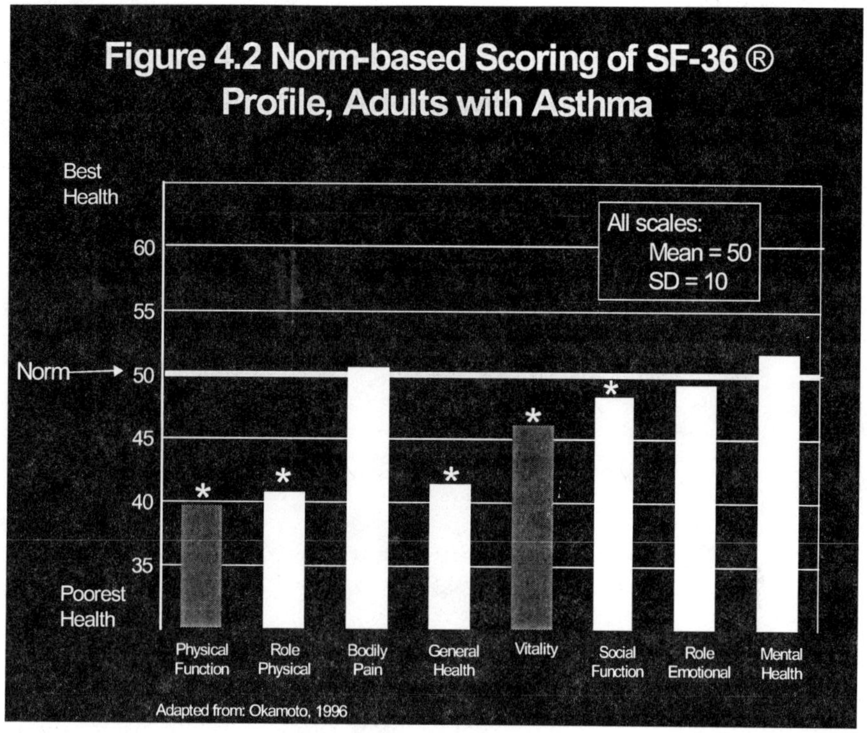

Other advantages of norm-based scoring are shown in Figure 4.3. Results for physical and mental summary measurers, which have always been scored in relation to norms, can be compared directly with results for the eight scales when all are standardized in relation to population norms.

Because the Physical (PCS) and Mental (MCS) component summary measures take into account the correlations among the eight SF-36 scales, it is clear from the example in Figure 4.3 that asthma has a very broad impact on the physical component of health (from the profile in Figure 4.2 with five significant differences) and from the physical summary measure (see Figure 4.3).

The application of norm-based scoring to a clinical trial of treatment effects is also illustrated in Figure 4.3. Patients treated using an inhaler showed statistically significant improvements (white bars with *) relative to baseline (shaded bars) after 16 weeks of treatment on three of the eight SF-36 scales, those most closely associated with physical functioning. As expected, the physical summary measure also improved significantly.

Norm-Based Scoring

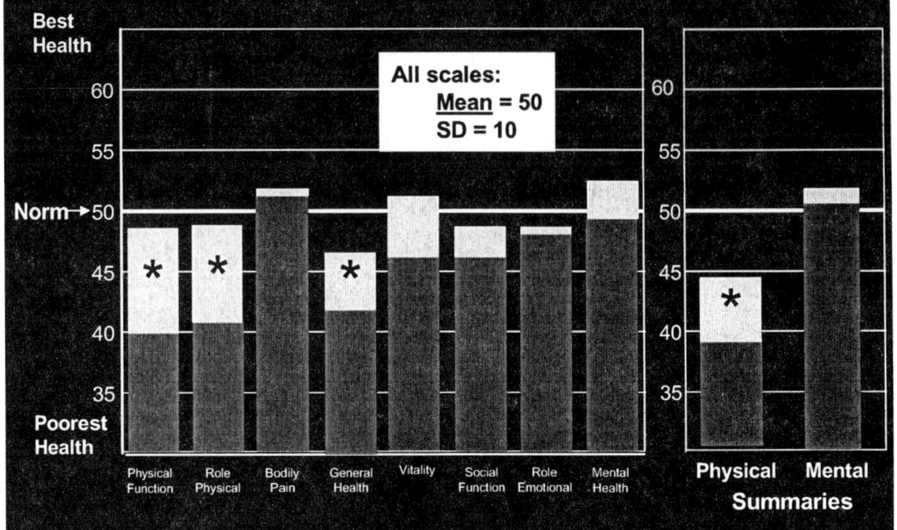

Figure 4.3 Interpreting Treatment Outcomes Among Adults with Asthma

Asthma: After inhaler treatment (one year follow-up). * Significant improvement with treatment

Conclusion

In summary, the main advantage of norm-based scoring of the SF-36 is easier interpretation. When interpreting the scores you no longer have to remember the norms for 8 scales. In norm-based scoring, the general population norm is built into the scoring algorithm. All scores above or below 50 can be interpreted as above or below the general population norm. And because the standard deviations for each scale are equalized at 10, it's easier to see exactly how far above (or below) the mean the score is in standard deviation units. Furthermore, since all 8 scales are scored to have the same standard deviation, comparisons in scores across scales and summary measures can be made directly.

Norm-based scoring has another very important advantage. It provides a basis for direct comparisons between scores from the original version of the SF-36 (v1) & Version 2 (v2). To facilitate such comparisons, we have made available a service for Version 1 scoring of scales and summary measures using the 1998 norms. In addition to providing much more up-to-date norms for use in interpreting Version 1 scales and summary measures, this scoring service assures the comparability of results for both versions of the SF-36 Health Survey. For more information, visit www.SF-36.com.

Again, we take this opportunity to underscore the importance of carefully documenting the SF-36 form (v1), norms and scoring algorithms used in reports of "Study Methods" accompanying results based on the 1998 SF-36 (v1) U.S. population norms. Further, because tables and figures are sometimes distributed separately, we also recommend inclusion of explicit references to "1998 SF-36 (v1) U.S. population norms" and to "norm-based scoring (NBS)" in tables and figures presenting results based on the new 1998 U.S. population norms.

Chapter 5: Norm-Based Scoring Of SF-36 Scales

This chapter provides instructions for the norm-based scoring of the eight multi-item scales of the SF-36 Health Survey. Algorithms are provided for both standard (4-week) and acute (1-week) recall survey forms. The instructions provided in this chapter assume that each of the eight SF-36 scales have already been scored on the 0-100 scale according to standard formulas for item aggregation and transformation of scores to a 0-100 scale published in the SF-36 Manual and Interpretation (Ware, Snow, Kosinski, Gandek, 1993).

Following the 0-100 score transformation is the norm-based scoring of each scale to have a mean of 50 and a standard deviation of 10 in the 1998 general U.S. population. Norm-based scoring methods of scales from standard (4-week recall) and acute (1 week recall) forms are presented separately. Finally, formal checks for errors in scoring are explained. A test dataset is available upon request (info@qualitymetric.com) to confirm successful reproduction of the scoring methods outlined in this chapter.

Importance Of Standardization

As with all standardized tests, standardization of content and scoring is what makes interpretation of SF-36 scales possible. The content of the SF-36 form and the scoring algorithms were selected and standardized following careful study of many options. The algorithms described in this chapter were chosen to be as simple as possible, satisfy the assumptions of the methods used to construct SF-36 scales, and to achieve the nearly perfect linear association with the original SF-36 scores, necessary to preserve their original interpretations.

Changes in the content of the survey or in the scoring method may compromise the reliability and validity of scores. Changes are also likely to bias scores sufficiently to invalidate normative comparisons and to prevent comparisons of results across studies.

There are at least two good reasons to adhere to the standards of content and scoring described in this manual. First, they are most likely to produce scores with the same reliability and validity as those previously reported for SF-36 scales. Second, comparisons of results across studies are made possible to the benefit of all who use these content and scoring standards. Third, differences in scores will have the same interpretations.

Prior to using the SF-36 scoring rules, it is essential to verify that the questionnaires being scored, including the questions asked (item stems), response choices and numbers assigned to response choices at the time of data entry, have been reproduced exactly. The scoring rules documented in the SF-36 Manual and Interpretation Guide are appropriate for the standard SF-36 survey questions, response choices, and numbers assigned to response choices.

Norm-Based Scoring Of Scale Scores, Standard Form (4-Week Recall)

Once each SF-36 scale has been scored on a 0-100 scale, the next step involves the norm-based scoring of each scale using the formulas shown below. Table 5.1 provides the information necessary to apply these formulas to each SF-36 scale from the standard form (4 week recall). The means and standard deviations (Table 5.1) used in norm-based scoring come from the 1998 general U.S. population. A linear z-score transformation is used so that all eight SF-36 scales have a mean of 50 and a standard deviation of 10 in the 1998 general U.S. population.

The advantage of the standardization and norm-based scoring of the 8 SF-36 scales is that results for one scale can be meaningfully compared with the other scales and their scores have a direct interpretation in relation to the distribution of scores in the 1998 general U.S. population. Specifically, all scores above or below 50 are above or below the average, respectively, in the 1998 general U.S. population. Because the standard deviation is 10 for all 8 scales, each one point difference or change in scores also has a direct interpretation. A one point difference or change is one-tenth of a standard deviation unit or an effect size of 0.10. Lastly, norm-based scoring provides the basis for comparing scale scores across Version 1.0 and Version 2.0 standard forms.

The first step in norm-based scoring consists of standardizing each SF-36 scale using a z-score transformation. A z-score for each scale is computed by subtracting the 1998 general U.S. population mean (Table 5.1) for each SF-36 scale and dividing the difference by the corresponding scale standard deviation (Table 5.1) from the 1998 general U.S. population. Formulas are listed below.

STEP 1. FORMULAS FOR Z-SCORE STANDARDIZATION OF SF-36 SCALES (STANDARD FORM)

PF_Z = (PF – 82.96845) / 23.83795
RP_Z = (RP – 77.93107) / 35.34865
BP_Z = (BP – 70.22865) / 23.35310
GH_Z = (GH – 70.10060) / 21.35900
VT_Z = (VT – 56.99917) / 21.12677
SF_Z = (SF – 83.56494) / 23.02758
RE_Z = (RE – 83.10276) / 31.64149
MH_Z = (MH – 75.21913) / 17.60698

Means and standard deviations are from Table 5.1.

TABLE 5.1 1998 GENERAL U.S. POPULATION MEANS AND STANDARD DEVIATIONS USED TO DERIVE SF-36 Z-SCORES (STANDARD FORM)

SF-36 SCALE	MEAN*	STANDARD DEVIATION
PHYSICAL FUNCTIONING	82.96845	23.83795
ROLE PHYSICAL	77.93107	35.34865
BODILY PAIN	70.22865	23.35310
GENERAL HEALTH	70.10060	21.35900
VITALITY	56.99917	21.12677
SOCIAL FUNCTIONING	83.56494	23.02758
ROLE EMOTIONAL	83.10276	31.64149
MENTAL HEALTH	75.21913	17.60698

*__Note__: The means and standard deviations for each SF-36 scale are based on the 0-100 scoring.

The second step involves transforming each SF-36 z-score to the norm-based (50, 10) scoring. This is accomplished by multiplying each z-score from Step 1 by 10 and adding the resulting product to 50. Formulas are listed below.

STEP 2. NORM-BASED TRANSFORMATION OF SF-36 Z-SCORES (STANDARD FORM):

Norm-Based PF: PF = 50 + (PF_Z * 10)
Norm-Based RP: RP = 50 + (RP_Z * 10)
Norm-Based BP: BP = 50 + (BP_Z * 10)
Norm-Based GH:GH = 50 + (GH_Z * 10)
Norm-Based VT: VT = 50 + (VT_Z * 10)
Norm-Based SF: SF = 50 + (SF_Z * 10)
Norm-Based RE: RE = 50 + (RE_Z * 10)
Norm-Based MH: MH = 50 + (MH_Z * 10)

Scoring Checks

Because of errors in reproducing a form, entering data, programming or processing, which can lead to inaccurate scale scores, we strongly recommend formal scoring checks prior to using the scales. Any discrepancies observed during the following checks should be investigated for scoring errors:

1. Calculate SF-36 scale scores by hand for several respondents and compare the results to those produced by your scale scoring computer software.

2. After items have been coded into their final item values, inspect the frequency distributions for the items to verify that only the final item values shown in Tables 6.1 through 6.8 in the SF-36 Manual and Interpretation Guide are observed. Discrepancies should be limited to respondents with values estimated for missing data as described in the manual.

3. After items have been recoded and scale scores have been computed, inspect the correlation between each scale and its component items to verify that all correlations are positive in direction and substantial in magnitude (0.30 or higher).

4. Check correlations between the General Health scale and the other seven scales to verify that all are positive; with rare exceptions they should also be substantial in magnitude (0.30 or higher).

5. For those familiar with principal factor or components analysis, inspect correlations between the eight scales and the first un-rotated factor or component extracted from the correlations among those scales. Regardless of extraction method, these correlations should be positive and substantial in magnitude (0.30 or higher).

Norm-Based Scoring Of Scale Scores, Acute Form (1-Week Recall)

After scoring the acute version SF-36 scales on a 0-100 scale, the next step involves the norm-based scoring (50/10) using the formulas shown below. Table 5.2 provides the information necessary to apply these formulas to each SF-36 scale from the Acute form (1 week recall). The means and standard deviations (Table 5.2) used in norm-based scoring come from the 1998 general U.S. population. A linear z-score transformation is used so that all eight SF-36 scales have a mean of 50 and a standard deviation of 10 in the 1998 general U.S. population.

The advantages of the norm-based scoring of the standard recall form above also apply to the acute version. The methods for transforming 0-100 scores on the acute scales to norm-based scores are also similar to those used for the standard form. The first step in norm-based scoring consists of standardizing each SF-36 scale using a z-score transformation. A z-score for each scale is computed by subtracting the 1998 general U.S. population mean (Table 5.2) for each acute form SF-36 scale and dividing the difference by the corresponding scale standard deviation (Table 5.2) from the 1998 general U.S. population. Formulas are listed below.

STEP 1. FORMULAS FOR Z-SCORE STANDARDIZATION OF SF-36 SCALES (ACUTE FORM)

PF_Z = (PF –82.34934) / 24.55363
RP_Z = (RP – 78.37950) / 35.25259
BP_Z = (BP – 73.37809) / 24.09701
GH_Z = (GH – 70.69938) / 21.60431
VT_Z = (VT – 57.64847) / 21.81907
SF_Z = (SF – 85.61860) / 22.83605
RE_Z = (RE – 82.44273) / 32.52898
MH_Z = (MH – 76.23511) / 17.25352

Means and standard deviations are from Table 5.2.

TABLE 5.2 1998 GENERAL U.S. POPULATION MEANS AND STANDARD DEVIATIONS USED TO DERIVE SF-36 Z-SCORES (ACUTE FORM)

SF-36 SCALE	MEAN*	SD
PHYSCIAL FUNCTIONING	82.34934	24.55363
ROLE PHYSICAL	78.37950	35.25259
BODILY PAIN	73.37809	24.09701
GENERAL HEALTH	70.69938	21.60431
VITALITY	57.64847	21.81907
SOCIAL FUNCTIONING	85.61860	22.83605
ROLE EMOTIONAL	82.44273	32.52898
MENTAL HEALTH	76.23511	17.25352

*__Note__: The means and standard deviations for each SF-36 scale are based on the 0-100 scoring.

Step 2. Norm-Based Transformation Of SF-36 Z-Scores (Acute Form)

The second step involves transforming each SF-36 z-score from Step 1 to the norm-based (50, 10) scoring. This is accomplished by multiplying each z-score by 10 and adding the resulting product to 50. Formulas are listed below.

STEP 2. NORM-BASED TRANSFORMATION OF SF-36 Z-SCORES (ACUTE FORM):

Norm-Based PF: PF = 50 + (PF_Z * 10)
Norm-Based RP: RP = 50 + (RP_Z * 10)
Norm-Based BP: BP = 50 + (BP_Z * 10)
Norm-Based GH: GH = 50 + (GH_Z * 10)
Norm-Based VT: VT = 50 + (VT_Z * 10)
Norm-Based SF: SF = 50 + (SF_Z * 10)
Norm-Based RE: RE = 50 + (RE_Z * 10)
Norm-Based MH: MH = 50 + (MH_Z * 10)

Scoring Checks

Because of errors in reproducing a form, entering data, programming or processing, which can lead to inaccurate scale scores, we strongly recommend formal scoring checks prior to using the scales. Any discrepancies observed during the following checks should be investigated for scoring errors.

1. Calculate SF-36v2 scale scores by hand for several respondents and compare the results to those produced by your scale scoring computer software.

2. After items have been coded into their final item values, inspect the frequency distributions for the items to verify that only the final item values shown in Tables 6.1 through 6.8 in the SF-36 Manual and Interpretation Guide are observed. Discrepancies should be limited to respondents with values estimated for missing data as described in the manual.

3. After items have been recoded and scale scores have been computed, inspect the correlation between each scale and its component items to verify that all correlations are positive in direction and substantial in magnitude (0.30 or higher).

4. Check correlations between the General Health scale and the other seven scales to verify that all are positive; with rare exceptions they should also be substantial in magnitude (0.30 or higher).

5. For those familiar with principal factor or components analysis, inspect correlations between the eight scales and the first unrotated factor or component extracted from the correlations among those scales. Regardless of extraction method, these correlations should be positive and substantial in magnitude (0.30 or higher).

Chapter 6: Norm-Based Scoring For Physical & Mental Summary Measures

This chapter provides scoring instructions for the SF-36 physical (PCS) and mental (MCS) component summary measures. Scoring of the SF-36 PCS and MCS summary measures involves three steps. First, the eight SF-36 scales are standardized using means and standard deviations from the 1998 general U.S. population. Second, they are aggregated using weights (factor score coefficients) from the 1990 general U.S. population. These are the same weights as those used to score PCS and MCS from the SF-36 Version in the first edition of this manual (Ware 1994). Finally, aggregate PCS and MCS scores are standardized using a linear T-score transformation to have a mean of 50 and a standard deviation of 10, in the 1998 general U.S. population. Norm-based scoring of the standard (4-week recall) and acute (1 week recall) forms is presented separately.

General U.S. population statistics used in the standardization and in the aggregation of SF-36 scale scores are presented in Table 6.1 for the standard form and in Table 6.2 for the acute form. Note that for both standard and acute forms the same factor score coefficients are used to score PCS and MCS. To make sure that the original coefficients used in this scoring "recipe" have the same affect in 1998, as in 1990, 1998 variances are utilized. Detailed information including formulas for scale aggregation and transformation of scores are presented below. Formal checks using a test dataset available upon request (info@qualitymetric.com) can be performed to confirm the successful reproduction of PCS and MCS scales, as discussed later in the chapter. We strongly recommend these tests.

Importance Of Standardization

As with the 1998 NBS scoring of SF-36 scales, which are aggregated to score the summary measures, standardization of the scoring of the PCS and MCS scales is vital to their interpretation. Any changes in scoring of the SF-36 scales or the algorithms for the summary measures may compromise their reliability and validity. Changes in scoring may also invalidate normative comparisons, based on the 1998 norms documented here.

The methods documented here achieve 1998 scores that are a nearly perfect transformation of the 1990 scores. For scales and summary measures, NBS based on 1998 norms only shifts the score distribution to better reflect the health of the US population in 1998. Otherwise, 1998 scores have the same interpretations as 1990 scores.

Norm-Based Scoring Of PCS And MCS, Standard Form (4-Week Recall)

Standard form PCS and MCS scales are scored using norm-based methods. The means and standard deviations used in scoring come from the 1998 general U.S. population and the factor score coefficients come from the 1990 general U.S. population (Ware et al. 1994). A linear T-score transformation method is used so that both the PCS and MCS have a mean of 50 and a standard deviation of 10 in the 1998 general U.S. population.

The advantage of the standardization and norm-based scoring of the PCS and MCS is that results for one can be meaningfully compared with the other and their scores have a direct interpretation in relation to the distribution of scores in the general U.S. population. Specifically, all scores above and below 50 are above and below the average, respectively, in the 1998 general U.S. population. Because the standard deviation is 10 for both PCS and MCS measures, each one point difference in scores also has a direct interpretation. A one point difference is one-tenth of a standard deviation.

TABLE 6.1 1998 GENERAL U.S. POPULATION MEANS, STANDARD DEVIATIONS AND 1990 FACTOR SCORE COEFFICIENTS USED TO DERIVE PCS AND MCS SCALE SCORES, STANDARD FORM

			Factor Score Coefficients	
SF-36 SCALE	**MEAN***	**STANDARD DEVIATION**	**PCS**	**MCS**
PF	82.96845	23.83795	0.42402	-0.22999
RP	77.93107	35.34865	0.35119	-0.12329
BP	70.22865	23.35310	0.31754	-0.09731
GH	70.10060	21.35900	0.24954	-0.01571
VT	56.99917	21.12677	0.02877	0.23534
SF	83.56494	23.02758	-0.00753	0.26876
RE	83.10276	31.64149	-0.19206	0.43407
MH	75.21913	17.60698	-0.22069	0.48581

***Note**: The means and standard deviations for each SF-36 scale are based on the 0-100 scoring.

It should be noted that mean scores for most of the scales vary substantially form those from the 1990 norms. For those scales that have been changed in any way from 1990 to 1998, several explanations are being explored (e.g., sampling bias in the 1990 study, downward temporal trends in physical health). Regardless of the explanations, these differences underscore the importance of using up-to-date norms and also the importance of using the same normative data when equating Versions 1 and 2 of the SF-36. 1998 norms for both make these comparisons possible.

Steps In Scoring

Following the scoring of the eight scales according to the standard SF-36 scoring algorithms (0-100 scale) explained in the SF-36 Manual and Interpretation Guide (Ware et al., 1993, PCS and MCS are scored in three steps as explained below:

Standardization Of Scales (Z-Scores), Standard Form

The first step in computing PCS and MCS consists of standardizing each of the 8 SF-36 scales using a z-score transformation. This is the same as Step 1 used in the norm-based scoring of the 8 SF-36 scales explained in Chapter 5. A z-score for each scale is computed by subtracting the mean 0-100 1998 general US population score (see Table 6.1) for each SF-36 scale and dividing the difference by the corresponding scale standard deviation. Note that the SF-36 scales scored on the 0-100 scale are used in step 1. Norm-based SF-36 scale scores are not used in this step. Formulas are listed below.

STEP 1. Formulas For Z-Score Standardization Of SF-36 Scales, (Standard Form)

PF_Z = (PF – 82.96845) / 23.83795
RP_Z = (RP – 77.93107) / 35.34865
BP_Z = (BP – 70.22865) / 23.35310
GH_Z = (GH – 70.10060) / 21.35900
VT_Z = (VT – 56.99917) / 21.12677
SF_Z = (SF – 83.56494) / 23.02758
RE_Z = (RE – 83.10276) / 31.64149
MH_Z = (MH – 75.21913) / 17.60698

Means and standard deviations are from Table 6.1.

Aggregation Of Scale Scores (Standard Form)

After a z-score has been computed for each SF-36 scale, the second step involves computation of aggregate scores for the physical and mental components using the physical and mental factor score coefficients from the 1990 general U.S. population as given in Table 6.1.

Computation of an aggregate physical component score consists of multiplying each SF-36 scale z-score by its respective physical factor score coefficient and summing the eight products, as shown below. Similarly, an aggregate mental component score is obtained by multiplying each SF-36 scale z-score by its respective mental factor score coefficient and summing the eight products.

STEP 2. Formulas For Aggregating Scales In Estimating Aggregate Physical And Mental Component Scores (Standard Form)

AGG_PHYS = (PF_Z*.42402) + (RP_Z*.35119) + (BP_Z*.31754) + (GH_Z*.24954) + (VT_Z * .02877) + (SF_Z*-.00753) + (RE_Z*-.19206) + (MH_Z*-.22069)

AGG_MENT= (PF_Z*-.22999) + (RP_Z*-.12329) + (BP_Z*-.09731) + (GH_Z*-.01571) + (VT_Z*.23534) + (SF_Z*.26876) + (RE_Z*.43407) + (MH_Z*.48581)

Transformation Of Summary Scores

The third step involves transforming each component score to the norm-based (50, 10) scoring. This is accomplished by multiplying each aggregate component scale score by 10 and adding the resulting product to 50. Formulas are shown in step 3.

STEP 3. FORMULAS FOR T-SCORE TRANSFORMATION OF COMPONENT SCORES (STANDARD FORM)

Transformed Physical (PCS) = 50 + (AGG_PHYS * 10)
Transformed Mental (MCS) = 50 + (AGG_MENT * 10)

Norm-Based Scoring Of PCS And MCS, Acute Form

Acute form PCS and MCS scales are scored using norm-based methods. The means and standard deviations used in scoring come from the 1998 general U.S. population and the factor score coefficients come from the 1990 general U.S. population documented in the first edition of this manual (Ware et al. 1994). A linear T-score transformation method is used so that both the PCS and MCS have a mean of 50 and a standard deviation of 10 in the 1998 general U.S. population.

The advantage of the standardization and norm-based scoring of the PCS and MCS is that results for one can be meaningfully compared with the other and their scores have a direct interpretation in relation to the distribution of scores in the general U.S. population. Specifically, all scores above and below 50 are above and below the average, respectively, in the 1998 general U.S. population. Because the standard deviation is 10 for both PCS and MCS measures, each one point difference in scores also has a direct interpretation. A one point difference is one-tenth of a standard deviation.

TABLE 6.2 1998 GENERAL U.S. POPULATION MEANS, STANDARD DEVIATIONS AND 1990 FACTOR SCORE COEFFICIENTS USED TO DERIVE PCS AND MCS SCALE SCORES, ACUTE FORM

			FACTOR SCORE COEFFICIENTS	
SF-36 SCALE	MEAN*	STANDARD DEVIATION	PCS	MCS
PF	82.34934	24.55363	0.42402	-0.22999
RP	78.37950	35.25259	0.35119	-0.12329
BP	73.37809	24.09701	0.31754	-0.09731
GH	70.69938	21.60431	0.24954	-0.01571
VT	57.64847	21.81907	0.02877	0.23534
SF	85.61860	22.83605	-0.00753	0.26876
RE	82.44273	32.52898	-0.19206	0.43407
MH	76.23511	17.25352	-0.22069	0.48581

***Note**: The means and standard deviations for each SF-36 are based on the 0-100 scoring.

Steps In Scoring

Following the scoring of the eight scales according to the standard SF-36 scoring algorithms (0-100 scale) explained earlier in SF-36 Manual and Interpretation Guide (Ware et al., 1993), PCS and MCS are scored in three steps as explained below:

Standardization Of Scales (Z-Scores), Acute Form

The first step in computing PCS and MCS consists of standardizing each of the 8 SF-36 scales using a z-score transformation. This is the same as Step 1 used in the norm-based scoring of the 8 SF-36 scales explained in Chapter 5. A z-score for each scale is computed by subtracting the mean 0-100 1998 general US population score (see Table 6.2) for each SF-36 scale and dividing the difference by the corresponding scale standard deviation. Note that the SF-36 scales scored on the 0-100 scale are used in step 1. Norm-based SF-36 scale scores are not used in this step. Formulas are listed below.

STEP 1. FORMULAS FOR Z-SCORE STANDARDIZATION OF SF-36 SCALES (ACUTE VERSION)

PF_Z = (PF –82.34934) / 24.55363
RP_Z = (RP – 78.37950) / 35.25259
BP_Z = (BP – 73.37809) / 24.09701
GH_Z = (GH – 70.69938) / 21.60431
VT_Z = (VT – 57.64847) / 21.81907
SF_Z = (SF – 85.61860) / 22.83605
RE_Z = (RE – 82.44273) / 32.52898
MH_Z = (MH – 76.23511) / 17.25352

Means and standard deviations are from Table 6.2

Aggregation Of Scale Scores (Acute Form)

After a z-score has been computed for each SF-36 scale, the second step involves computation of aggregate scores for the physical and mental components using the physical and mental factor score coefficients from the 1990 general U.S. population as given in Table 6.2.

Computation of an aggregate physical component score consists of multiplying each SF-36 scale z-score by its respective physical factor score coefficient and summing the eight products, as shown in step 2. Similarly, an aggregate mental component score is obtained by multiplying each SF-36 scale z-score by its respective mental factor score coefficient and summing the eight products.

STEP 2. FORMULAS FOR AGGREGATING STANDARDIZED SCALES IN ESTIMATING AGGREGATE PHYSICAL AND MENTAL COMPONENT SCORES (ACUTE FORM)

AGG_PHYS = (PF_Z * .42402) + (RP_Z * .35119) + (BP_Z * .31754) + (GH_Z * .24954) + (VT_Z * .02877) + (SF_Z * -.00753) + (RE_Z * -.19206) + (MH_Z * -.22069)

AGG_MENT = (PF_Z * -.22999) + (RP_Z * -.12329) + (BP_Z * -.09731) + (GH_Z * -.01571) + (VT_Z * .23534) + (SF_Z * .26876) + (RE_Z * .43407) + (MH_Z * .48581)

Transformation Of Summary Scores

The third step involves transforming each component score to the norm-based (50, 10) scoring. This is accomplished by multiplying each aggregate component scale score by 10 and adding the resulting product to 50. Formulas are shown in step 3.

STEP 3. FORMULAS FOR T-SCORE TRANSFORMATION OF COMPONENT SCORES

Transformed Physical (PCS) = 50 + (AGG_PHYS * 10)
Transformed Mental (MCS) = 50 + (AGG_MENT * 10)

Missing Data Estimation

Results from ongoing evaluations of options to score PCS and MCS when a respondent is missing any one of the eight SF-36 scales has shown considerable promise. Evaluation of missing data rates across general and clinical populations has shown that 50% of those who have missing PCS and MCS scores are missing PCS and MCS because of missing data on one SF-36 scale. QualityMetric Incorporated's Missing Data Estimator (MDE) will enable you to score PCS and MCS with data for 7 of the 8 SF-36 scales. PCS and MCS scores from MDE have proven to be reliable and valid (Ware et al., forthcoming). Further efforts are underway to evaluate options for scoring PCS and MCS when more than 1 SF-36 scale score is missing. More information will be available at these websites www.sf-36.com and www.qualitymetric.com.

Until QualityMetric Incorporated's MDE is made available, it is recommended that component scale scores be set to missing if the respondent is missing any one of the eight SF-36 scales. To minimize the number of component scores missing, we recommend estimating each of the eight scale scores if half or more of the items are complete, as documented earlier.

Features Of PCS And MCS Scores

The PCS and MCS were constructed and scored to achieve a number of advantages, in addition to reducing the SF-36 from an eight-scale profile to two summary measures without substantial loss of information. Features of the PCS and MCS scores, including their reliability, confidence intervals (CI), skewness (percent ceiling and floor), and number of levels observed in the general U.S. population, are summarized in Table 6.3. These results confirm some of the theoretical advantages of the two summary measures as compared to the eight SF-36 scales, including a very large increase in the number of levels defined, smaller confidence intervals relative to each of the eight scales, as well as the elimination of both floor and ceiling effects.

TABLE 6.3 COMPARISON OF FEATURES OF SF-36 SCALES AND SUMMARY MEASURES, 1998 GENERAL U.S. POPULATION

		SUMMARY MEASURES	
	SF-36 SCALES[b]	PCS	MCS
Reliability	.84 - .95	.95	.93
95% CI (±)	12 – 17	4.5	5.2
% Floor	0.0 – 2.1	0	0
% Ceiling	2.1 – 60.2	0	0
# of Levels[a]	8 - 20	486	494

[a] Scores rounded to first decimal place
[b] Statistics are presented as the range of results found across the eight SF-36 scales (standard and acute forms) in the 1998 general U.S. population.

Scoring Checks

Because errors can lead to inaccurate scale scores, we strongly recommend formal scoring checks of SF-36 scales prior to computing the SF-36 component summary scales. These formal scoring checks are explained in full detail in the SF-36 Manual and Interpretation Guide (Ware et al., 1993).

The following scoring checks are also strongly recommended for the SF-36 component summary scales. Any discrepancies should be investigated for scoring errors:

Check correlation's between the eight SF-36 scales and the PCS and MCS scales. The PF, RP, and BP scales should correlate highest with the PCS and lowest with the MCS. The MH, RE, and SF scales should correlate highest with the MCS and lowest with the PCS. The GH and VT scales should correlate moderately with both physical and mental component scales.

Check the correlation between the physical and mental component summary scales. The correlation should be very low, generally lower than 0.30.

Scoring Exercise

The test data set for the SF-36 and SF-36V2 are available in electronic format to purchasers of this manual – by sending an email request to info@qualitymetric.com. QualityMetric Incorporated also offers a Scoring & Data Quality Analysis service (information available at www.qualitymetric.com).

Table 6.4 presents descriptive statistics for the eight SF-36 scales (0-100 and norm-based) and the physical and mental component summary measures from the test dataset for the standard form. Table 6.5 presents descriptive statistics for the eight SF-36 scales (0-100 and norm-based) and the physical and mental component summary measures from the acute form.

After scoring the test dataset, you should observe the same means, standard deviations, and minimum and maximum observed values as those presented in Table 6.4 for the standard form and in Table 6.5 for the acute form.

TABLE 6.4 TEST DATASET DESCRIPTIVE STATISTICS*: SF-36 SCALES AND SUMMARY MEASURES (N = 100), STANDARD FORM

		0-100 SCORES				NORM-BASED SCORES			
	NO. OF CASES	MEAN	STANDARD DEVIATION	MIN. VALUE	MAX. VALUE	MEAN	STANDARD DEVIATION	MIN. VALUE	MAX. VALUE
Physical Functioning	100	82.55	23.74	5	100	49.82	9.96	17.29	57.14
Role Physical	100	78.25	35.82	0	100	50.09	10.13	27.95	56.24
Bodily Pain	100	70.34	23.11	0	100	50.05	9.90	19.93	62.75
General Health	100	65.32	22.72	0	100	47.76	10.63	17.18	63.99
Vitality	100	58.22	22.36	0	94	50.58	10.59	23.02	70.35
Social Functioning	100	83.00	22.79	0	100	49.75	9.90	13.71	57.14
Role Emotional	100	80.33	35.17	0	100	49.12	11.11	23.74	55.34
Mental Health	100	73.74	22.15	0	100	49.16	12.58	7.28	64.07
Physical Component Summary (PCS)	100	N/A	-	-	-	49.76	9.78	20.92	63.12
Mental Component Summary (MCS)	100	N/A	-	-	-	49.34	11.70	8.67	63.46

*All descriptive statistics are rounded to the second decimal point.

TABLE 6.5 TEST DATASET DESCRIPTIVE STATISTICS*: SF-36 SCALES AND SUMMARY MEASURES (N = 100), ACUTE FORM

		0-100 SCORES				NORM-BASED SCORES			
	NO. OF CASES	MEAN	STANDARD DEVIATION	MIN. VALUE	MAX. VALUE	MEAN	STANDARD DEVIATION	MIN. VALUE	MAX. VALUE
Physical Functioning	100	77.75	27.44	0	100	48.13	11.17	16.46	57.19
Role Physical	100	71.25	39.79	0	100	47.98	11.29	27.77	56.13
Bodily Pain	100	69.85	24.42	0	100	48.54	10.13	19.55	61.05
General Health	100	68.75	22.42	5	100	49.10	10.38	19.59	63.56
Vitality	100	59.98	22.51	0	100	51.07	10.32	23.58	69.41
Social Functioning	100	84.88	23.52	0	100	49.67	10.30	12.51	56.30
Role Emotional	100	83.67	31.96	0	100	50.38	9.82	24.66	55.40
Mental Health	100	78.35	15.85	8	100	51.23	9.19	10.45	63.77
Physical Component Summary (PCS)	100	47.49	10.87	19.00	63.13	47.49	10.87	19.00	63.13
Mental Component Summary (MCS)	100	51.76	8.61	13.43	62.06	51.76	8.61	13.44	62.07

*All descriptive statistics are rounded to the second decimal point.

SF-36 algorithms have been made available to computer software vendors and other organizations providing scoring and analysis services for the SF-36. Look for the symbol below.

This symbol is your assurance that computer software products and data processing services produce results that are comparable with this Manual and with other normative data and interpretation guidelines for the SF-36 Health Survey.

Chapter 7: Reliability And Statistical Power

Reliability estimates for the PCS and MCS scales were calculated using data from the Medical Outcomes Study (MOS), the 1990 and 1998 general U.S. populations, and data from general population surveys in Denmark, France, Italy, Netherlands, Norway, Spain, Sweden, and the U.K. As documented below, reliability estimates based on both internal consistency and test-retest methods have been high, ranging from 0.89 to 0.94 for the PCS and from 0.74 to 0.91 for the MCS studies of patients in the U.S. and in general population studies across countries. While in previous studies of the eight SF-36 scales (McHorney, Ware, Lu, et al., 1994), reliability estimates were slightly lower for more disadvantaged study participants, PCS and MCS reliability estimates were similar for disadvantaged and more advantaged groups.

Background

Indices of reliability give an indication of the extent to which the scores produced by a particular measurement procedure are consistent and reproducible. A measurement procedure is reliable to the extent that items within the same scale give the same results or to the extent that an individual scores the same across repeated administrations of the scale (Nunnally & Bernstein, 1994). A reliability coefficient is an estimate of how much of the variation in a score is real or truth, as opposed to chance or random errors. For example, a reliability coefficient of 0.80 indicates that 80% of the total measured variance is true score. Suggested levels of reliability are 0.70 or greater for scales used in group-level analyses and 0.90 or greater for scales used in decisions at the individual level (Nunnally & Bernstein, 1994).

There are several methods that can be used to estimate reliability. Reliability can be estimated by correlating scores from one administration with scores from another (test-retest reliability), or by correlating scores and testing the equivalence of individual answers across alternative forms of an instrument (alternative forms reliability), or by examining the equivalence of responses within the same test from a single administration (internal consistency reliability) (Nunnally & Bernstein, 1994). Most studies to date have used the internal consistency method and Cronbach's coefficient alpha to estimate the reliability of SF-36 scales, although all three methods listed above have been used in one or more studies (Ware, Snow, Kosinski, et al., 1993; McHorney & Ware, 1995).

Estimation Of Reliability

Both test-retest and internal consistency methods have been used in estimating the reliability of the PCS and MCS scales. Because the PCS and MCS scales are a linear combination of eight scales measuring distinct health constructs, it is necessary to take into account the reliability of each scale as well as the covariances among them in estimating reliability using the internal consistency method (Nunnally & Bernstein, 1994). Using the covariance matrix of SF-36 scales from each sample, and the physical and mental factor score coefficients from the general U.S. population, reliability is estimated in the following steps: (1) each off-diagonal covariance is multiplied by the product of its respective factor score coefficient, summed, and multiplied by two (two sides of the matrix); (2) the observed score variance is calculated by multiplying each diagonal of the covariance matrix by the squared factor score coefficient; (3) total score variance is calculated by summing the products of steps one and two; (4) true score variance is calculated by multiplying each diagonal entry computed in step #2 by the respective SF-36 scale reliability; and (5) each component summary reliability is computed by subtracting the true score variance (step #4) from the observed variance (step #2) divided by the total score variance (step #3), the result of which is subtracted from one.

Summary Of Reliability Estimates

General Population

Reliability coefficients for the PCS and MCS scales have been estimated using the internal consistency method for respondents to general population surveys in ten countries (Denmark, France, Germany, Italy, Netherlands, Norway, Spain, Sweden, The U.K., and the U.S.). Table 7.1 summarizes these results. The sampling methods for these surveys and the characteristics of respondents are documented elsewhere (Ware, Keller, Gandek, et al., 1995). Return rates ranged from 62.5% to 83.1%. Table 7.1 also presents test-retest reliability estimates for PCS and MCS in the general U.S. and U.K. populations.

TABLE 7.1 RELIABILITY ESTIMATES FOR PCS AND MCS SCALES IN GENERAL POPULATION FROM TEN COUNTRIES

COUNTRIES	(N)	PCS	MCS
Denmark	4,084	.91	.85
France	3,656	.90	.88
Germany	2,914	.94	.87
Italy	1,483	.90	.86
Netherlands	1,771	.92	.89
Norway	2,323	.92	.89
Spain	9,151	.94	.90
Sweden	8,930	.92	.88
U.K.	2,056	.93	.88
U.S. (1990)	2,474	.92	.89
U.S. (1998) 4-week recall	1,982	.94	.89
U.S. (1998) 1-week recall	1,646	.94	.89
U.K. Test-Retest	180	.89	.80
U.S. Test-Retest	540	.87	.74

Internal consistency reliability coefficients ranged from 0.90 to 0.94 for the PCS scale and 0.85 to 0.90 for the MCS scale. These results suggest that the underlying two dimensions of health measured by the SF-36 Health Survey can be reliably scored for the purpose of summarizing SF-36 scale score data in general populations studied to date.

Test-retest reliability for an interval of two weeks between administrations has also been estimated using data from the U.K. (Brazier, Harper, Jones, et al., 1992). The correlations between scores from administrations two weeks apart were 0.89 for the PCS and 0.80 for the MCS (N = 180). In the U.S., these correlations were 0.87 and 0.74, respectively (N=540).

These data demonstrate that the component summary measures have reliabilities that generally equal or exceed those of the eight scales.

TABLE 7.2 RELIABILITY ESTIMATES FOR PCS AND MCS SCALES: MOS PATIENT SUBGROUPS (N = 3,445)

		N	PCS	MCS
TOTAL SAMPLE			.92	.90
AGE	<65	2456	.91	.91
	65 – 74	700	.92	.86
	75+	287	.91	.86
GENDER	Female	2126	.92	.90
	Male	1319	.91	.90
RACE	White	2625	.92	.90
	Black	481	.90	.88
	Other	221	.90	.89
EDUCATION	<8	209	.94	.89
	9 – 11	313	.93	.90
	12	1005	.91	.89
	>12	1791	.91	.91
POVERTY STATUS	Poverty	253	.93	.91
	Non-Poverty	2864	.93	.90
DIAGNOSIS	Hypertension	2089	.92	.86
	Diabetes	624	.92	.86
	CHF	216	.91	.88
	MI	107	.89	.84
	Clinical Depression	503	.92	.88
	Symptomatic Depression	785	.91	.87
DISEASE SEVERITY	Uncomplicated Medical	1136	.90	.85
	Complicated Medical	289	.91	.86
	Psychiatric and Medical	300	.89	.86

NOTE: Estimates based on internal consistency method (see text).

Patient Subgroups

The reliability of the PCS and MCS scales was also estimated using the internal consistency method for 23 subgroups of patients participating in the MOS and for the total MOS sample. These patients (N = 3,445) differed in socio-demographic characteristics, diagnosis, and disease severity, as defined elsewhere (McHorney, Ware, Lu et al., 1994). Table 7.2 summarizes these results. Estimates of reliability for the SF-36 component summary scale scores varied very little across the groups, with a range of coefficients from 0.89 to 0.94 for the PCS and from 0.84 to 0.91 for the MCS. Estimates of reliability tended to be higher for the PCS relative to the MCS. Minimum standards of reliability for purposes of group comparisons (r > .70) were satisfied in all 23 patient subgroups for both physical and mental component scales. Minimum reliability standards required for comparisons of individual patients (r > .90) were met in 21 out of 23 patient groups for the physical component scale and for one-third of the patient groups for the mental component scale.

General Population Subgroups

The internal consistency reliability of the PCS and MCS scales was also estimated for 12 subgroups of respondents from the general U.S. population sample. As shown in Table 7.3, reliability coefficients varied very little across the 12 subgroups, with a range of 0.90 to 0.94 for the physical component scale and a range of 0.85 to 0.89 for the mental component scale.

TABLE 7.3 RELIABILITY ESTIMATES FOR PCS AND MCS SCALES: GENERAL U.S. POPULATION SUBGROUPS (N = 2,474)

		N	PCS	MCS
TOTAL SAMPLE			.93	.88
AGE	<65	1757	.92	.87
	65 – 74	442	.93	.85
	75+	264	.91	.89
GENDER	Female	1414	.93	.88
	Male	1055	.93	.87
RACE	White	2077	.93	.88
	Black	223	.94	.85
	Other	174	.90	.88
EDUCATION	<8	215	.93	.88
	9 – 11	277	.93	.86
	12	820	.93	.89
	>12	1162	.92	.87

NOTE: Estimates based on internal consistency method (see text).

Minimum standards of reliability for group comparisons were satisfied for both component scales across all subgroups. Minimum reliability standards recommended for individual respondents were met for the physical component summary scale for all subgroups; and were approached, though not achieved, for the mental component summary.

Statistical Power

Statistical power, the probability that a difference will be found when there is one, is largely determined by features of the sample design, such as the effect size under study and sample size. Statistical power is also determined by measurement reliability, because noisy measures have greater error variance relative to systematic variance, and thus less statistical power. Results of previous studies (McHorney, Ware, Rogers, et al., 1992) have shown that measures that reliably define more levels of health are more precise in detecting differences between groups of patients differing in health. Since the PCS and MCS measures define *many* more levels of health than any of the SF-36 scales and have been shown to be as reliable or more reliable, one can expect them to achieve greater statistical power in detecting differences in physical and mental health, with some exceptions discussed in Chapter 8.

Tables 7.4 through 7.8 present estimates of sample sizes necessary to detect average group differences in the PCS and MCS scores equal to 1, 2, 5, 10, and 20 points. We relied upon formulas published by Cohen (1988) and variance estimates from general U.S. population studies in estimating these sample sizes. We estimated sample sizes for five different study designs beginning with the most powerful design, an experimental comparison between two randomly formed groups with comparisons between repeated assessments over time, to the least powerful, a simple comparison between two group means. A non-directional hypothesis (two-tailed test) with a false rejection rate of 5%, and with a statistical power of 80%, was assumed for all estimates.

In comparing these sample size tables to those presented for the eight scales in the *SF-36® Health Survey Manual and Interpretation Guide* (Ware, Snow, Kosinski, et al., 1993), one should keep in mind that the number of points used to define each difference are not comparable (in standard deviation units) between the components and the eight scales. For example, a 10-point difference represents one standard deviation unit for both the PCS and MCS, but only half to one-third that amount for each of the eight scales. Thus, 10 points, as measured by the PCS or MCS is comparable to approximately 20 points or 30 points as measured by each of the eight scales.

Experimental Studies

Tables 7.4 and 7.5 present sample size estimates for two experimental study designs: two randomly formed groups with repeated assessments and two randomly formed groups with post-intervention assessments only. The repeated measures experimental design and all other repeated measures designs discussed in the following section assume a correlation of 0.70 between administrations. This is a conservative assumption given that correlations for the PCS and MCS scales are 0.89 and 0.80, respectively, in a test-retest study (Brazier, Harper, Jones, et al., 1992). The MOS has observed correlations for the PCS and MCS scales of 0.73 and 0.69, respectively, between repeated administrations six months apart.

Table 7.4 presents sample size estimates for a two-group randomized groups experiment with repeated SF-36 measures. As this table illustrates, it takes many more subjects to detect a one-point difference than to detect a very large difference of 10 points. In comparison to the best SF-36 scales measuring physical (PF) and mental (MH) health, the component summary scales reduce considerably the number of subjects required to detect small and large differences. For example, a sample size of 1,364 subjects in each randomly formed group is required to detect a two-point difference ($p < 0.05$, 80% power) in the SF-36 PF scale, in comparison with a sample size of 201 subjects in each randomly formed group for the PCS scale. However, this comparison is misleading. Two points on the PF scale is much smaller than two points on the PCS, in standard deviation (SD) terms. Taking into account this difference, it would be more appropriate to compare the power of the PCS in detecting a one-point difference (i.e., 0.1 SD unit) relative to the power of the PF scale to detect a two-point difference, which is much closer to a difference of 0.1 SD units. More than 1,300 people per group would be required to detect a two-point difference in the PF scale and the two other best SF-36 physical health scales (RP, BP) (see Table 7.4, Ware, Snow, Kosinski, et al., 1993). A one-point difference (0.1 SD unit) in the PCS is detectable with 801 people per group.

TABLE 7.4 SAMPLE SIZES NEEDED TO DETECT DIFFERENCES BETWEEN POST-INTERVENTION SCORES OF TWO EXPERIMENTAL GROUPS WITH PRE-INTERVENTION SCORES AS COVARIATES

	NUMBER OF POINTS DIFFERENCE				
	1	2	5	10	20
Physical Component Summary	801	201	33	9	5
Mental Component Summary	801	201	33	9	5

NOTE: Estimates assume alpha = 0.05, two-tailed test, power = 80% (Cohen, 1988), and an inter-temporal correlation of .70.

Table 7.5 presents sample size estimates for comparisons between two experimental groups with post-intervention PCS and MCS measures only. Comparisons between the sample sizes in Table 7.5 and Table 7.4 reveal gains in statistical power from a repeated measures experimental design relative to one with post-intervention measures only. About twice as many subjects are required to detect the same difference in scores with a post-intervention design than with a repeated measures design. For example, 1,571 subjects are required to detect the smallest difference (one point) in the PCS and MCS scores in Table 7.5 compared with only 801 subjects in Table 7.4.

TABLE 7.5 SAMPLE SIZES NEEDED TO DETECT DIFFERENCES BETWEEN TWO EXPERIMENTAL GROUPS, POST-INTERVENTION SCORES ONLY

	NUMBER OF POINTS DIFFERENCE				
	1	2	5	10	20
Physical Component Summary	1571	393	64	17	5
Mental Component Summary	1571	393	64	17	5

NOTE: Estimates assume alpha = 0.05, two-tailed test, power = 80% (Cohen, 1988), and an inter-temporal correlation of .70.

Non-Experimental Studies

Tables 7.6 to 7.8 present sample size estimates for three non-experimental comparisons involving SF-36 component summary scales: (1) comparisons between two self-selected groups with administrations before and after intervention(s) (Table 7.6); (2) repeated measures over time for a single group (Table 7.7); and (3) a comparison between a group mean score and a fixed score, such as the general population norm (Table 7.8).

The sample size estimates in Table 7.6 for a non-experimental, two-group study with repeated measures assumes that difference scores will be analyzed to maximize the internal validity of the study design. Comparisons between the sample sizes presented in Table 7.6 and Table 7.4 illustrate the power gained from an experimental versus a non-experimental two-group comparison. The power gained is approximately 29% for the smallest difference (one point) in the PCS and MCS scores.

Table 7.7 presents the sample sizes required to detect differences in the PCS and MCS scores over time within one group. As Table 7.7 illustrates, the sample size required to detect a change in the PCS and MCS scale scores over time within one group is smaller than the sample sizes required in the other study designs. However, the results are more difficult to interpret than the results for study designs that compare scores between two groups receiving different interventions (Cook & Campbell, 1979).

Estimates of sample sizes required to compare average PCS and MCS scores to a fixed norm, such as the general population, are presented in Table 7.8. As illustrated, a difference of five points on the PCS and MCS scales between a sample mean and a norm can be detected with only 32 subjects in the sample, compared with 197 subjects for a difference of two points. These estimates of sample sizes are less than those required for most of the SF-36 scales for similar comparisons (in terms of SD units). For example, to detect a 10-point difference in a PF scale score (i.e., one-half SD unit) between a sample and a norm requires 44 subjects.

Power Advantages Of PCS And MCS

Comparable effect size comparisons between the sample sizes needed to detect differences with the eight SF-36 scales, as compared to the PCS and MCS scales show a consistent advantage of the summaries. This is due to the summaries' generally higher or equal reliabilities in combination with the increased precision from defining many more scale levels. The power advantage of the components relative to the eight scales will be largest for SF-36 scales with the highest standard deviations (e.g., RP, RE) and less for others (e.g., MH, GH, VT). However, these analyses have not addressed another important consideration, namely, validity (see Chapter 8). It is also important to keep in mind that comparisons between SF-36 scales and the PCS and MCS should be made in comparable units, taking into account differences in their standard deviations.

TABLE 7.6 SAMPLE SIZES NEEDED TO DETECT DIFFERENCES BETWEEN TWO SELF-SELECTED GROUPS, REPEATED MEASURES DESIGN

	NUMBER OF POINTS DIFFERENCE				
	1	2	5	10	20
Physical Component Summary	1122	281	46	12	4
Mental Component Summary	1122	281	46	12	4

TABLE 7.7 SAMPLE SIZES NEEDED TO DETECT DIFFERENCES OVER TIME WITHIN ONE GROUP

	NUMBER OF POINTS DIFFERENCE				
	1	2	5	10	20
Physical Component Summary	561	140	23	6	2
Mental Component Summary	561	140	23	6	2

TABLE 7.8 SAMPLE SIZES NEEDED TO DETECT DIFFERENCES BETWEEN A GROUP MEAN AND A FIXED NORM

	NUMBER OF POINTS DIFFERENCE				
	1	2	5	10	20
Physical Component Summary	786	197	32	9	3
Mental Component Summary	786	197	32	9	3

NOTE: Estimates assume alpha = 0.05, two-tailed test, power = 80% (Cohen, 1988), and an inter-temporal correlation of .70.

Confidence Intervals For Individual Scores

Confidence intervals provide valuable information about the amount of fluctuation that can be expected in a single score due to measurement error. A confidence interval around an individual score is a function of the standard deviation (SD) of the score distribution and the standard error of measurement (SEM). The size of the SEM is a function of the reliability of that score (Nunn ally, 1978).

Two attributes of the SF-36 PCS and MCS scales (relatively small standard deviations and high reliability) lead to reductions in confidence intervals around individual scores of about one-half to one-fifth relative to those for the eight SF-36 scales. With smaller confidence intervals, fluctuations in an individual patient score due to chance are less likely, facilitating their use in monitoring individual patients in clinical practice.

Table 7.9 compares estimates of confidence intervals for the eight SF-36 scales and the PCS and MCS scales for an individual respondent's score. These estimates are based on the reliability and standard deviation (SD) of each scale in the general U.S. population. If either the reliability or SD varies substantially in a sample, confidence intervals should be re-estimated using published formulas (e.g., Nunn ally & Bernstein, 1994). It is also important to keep in mind that estimates of confidence intervals are not always symmetrical around the *observed* score.

The confidence intervals in Table 7.9 can be used to take into account fluctuations due to measurement error when interpreting scores for one patient or other respondents. Intervals for three levels of confidence are presented in Table 7.9: 68% (1 SEM), 90% (1.64 SEM), and 95% (2 SEM). Examples of how confidence intervals can be used to interpret individual scores are presented below. Appendix D presents norms for changes in scores for patients participating in the MOS. Chapter 12 discusses their use in clinical practice.

According to Table 7.9, individual patient scores on the PCS and MCS would be expected to fall within 2.8 and 3.2 points, respectively, about 68% of the time. To be much more certain about an individual's PCS and MCS score, use the 95% confidence interval, which is 5.7 points for the PCS and 6.3 points for the MCS. Compared to the SF-36 scales, the PCS and MCS scales make it possible to monitor the scores of individual patients with a much higher degree of confidence. As discussed in the preceding section, however, the gains are not as large (in SD units) as they appear to be.

TABLE 7.9 CONFIDENCE INTERVALS FOR INDIVIDUAL PATIENT SCORES

SCALE	LABEL	CONFIDENCE INTERVALS (CI) 68%[a]	90%[b]	95%[c]
Physical Functioning	PF	2.4	4.0	4.8
Role Physical	RP	3.3	5.4	6.5
Bodily Pain	BP	3.1	5.2	6.1
General Health	GH	4.0	6.5	7.8
Vitality	VT	3.4	5.7	6.7
Social Functioning	SF	3.7	6.0	7.3
Role Emotional	RE	4.1	6.7	8.0
Mental Health	MH	3.9	6.3	7.6
Physical Component Summary	PCS	2.4	4.0	4.8
Mental Component Summary	MCS	3.3	5.4	6.5

A 68% CI equals 1 SEM

b 90% CI equals 1.64 SEM

c 95% CI equals 2 SEM

NOTE: These estimates are based on reliability estimates and standard deviations for SF-36 scales and the PCS and MCS in the 1998 general U.S. population.

Individual scores on the PCS and MCS can be compared to general U.S. population norms or to norms for diagnostic groups by using the confidence levels presented in Table 7.9. Suppose that a clinician wanted to know whether a PCS score of 44 for a 40-year-old male patient was below that of the general U.S. population. Because the mean and SD are 50 and 10, respectively, for the PCS in the general U.S. population, it is obvious that the patient is well below the norm. Using the norms presented in Table 14.5 for males age 40, it is apparent that a score of 44 is well below the norm of 52.1 for a 40-year-old male in the general U.S. population (52.1 - 44 = 8.1). Because 8.1 is greater than the 95% confidence interval of 5.7 (from Table 5.9), the clinician can be confident that the patient's score of 44 is below the norm for men of a similar age in the general U.S. population, more than would be expected due to measurement error. These examples and other considerations are discussed in Chapter 12.

Chapter 8: Empirical Validation

Studies of validity are about the meaning of scores and whether or not they have their intended interpretations. The methods we have used in studies of the SF-36 have followed guidelines recommended for use in validating psychological and educational measures by the American Psychological Association, the American Educational Research Association, and the National Council on Measurement in Education (American Psychological Association, 1985). The same methods were used to study validity and to establish interpretation guidelines for the eight SF-36 scales, as discussed in the original *SF-36® User's Manual* (Ware, Snow, Kosinski, et al., 1993). That manual explains the methods, beginning with comparisons of the content of the SF-36 with other widely used measures. The content analysis, which has been subsequently updated and extended (Ware, 1995) revealed that the SF-36 includes eight of the health concepts most frequently represented in widely used health status measures. The SF-36 differs from most other measures in that it attempts to represent a wider range of levels for most of those concepts.

This chapter is divided into three sections, beginning with a summary of results from the first published tests of the validity of the PCS and MCS scales relative to the eight-scale SF-36 profile. The PCS and MCS scales performed in the 80-100 percent range relative to the best SF-36 scale in empirical tests of validity. These results, which are summarized elsewhere, (Ware, Kosinski, Bayliss, et al., 1995), constitute strong support of the usefulness of the PCS and MCS in summarizing and interpreting results. Detailed results, including nine tables not previously published, are presented here.

The second section extends the empirical evaluation of the validity of the PCS and MCS scales by replicating the original "four-group" tests that demonstrated the validity of the eight SF-36 scales in discriminating among MOS patient groups known to differ in severity of physical and/or mental condition, as defined clinically (McHorney, Ware, & Raczek, 1993). When the same tests were applied to the PCS and MCS, the summary scales never missed a difference captured by an SF-36 scale and performed in the 70-100 percent range in tests of empirical validity, relative to the best SF-36 scale. These tests call attention to the tradeoffs involved with the simplicity of two summary measures relative to the richness of the eight-scale SF-36 profile.

A third section summarizes results of correlational analyses of the validity of the PCS and MCS in relation to 33 health status scales and summary scales developed during the course of the MOS (Stewart & Ware, 1992) and measures of the frequency of 19 specific symptoms in four categories (Ware, Snow, Kosinski, et al., 1993). These results provide information useful in deciding which measures are most likely to add information beyond what can be known from the two summary measures, and demonstrate the sensitivity of the PCS and/or MCS to most specific symptoms.

Initial Validation Studies

The first round of validation studies of the two summary measures focused on their empirical validity relative to that of the profile of eight scales constructed from the SF-36. Although there has been some debate regarding the tradeoffs involved with these two approaches (Ware, 1984; Bergner & Rothman, 1987; Patrick & Erickson, 1993), their implications have not been explored empirically, with two exceptions based on single criteria (Katz, Larson, Phillips, et al., 1992; Beaton, Bombardier, & Hogg-Johnson, 1994). To evaluate these tradeoffs, we used the logic of "known groups" validity (Kerlinger, 1964) and defined "criterion" groups of patients differing in ways that impact on physical or mental health status. To test the generalizability of results, 16 tests were performed involving both cross-sectional and longitudinal study designs. Results are presented elsewhere and are summarized here; nine tables of specific findings not included in the original publication are appended (see Appendix B).

Comparisons between the summary measures and the SF-36 eight-scale profile were designed to approximate as closely as possible their intended use and circumstances that might affect conclusions. Several considerations guided selection of criteria used in defining groups reported here: (a) a strong theoretical foundation for hypotheses, including both direction of differences and whether physical or mental dimensions of health should be most affected; and (b) replication across both cross-sectional and longitudinal designs. Conclusions about different methods should be based on multiple tests. Criteria known to involve physical more than mental health differences, as well as the reverse pattern, were selected. Finally, data from both cross-sectional and longitudinal study designs were analyzed. Although measures that do best in discriminating the effects of differences at a point in time should also be most responsive to the impact of those changes over time, this principal has been questioned (Guyatt, Walter, & Norman, 1987).

Seven categories of comparisons were performed, involving groups of patients differing in: (1) presence of chronic medical conditions (four conditions); (2) severity of hypertension (two levels), diabetes (four levels), and severity of congestive heart failure (two levels); (3) the presence of any one of 16 comorbid conditions (and a count of 10 others); (4) frequency of acute symptoms in four clusters (ear, nose, and throat (ENT), central nervous system (CNS), musculoskeletal, and gastrointestinal and genitourinary (GI/GU)); (5) cross-sectional and longitudinal comparisons of age effects among the most well group available, patients with uncomplicated hypertension; (6) longitudinal comparisons of patients classified at one-year follow-up according to self-reported changes in physical, mental, and general health status (five categories each); and (7) cross-sectional comparison of patients with and without clinical depression and longitudinal comparison of patients recovering from depression. All tests were based on clinical data used in previous MOS reports (Wells, Hays, Burnam, et al., 1989; Wells, Stewart, Hays, et al., 1989; Kravitz, Greenfield, Rogers, et al., 1992; McHorney, Ware, & Raczek, 1993). Specific clinical definitions are documented in Appendix A.

Hypotheses

A strong theoretical foundation for generating hypotheses makes it easier to draw conclusions about measurement validity (Kerlinger, 1964). The result that would be expected for a valid measure must be known in advance for each test. We hypothesized that: (a) patients with more severe conditions, such as congestive heart failure, would score worse, particularly in physical health, than those with uncomplicated hypertension; (b) patients at more advanced levels of disease severity or with comorbid conditions would score lower; (c) scores would be lower for patients reporting a greater frequency of acute symptoms; (d) self-reported changes in physical, mental, and general health at one-year follow-up would be most related to changes estimated from repeated measures of the same concepts; (e) physical health (but not mental health) would decline with age; and (f) mental health would be better for patients without clinical depression and improve with clinical recovery from major depression.

Analysis Plan

Analyses of groups in the first three categories used ordinary least squares multiple regression techniques (SAS Institute, 1989) with statistical adjustment for differences in age, gender, race, poverty, study site, health care setting, and season of the year, to maintain comparability with previous MOS analyses (Wells, Burnam, Rogers, et al., 1992; Rogers, Wells, Meredith, et al., 1993). Longitudinal analyses and other cross-sectional analyses used the same statistical methods but without adjustments for baseline patient characteristics. All analyses of SF-36 profiles used multivariate analysis of variance (MANOVA) (Stevens, 1992), which provides an overall test of whether average scores (cross-sectional) or average changes in scores (longitudinal) for any of the eight SF-36 scales differed across any of the groups being compared. For those tests that yielded a significant MANOVA F-ratio, regression models were estimated to test the relative validity (RV) of each scale. Thus, according to this convention, only those scales that met two statistical criteria were considered valid: (a) significant overall MANOVA F for the set of criterion variables (defining patient groups) in relation to the profile of eight scales; and (b) significant univariate F for the same set of criterion variables and the scale in question.

To estimate the RV for each scale in relation to the best of the eight SF-36 scales, ratios of F-statistics were compared as in previous MOS studies (McHorney, Ware, & Raczek, 1993). The F-statistic for each measure is a ratio of the variance in scores due to differences among independent groups or between repeated assessments for the same group, relative to the within group (error) variance. The F-statistic for a given measure in a given test would be larger when the measure yields a larger average separation in mean scores being compared and/or a smaller error variance. The RV estimate for each measure in each test indicates in proportional terms the empirical validity of the scale in question relative to the most valid scale in that test (Liang, Larsen, Cullen, et al., 1985; Winer, Brown, & Michels, 1991; McHorney, Ware, & Raczek, 1993).

When one measure performs exceptionally well, estimates (based on RV) of the usefulness of other measures sometimes appear relatively low to the point of being misleading (Ware, Snow, Kosinski, et al., 1993). Therefore, standardized estimates of effect size (ES) (Kazis, Anderson, &

Meenan, 1989) were also computed by dividing the average difference for each measure by the standard deviation (SD) for that measure, using SD estimates from the general U.S. population, as published elsewhere (Ware, Snow, Kosinski, et al., 1993).

Summary Of Results: First Round

Table 8.1 summarizes RV coefficients for the two summary measures and the eight-scale SF-36 profile across all 16 tests, as published elsewhere (Ware, Kosinski, Bayliss, et al., 1995). The first 12 columns include criterion variables defining differences in physical health, and the last three columns are tests for differences in mental health. (An exception is the ninth column (GI/GU symptom cluster) shown previously to impact most on mental health (Stewart, Greenfield, Hays, et al., 1989).) For each test, the "best" of the eight SF-36 scales (with the highest F-ratio) is labeled RV = 1.00 and is boldfaced. Horizontal lines in Table 8.1 distinguish SF-36 scales hypothesized to be most valid in measuring physical health (PF, RP, and BP) versus mental health (MH, RE, and SF). The two more general scales (GH and VT) are in the middle grouping. F-ratios for the eight-scale MANOVA

Tests are presented for each criterion, followed by results for the two summary measures (PCS and MCS). Blanks in Table 8.1 indicate a non-significant MANOVA F-statistic for the eight scales in that test or a non-significant univariate F-statistic for a particular scale in that test. RV coefficients were not estimated for measures with non-significant F-statistics.

The two summary measures did well in these tests relative to the profile of eight SF-36 scales. In comparisons that involved physical health "criteria" and yielded significant differences for any of the three physical scales (PF, RP, and BP), statistical conclusions based on the PCS agreed nine of nine times (RV coefficients for the PCS ranged from 0.20 to 0.89, median = 0.79).

Differences in either or both of the two "general" scales (GH and VT) were significant in 13 of the 16 tests, including five with RV = 1.00. In nearly all instances, the PCS and/or MCS also performed well. The PCS captured 12 of 13 of the significant differences captured by a general scale (range of RV coefficients 0.01 to 0.89, median = .72); the MCS detected 11 of 13 (RV = 0.03-1.47, median = 0.35).

The three best mental health scales (MH, RE, and SF) yielded one or more significant results in 13 of the 16 tests (RV coefficients ranged from 0.03 - 1.00, median = 0.40). For 12 of 13, the MCS also produced statistically significant results (RV = .03 - 1.47, median = .43). Some coefficients were low because both physical and mental tests were included. For the four mental health tests (three right-hand columns in Table 8.1 and GI/GU symptoms), RV was 0.98 - 1.00 for the MH scale. For the MCS in these four tests, RV's of 1.02, 1.03, 1.47, and 0.93, respectively, were observed.

Table 8.1 also documents instances in which statistical conclusions varied across analyses of profiles and summary measures. Effects of GI/GU symptoms detected by the PF and BP scales were missed by the PCS; they were detected by the MCS. PCS scores differed significantly across levels of severity of diabetes, but were missed by the eight-scale profile. Differences in the SF-36 profile were significant across levels of hypertension severity, but the univariate F-statistics were not significant for any of the eight scales.

Results from tests involving the severity of acute symptoms suggest that the validity of the two summary measures varies substantially across symptom clusters. For example, the impact of ENT symptoms was best detected by the PCS. The impact of the CNS symptoms was detected by both summary measures, with the MCS performing better than the PCS. Musculoskeletal symptoms were reflected in scores for both summary measures, with the PCS clearly more affected than the MCS.

TABLE 8.1 SUMMARY OF RELATIVE VALIDITY COEFFICIENTS FOR SF-36 PROFILES AND SUMMARY MEASURES, SIXTEEN COMPARISONS USED TO TEST VALIDITY

		SEVERITY OF DISEASE				SYMPTOM CLUSTERS				AGE DIFFERENCES		SELF-REPORTED CHANGE			CLINICAL DEPRESSION	
MEASURES	CHRONIC CONDITIONS	HYPER-TENSION	DIABETES	CHF	COMORBID CONDITIONS	EAR, NOSE & THROAT	CENTRAL NERVOUS SYSTEM	MUSCULO SKELETAL	GI/GU[a]	CROSS-SECTIONAL	LONGI-TUDINAL	PHYSICAL	GENERAL	MENTAL	CROSS-SECTIONAL	LONGI-TUDINAL
PF	.87***			1.00***	.57***	1.00***	.75***	.28***	.43*	1.00***	.62***	1.00***	.79***	.19***	.00	
RP	.43***			.82***	.44***	.32*	.36***	.27***		.42***		.39***	.40***	.11***	.05***	.23***
BP	.12*			.25*	1.00***		.23***	1.00***	.39*	.14**		.20***	.21***	.09***	.06***	
GH	1.00***			.82***	.87***	.42**	.38***	.11***		.08*	1.00***	.74***	1.00***	.39***	.07***	.16***
VT	.46***			.64***	.53***		1.00 ***	.13***			.41***	.30***	.49***	.34***	.24***	1.00***
SF	.21***			.27*	.25***		.44***	.08***	.82***			.61***	.65***	.53***	.58***	.52***
RE	.12*			.34**	.13*		.38***	.03***	.36*			.11***	.11***	.46***	.41***	.84***
MH	.12*			.25*	.30***	.91***	.84***		1.00***	.20***		.26***	.46***	1.00***	1.00***	.98***
MANOVA F 8 SCALES	6.61***	2.17*	NS[b]	3.42***	5.14***	3.57***	9.96***	3.07***	28.14***	7.65***	2.60**	9.35***	12.91***	10.97***	165.85***	4.89***
PCS	.71***		1.00*	.83***	.89***	.86***	.61***	.55***		.82***	.20**	.79***	.74***	.05**	.01*	
MCS				.24*	.13*	.51***	.86***	.03***	.93***	.35***		.18***	.29***	1.02***	1.03***	1.47***

Summary Of Results: Second Round

Tables 8.2 - 8.4 present unpublished analyses of tests of the validity of the PCS and MCS in discriminating among four mutually exclusive groups of MOS patients known to differ in severity of medical (physical) and psychiatric conditions. The top panels of Tables 8.2 - 8.4 repeat results from analyses of the eight-scale SF-36 profile in the same tests as reported elsewhere (McHorney, Ware, & Raczek, 1993), and the bottom panel extends the comparisons to include the PCS and MCS scales. Tables 8.3 and 8.4 add columns to standardize effect size (ES) estimates in addition to mean differences, F-ratios, and RV estimates. Data in the top panel differ in some instances from the previous publication due to slight improvements in the definitions of clinical status.

TABLE 8.2 COMPARISON OF MEANS FOR SF-36 SCALES AND SUMMARY MEASURES, MOS PATIENTS DIFFERING IN MEDICAL AND PSYCHIATRIC CONDITIONS (N = 1,150)

	COMPARISON GROUPS			
SCALE	MINOR MEDICAL (N = 697)	SERIOUS MEDICAL (N = 162)	PSYCHIATRIC ONLY (N = 242)	PSYCHIATRIC & SERIOUS MEDICAL (N = 49)
Physical Functioning	80.14 (0.8)	57.07 (2.1)	79.90 (1.5)	45.28 (4.1)
Role Physical	69.55 (1.4)	40.28 (3.1)	56.20 (2.5)	22.95 (4.5)
Bodily Pain	76.01 (0.8)	65.10 (2.0)	66.02 (1.5)	48.71 (3.5)
General Health	67.26 (0.7)	47.62 (1.7)	57.65 (1.4)	40.61 (2.5)
Vitality	62.19 (0.7)	47.45 (1.7)	44.28 (1.4)	37.41 (3.1)
Social Functioning	91.62 (0.6)	78.63 (2.0)	67.04 (1.7)	60.71 (3.7)
Role Emotional	84.12 (1.2)	72.63 (3.1)	45.04 (2.6)	44.22 (5.7)
Mental Health	82.06 (0.5)	77.18 (1.3)	54.01 (1.3)	54.67 (3.1)
Physical Component Summary	46.37 (0.4)	36.27 (0.9)	47.95 (0.7)	33.54 (1.4)
Mental Component Summary	54.29 (0.3)	52.23 (0.8)	37.62 (0.8)	41.69 (1.6)

NOTE: Table entries are means (standard errors), comparison groups are defined as in previous MOS validity studies (McHorney, Ware, & Raczek, 1993)

The results in Tables 8.3 and 8.4 largely replicate results and lead to conclusions similar to those from the first round of validity studies of the PCS and MCS. Comparisons between groups known (by clinical diagnosis) to differ from the minor medical group in terms of serious medical (physical) morbidity (the first set of columns in Table 8.3 and the second set of columns in Table 6.4) involve the most pure *physical* differences. In these tests, the PCS yielded very large differences (RV = 0.94 and 0.82) relative to the best SF-36 scale (GH and PF, respectively). In both of these tests, the MCS yielded significant, but small, group differences as well as small RV and ES estimates, as hypothesized (RV = 0.06, ES = 0.21 and RV = 0.05, ES = 0.41).

In the two validity tests involving relatively pure mental health comparisons (second set of columns in Table 8.3 and first set of columns in Table 8.4) large differences in group means, RV and ES estimates were observed for the MCS (RV = 1.06, ES = 1.67 and RV = 0.69 and ES = 1.05, respectively), relative to the best SF-36 scale (MH in both tests). In both tests for differences in mental health criteria, PCS yielded very small differences and RV and ES estimates in the first set (0.01 and 0.16, respectively) and insignificant differences in the second.

When physical and mental differences are confounded (third sets of columns in both Table 8.3 and 8.4), both the PCS and MCS revealed significant differences with large ES estimates (1.17 to 1.46 SD units), and with RV estimates ranging from 0.48 to 1.07, relative to the best SF-36 scale (SF and MH, respectively).

TABLE 8.3 SUMMARY OF CLINICAL VALIDITY TESTS INVOLVING MINOR MEDICAL PATIENTS

	SERIOUS MEDICAL vs. MINOR MEDICAL				PSYCHIATRIC vs. MINOR MEDICAL				BOTH SERIOUS MEDICAL & PSYCHIATRIC vs. MINOR MEDICAL			
	MEAN DIFFERENCE	ES[1]	F	RV[2]	MEAN DIFFERENCE	ES	F	RV	MEAN DIFFERENCE	ES	F	RV
PF	-23.06	0.99	130.19[a]	0.91	-0.23	0.01	0.02	0.00	-34.86	1.50	109.41[a]	0.64
RP	-29.27	0.86	83.36[a]	0.58	-13.35	0.39	23.72	0.04	-46.59	1.37	77.97[a]	0.46
BP	-10.91	1.29	10.90[a]	0.08	-9.99	0.42	35.40	0.07	-27.30	1.15	70.06[a]	0.41
GH	-19.65	0.97	144.00[a]	1.00	-9.60	0.47	44.62	0.08	-26.65	1.31	100.60[a]	0.59
VT	-14.75	0.70	69.39[a]	0.48	-17.91	0.85	139.24	0.26	-24.78	1.18	69.89[a]	0.41
SF	-13.00	0.59	71.91[a]	0.50	-24.58	1.08	315.04	0.59	-30.91	1.36	169.52[a]	1.00
RE	-11.49	0.35	16.48[a]	0.11	-39.08	1.18	243.67	0.46	-39.90	1.21	74.65[a]	0.44
MH	-4.88	0.27	14.36[a]	0.10	-28.05	1.55	530.38	1.00	-27.39	1.52	153.02[a]	0.90
PCS	-10.10	1.01	135.26[a]	0.94	1.58	0.16	4.45[c]	0.01	-12.83	1.28	80.82[a]	0.48
MCS	-2.06	0.21	8.24[b]	0.06	-16.67	1.67	561.69[c]	1.06	-12.60	1.26	110.46[a]	0.65

a P< .001 b p< .01 c p< .05

1 Effect Size (ES) = means difference/SD, where SD comes from the general U.S. population

2 RV = relative validity (see text)

TABLE 8.4 SUMMARY OF CLINICAL VALIDITY TESTS INVOLVING CHRONICALLY ILL PATIENTS

	PSYCHIATRIC AND SERIOUS MEDICAL vs. SERIOUS MEDICAL ONLY				PSYCHIATRIC AND SERIOUS MEDICAL vs. PSYCHIATRIC ONLY				PSYCHIATRIC vs. SERIOUS MEDICAL			
	MEAN DIFFERENCE	ES[1]	F	RV[2]	MEAN DIFFERENC E	ES	F	RV	MEAN DIFFERENCE	ES	F	RV
PF	-11.80	0.51	6.76[b]	0.11	-34.62	1.49	85.75[a]	1.00	22.10	0.95	82.62[a]	0.59
RP	-17.32	0.51	7.78[b]	0.13	-33.23	0.98	31.92[a]	0.37	15.92	0.47	16.00[a]	0.11
BP	-16.39	0.69	15.76[a]	0.26	-17.31	0.73	20.70[a]	0.24	0.92	0.04	0.14	0.00
GH	-7.01	0.34	4.28[c]	0.07	-17.05	0.84	25.00[a]	0.29	10.05	0.49	19.80[a]	0.14
VT	-10.04	0.48	8.12[b]	0.13	-6.87	0.33	4.20[c]	0.05	-3.17	0.15	2.10	0.01
SF	-17.91	0.79	18.23[a]	0.30	-6.33	0.28	2.40	0.03	-11.58	0.51	19.45[a]	0.14
RE	-28.41	0.86	19.36[a]	0.32	-0.82	0.02	0.02	0.00	-27.59	0.83	45.43[a]	0.32
MH	-22.51	1.25	60.37[a]	1.00	0.65	0.04	0.04	0.00	-23.17	1.28	140.66[a]	1.00
PCS	-2.73	0.27	2.31	0.04	-14.41	1.44	70.06[a]	0.82	11.68	1.17	105.06[a]	0.75
MCS	-10.54	1.05	41.47[a]	0.69	4.08	0.41	4.24[c]	0.05	-14.61	1.46	150.55[a]	1.07

a P< .001 b p< .01 c p< .05

1 Effect Size (ES) = means difference/SD, where SD comes from the general U.S. population

2 RV = relative validity (see text)

Advantages And Disadvantages Of PCS And MCS

The two summary measures reduced the number of statistical analyses to 32 from 128 (8 scales times 16 tests), illustrating their advantage in reducing the number of statistical comparisons. The summary measures proved to be very useful in most of these tests. In both cross-sectional and longitudinal tests, the PCS rarely missed a difference it was expected to capture, and it was the only measure to detect the impact of differences in the severity of diabetes.

The PCS consistently performed below the best physical health scale in the physical health tests, although usually with an RV □ 0.80, relative to the best of the eight scales. The simplicity of a single measure of physical health appears to go hand-in-hand with an empirical validity that is about 80% of that achieved by the best SF-36 scale. The MCS consistently performed as well as or better than the best scale in mental health tests. Thus, these analyses revealed little or no tradeoff involved in relying on the MCS in testing hypotheses about mental health.

The PCS and MCS were also expected to have an advantage in interpretation as physical versus mental health measures, respectively. Because most of the eight scales are substantially inter-correlated and most have complicated physical and mental factor content, most have more than one interpretation. Interpretation has been shown to be least complicated for the PF and MH scales and most complicated for the VT scale (McHorney, Ware, & Raczek, 1993; Ware, Snow, Kosinski, et al., 1993; see also Chapter 3). A difference or change in VT scores could reflect changes in physical or mental health or both. The problem this presents in interpretation was illustrated in the first round of validity studies (see Appendix B, Table B.1). Those studies revealed a large difference in average VT scores favoring patients with uncomplicated hypertension over those with CHF ($\Delta = 14.1$, $t = 5.97$, $p < 0.001$), a comparison of groups known to differ in physical health. The average change in VT scores for patients who recovered from clinical depression was also large ($\Delta = 14.4$, $t = 8.6$, $p < 0.001$). Are these differences in physical or mental health? Because the pattern of differences was the same for VT in both tests, it is not clear whether they have the same interpretation. However, the PCS and MCS produced different results suggesting that changes in physical and mental health were involved, respectively. The impact of CHF was significant for the PCS ($\Delta = 8.9$, $t = 6.96$, $p < 0.001$), but not for the MCS ($\Delta = 1.6$, $t = 1.55$, $p > 0.05$), suggesting a *physical* health difference. The MCS improved ($\Delta = 9.8$, $t = 9.42$, $p < 0.001$) with recovery from depression and the PCS did not ($\Delta = 1.4$, $t = <1$, $p > 0.05$), suggesting a *mental* health difference. These results illustrate an advantage of the PCS and MCS in interpreting health outcomes.

Correlations With Specific Symptoms

Table 8.5 presents correlations between the PCS and MCS and self-reported frequency of symptoms in the MOS. Symptoms were reported for the prior four-week period. Symptoms are grouped into four categories: (1) those correlating highly (0.30 or better) with the PCS only; (2) those that correlate 0.30 or better with the MCS scale; (3) those correlating 0.30 or better with both the PCS and MCS scales; and (4) symptoms correlating less than 0.30 with both the PCS and MCS. All table entries are product-moment correlations.

A number of overall patterns of results are apparent in Table 8.5. The symptoms most strongly associated with the PCS scores include shortness of breath, stiffness and pain in muscles, backaches or lower back pain, and chest pain. Correlations were highest with the MCS for headaches more than usual, waking up early/unable to sleep, and being dizzy when standing up. Other symptoms correlating highest with the MCS (lightheaded while on feet and feeling drowsy or sedated) also correlated equally highly with the PCS. It is interesting that the same four groupings of symptoms was formed when these criteria were applied to the PF and MH scales in analyses of these symptoms reported in the original *SF-36® User's Manual* (Ware, Snow, Kosinski, et al., 1993; Table 6.16).

Other correlations in the last category are noteworthy, including significant associations between the PCS and sudden weakness, urinating more than usual, acid indigestion after meals, and coughing that produced sputum. Sudden weakness and acid indigestion also correlated highest with the MCS.

The results presented in Table 8.5 are useful in speculating about the symptoms most likely to be underlying differences in the PCS and MCS scores. These results suggest that the PCS and/or MCS are sensitive to differences in self-reports of the frequency of a wide range of different symptoms, including all 19 symptoms shown in Table 8.5.

TABLE 8.5 CORRELATIONS BETWEEN THE PCS AND MCS AND SPECIFIC SYMPTOMS IN FOUR CATEGORIES

			COMPONENT SUMMARIES	
SPECIFIC SYMPTOMS	**MEAN[a]**	**SD**	**PCS[b]**	**MCS[b]**
Shortness of breath (climbing stairs)	1.89	1.2	-.55	-.19
Stiffness, pain in muscles	2.89	1.4	-.53	-.12
Backaches or lower back pain	2.41	1.4	-.42	-.16
Chest pains brought on by activities	1.48	0.9	-.40	-.18
Pins and needles in your feet	1.75	1.2	-.38	-.14
Dry mouth	2.16	1.3	-.37	-.26
Heart pounding or palpitations	1.58	1.0	-.32	-.27
Blurred vision	1.53	1.0	-.30	-.24
Headaches more than usual	1.69	1.1	-.23	-.38
Waking up early, unable to sleep	2.34	1.3	-.29	-.35
Dizzy when standing up	1.61	0.9	-.27	-.32
Lightheaded while on feet	1.63	0.9	-.38	-.32
Drowsy or sedated	1.87	1.1	-.33	-.38
Urinating more than usual	1.78	1.2	-.28	-.15
Sudden weakness relieved by eating	1.39	0.8	-.28	-.26
Acid indigestion after meals	2.20	1.2	-.25	-.25
Coughing that produced sputum	1.82	1.2	-.22	-.15
Trouble passing urine	1.22	0.7	-.15	-.14
Fainting or passing out	1.03	0.2	-.09	-.09

a 1 = never, 2 = once or twice, 3 = a few times, 4 = fairly often, 5 = very often

b Note: short form versions of PF, BP, and SF scales were used to construct the PCS and MCS

Correlations With Other MOS Scales

Correlations between the PCS and MCS scales and other measures of known validity can be useful in evaluating their validity. Table 8.6 summarizes previously unpublished associations for 33 measures studied in the MOS. These measures are grouped into 10 different categories. The labels used to identify them, as well as their construction and scoring, are documented elsewhere (Stewart & Ware, 1992, specifically in Chapter 20 [Tables 20-2 and 20-3, pp. 350-360]). It is important to keep in mind when interpreting this table that in many instances one or more SF-36 items are also included in the MOS measure being correlated with the PCS or MCS. The resulting correlations, which are inflated, are labeled in the table.

The correlations in Table 8.6 indicated how well the PCS and MCS scales reproduce longer-form measures (e.g., MHI 32) and how well they reflect measures not directly represented in the SF-36 (e.g., sexual functioning). The scoring of the MOS scales is indicated in parentheses after each variable name. As would be expected, correlations between unfavorably scored measures and the PCS and MCS, which are scored positively, are negative.

The entries in Table 8.6 can be very useful in judging the value of adding measures of other concepts to supplement the SF-36. For example, based on substantial correlations (0.53 to 0.63), it is clear that the PCS well reflects overall satisfaction with physical ability and mobility. Both the PCS and MCS correlate substantially with the summary of eight physical and psycho-physiologic symptoms measured in the MOS (-0.55 and -0.41, respectively).

Among the measures not included in the SF-36, the MOS cognitive functioning scale had a very high correlation with the MCS (r = 0.70). Also, variations in sleep, as measured by the MOS sleep problems index, correlate substantially with the MCS (r = -0.57). In contrast, correlations between the SF-36 scales and sexual functioning (problems) tended to be low. Given that the same pattern was observed for the eight SF-36 scales (Ware, Snow, Kosinski, et al., 1993), these results suggest that variations in sexual functioning are not well represented in the SF-36 scales. Thus, sexual functioning is a candidate for inclusion in a generic health battery designed to supplement the SF-36. Accordingly, two large NIH-sponsored clinical trials using the SF-36 to monitor outcomes of treatment for women at high risk of breast cancer and men with prostate disease supplement the SF-36 with the MOS Sexual Problems Scale (see Stewart & Ware, 1992).

TABLE 8.6 CORRELATIONS BETWEEN THE PCS AND MCS AND MOS FUNCTIONING AND WELL-BEING MEASURES

MEASURE		k^1	PCS^b	MCS^b
Physical Functioning	Satisfaction w/ Physical Ability (+)[2]	1	0.63	0.34
	Mobility (+)	2	0.53	0.23
Role Functioning	Role Limitations due to Physical Health (-)	7	-0.77	-0.34
	Role Limitations due to Emotional Problems (-)	3	-0.15	-0.81
	Unable to do Work due to Health (-)	1	-0.23	-0.06
	Unable to do Housework due to Health (-)	1	-0.23	-0.22
Social, Family, Sexual Functioning	Social Activity Limitations due to Health (+)	4	0.41	0.67
	Sexual Problems (-)	5	-0.13	-0.28
	Satisfaction with Family Life (+)	3	0.02	0.48
	Overall Happiness w/ Family Life	1	0.02	0.52
	Marital Functioning (+)	6	0.03	0.43
Psychological Distress/Well-Being	Anxiety (-)	6	-0.11	-0.78
	Depression/Behavioral-Emotional Control (-)	13	-0.07	-0.88
	Positive Affect (+)	7	0.12	0.83
	Feelings of Belonging (+)	3	0.02	0.38
	Psychological Well-Being (+)	10	0.09	0.81
	Mental Health Index (+)	32	0.09	0.90
	Mental Health Index II (+)	17	0.08	0.90
Cognitive Functioning	Cognitive Functioning (+)	6	0.18	0.70
Health Perceptions	Current Health (+)	7	0.65	0.45
	Prior Health (+)	3	0.36	0.14
	Health Outlook (+)	6	0.41	0.22
	Health Concern (-)	4	-0.22	-0.12
	Resistance to Illness (+)	4	0.28	0.32
	General Health Rating Index (+)	19	0.60	0.42
	Health Distress (-)	6	-0.45	-0.57
Sleep	Sleep Problems Index (-)	9	-0.34	-0.57
Pain	Effects of Pain (-)	6	-0.67	-0.38
	Pain Severity (-)	5	-0.61	-0.24
	Days Pain Interfered (-)	1	-0.56	-0.26
	Overall Pain Index (-)	12	-0.70	-0.34
Physical/Psycho-Physiologic Symptoms	Physical/Psycho-Physiologic Symptoms (-)	8	-0.55	-0.41
Quality of Life	Life Satisfaction (+)	1	0.11	0.68

1 K = number of items

2 (+) scale scores from low to high reflect positive status, (-) scale scores from low to high reflect negative status

a Correlations between scales and summary measures are not significant ($p < .05$)

b Correlation is inflated because measure includes one or more SF-36 items

Chapter 9: Interpretation: Content And Criterion-Based

Background

Traditional analyses of validity include empirical tests of "whether" and "how" valid a measure is, and results are most often expressed in terms of correlation coefficients. In contrast to such correlational analyses, analyses presented here were designed to yield interpretation guidelines for differences in PCS and MCS scores of specific amounts. Two kinds of results are presented. The first includes plots of responses to specific SF-36 items to establish content-based interpretation guidelines for differences throughout the range of PCS and MCS scores. The second includes results based on analyses of external "criteria," such as comparisons between groups differing in chronic conditions, and analyses using PCS and MCS scores to predict job loss due to health problems, utilization of health care services, and five-year mortality rates. Analyses of chronic conditions yield interpretation guidelines based on the hypothesized impact of specific conditions on PCS and MCS scores. Plots of results from predictive tests of validity yield interpretation guidelines based on the consequences of PCS and MCS scores and particularly the social relevance of differences in scores.

Content-Based Interpretation

Content-based interpretation guidelines are based on analyses of the content of SF-36 items as a way of understanding the meaning and interpretation of differences in PCS and MCS scores in between the extremes. This is accomplished by plotting specific item responses across levels of the PCS and MCS as they were plotted for the eight SF-36 scales (see Ware, Snow, Kosinski, et al., 1993 for a further discussion). For example, it is useful to know that about 90% of those within or below a PCS score of 40-44 in the general U.S. population report health-related limitations in their performance of vigorous physical activities.

Meaning Of High And Low Scores

Table 9.1 presents content-based descriptions of the health states associated with very high and very low scores on the PCS and MCS scales. These descriptions, which are based on the known contributions of the eight SF-36 scales to the definition of those health states (from Chapters 3 and 4), can be used in summarizing what the PCS and MCS measure.

Very high or very low scores for the PCS and MCS reflect a combination of physical and mental *function* and *well-being*, the extent of social and role *disability*, and *personal evaluation* of health status. The lowest state of health reflects substantial functional limitation, severe social and role disability, distress, *and* very unfavorable evaluations of health status and outlook. Very high scores are earned only in the absence of limitations, in the absence of disability in social or usual role activities, and with high levels of well-being and very favorable personal health evaluations.

TABLE 9.1 DESCRIPTION OF VERY HIGH AND VERY LOW PCS AND MCS HEALTH STATUS LEVELS

SCALE	VERY LOW	VERY HIGH
PCS	Substantial limitations in self care, physical, social, and role activities; sever bodily pain; frequent tiredness; health rated "poor"	No physical limitations, disabilities, or decrements in well-being; high energy level; health rated "excellent"
MCS	Frequent psychological distress, substantial social and role disability due to emotional problems; health in general rated "poor"	Frequent positive affect; absence of psychological distress and limitations in usual social/role activities due to emotional problems; health rated "excellent"

Although operational definitions are similar for some of the physical and mental health items, they are distinct both conceptually and empirically. The PCS reflects *physical morbidity* and *etiology*, whereas the MCS reflects *psychological or mental morbidity* and *etiology*. It is important to note that a very high PCS score requires more than freedom from physical limitations and social and role disability; it requires an evaluation of current health as "excellent." Likewise, the most favorable personal evaluation of health as "excellent" is not enough for a very high score; PCS scores are lower with limitations or disabilities in the physical spectrum, reflecting the consequences of such limitations and disabilities in physical health. The same logic is reflected in the scoring of the MCS. Both the PCS and MCS place high weights on both the personal and the social implications of different health states. For these reasons, the PCS and MCS are unique in their comprehensiveness as summary health measures.

How To Use These Tables

To facilitate the interpretation of tables of results presented in Chapter 9, the same format is used for all tables. This format is explained in detail for Table 9.2, which presents 10 content-based interpretation guidelines for scores at eight levels of the PCS scale. The range of scores defining each of the eight levels, the mean PCS score for each level, and the sample size are presented in the left-most columns. The eight levels represent five-point intervals throughout the range of PCS scores observed to date in the general U.S. population. Scores at the highest and lowest levels have been collapsed to maintain sample sizes above 100.

Content-based interpretation guidelines were prepared in several steps. First, items with good face validity, and representing scales most highly correlated with the PCS, such as the 10 items in Table 9.2, were selected from the SF-36. Second, responses to each item were dichotomized in a way that is meaningful and that reveals differences across levels of the scale in the score ranges of interest. Third, the percentage of responses to each dichotomous item at each PCS level being interpreted was estimated and plotted.

All table entries are percentages. The first pair of columns headed "%" presents the percentage of the general U.S. population (N = 2,474) at each level of PCS scale scores who reported any limitations in "vigorous activities." The second column in the first pair of columns, headed "Δ/Δ," presents "difference ratios," defined as the percentage point change in each "criterion" item associated with a one-point change in PCS scores, from one particular level to an adjacent level. For example, from level one to level two (an average change of about five on the PCS scale), limitations in vigorous activities increased by 8 percentage points, or about 1.6 percentage points for each PCS point (8.2/5.1 = 1.6). Comparison of difference ratios across levels of PCS illustrate that the vigorous activity item is most useful for interpreting differences in the PCS scores at the top levels, whereas "walking one block" is most useful at the lower levels.

When one or more scores being compared across levels are close to the extremes of the range defining a particular level, or where difference ratios vary inconsistently, it is necessary to interpolate, using the Δ/Δ column entries across adjacent rows. For example, a 3-point change in PCS in the 45-54 range is associated with about 13.8% (3 x 4.6) change in the probability of a limitation in vigorous activities.

As hypothesized (Ware, Snow, Kosinski, et al., 1993), these scale scores have monotonic relationships with the variables used to establish validity and interpretation guidelines. Accordingly, the Δ/Δ columns nearly always reflect a smooth monotonic trend showing increasing and decreasing unit changes without inconsistent reversals. Most of the exceptions are apparent in Table 9.2. We have chosen not to collapse adjacent levels to "smooth out" these trends because for nearly all other interpretation guidelines substantial information would be lost. Complete documentation makes it possible to choose the most appropriate way to interpolate in handling such situations. Numerous examples are explained in Chapter 9.

TABLE 9.2 PERCENTAGE OF ADULTS ENDORSING SELECTED SF-36 ITEMS AT EIGHT LEVELS OF PCS SCORES: GENERAL U.S. POPULATION

PCS SCORES				PHYSICAL LIMITATIONS						ROLE DISABILITY				PAIN		VITALITY				GENERAL HEALTH			
				1 Vigorous Activities		2 Walking 1 Block		3 Climbing Stairs		4 Difficulty at Work		5 Cut Down Worktime		6 Very Severe		7 Have Lot of Energy		8 Feeling Tired		9 Excellent Health		10 Fair/Poor Health	
LEVELS	RANGE	MEAN	(N)	%	Δ/Δ	%	Δ/Δ	%	Δ/Δ	%	Δ/Δ	%	Δ/Δ	%	Δ/Δ	%	Δ/Δ	%	Δ/Δ	%	Δ/Δ	%	Δ/Δ
1	60 - 73	61.9	157	20.0		0.6		0.6		0.0		0.0		0.0		40.1		10.2		47.4		1.9	
					1.6		-0.1		0.0		0.2		0.1		0.0		-4.1		0.9		2.6		0.0
2	55 - 59	56.8	691	28.2		0.3		0.6		1.2		0.4		0.0		61.2		5.5		34.2		2.0	
					7.5		0.1		0.6		0.7		0.8		0.2		2.7		0.3		4.6		0.7
3	50 - 54	52.3	565	61.9		0.9		3.2		4.4		4.1		1.0		48.9		6.7		13.4		5.3	
					4.6		1.5		1.9		2.4		1.1		0.2		3.0		0.4		1.8		1.5
4	45 - 49	47.3	304	85.1		8.2		12.9		16.6		9.5		2.3		33.9		8.6		4.3		12.8	
					1.2		1.8		2.9		6.0		3.0		0.3		1.7		1.1		0.0		1.9
5	40 - 44	42.2	194	91.0		17.3		27.7		47.2		24.9		4.1		25.3		14.5		4.2		22.3	
					-0.2		4.1		3.0		4.0		4.9		1.6		1.3		2.3		-0.1		3.0
6	35 - 39	37.1	161	89.9		38.4		43.2		67.5		49.7		12.4		18.7		26.1		3.7		37.5	
					1.1		1.2		4.7		4.2		3.1		1.8		1.8		2.3		0.7		4.6
7	30 - 34	32.1	131	95.3		44.5		66.9		88.5		65.1		21.4		9.9		37.4		0.0		60.5	
					0.3		4.2		2.8		0.7		1.9		3.1		0.5		0.9		-0.1		1.8
8	8 - 29	23.3	190	97.9		81.6		92.0		94.7		81.9		48.4		5.3		45.0		0.5		76.7	

NOTE: All table entries are percentages

KEY TO COLUMN DEFINITIONS

1 % any limitations in vigorous activities (PF01)
2 % any limitations in walking one block (PF09)
3 % any limitations in climbing one flight of stairs (PF05)
4 % reporting difficulty performing at work due to physical health (RP4)
5 % reporting cutting down amount of time spent on work due to physical health (RP1)
6 % reporting very severe or severe bodily pain (BP1)
7 % reporting having a lot of energy all or most of the time (VT2)
8 % reporting feeling tiered all or most of the time (VT4)
9 % reporting excellent health (GH1)
10 % reporting fair or poor health (GH1)

Vigorous Physical Activities And PCS

As shown in the first column of percentages, from 90-98% of those at the lowest four PCS levels (levels 5-8) reported limitations in vigorous physical activities. Across the four higher PCS levels (levels 1-4) these percentages decline from 85%, 62%, 28%, to 20%. Thus, a five-point increase in the PCS from the midpoint of Level 4 (45-49), which is just below the mean, to the midpoint of the next level (50-54) represents a substantial decline (from 85.1% to 61.9%) in the percentage who are limited in vigorous activities.

Walking One Block/ Climbing Stairs And PCS

The second and third pairs of columns of Table 9.2 present the percentage of the general U.S. population who are limited in walking one block and climbing one flight of stairs at each of eight levels of the PCS. The pattern of results across levels is similar for both items. At the bottom of the PCS range (levels 6-8) 38% - 82% reported limitations in walking one block and 43% - 92% reported limitations in climbing one flight of stairs. Very few respondents (3.2% or less) reported either limitation at the top of the range (levels 1-3 of the PCS scores). Thus, these two items appear to be most useful for interpreting and explaining differences in scale scores at the middle and lower levels of the PCS score distribution.

Role Disability And PCS

Pairs of columns numbered (4) and (5) present the percentage of the general U.S. population who reported difficulty performing at work and the need to cut down the amount of time at work because of physical health problems. For both items, these limitations were absent at the top levels of the PCS and were very prevalent at the bottom levels of the PCS.

Bodily Pain And PCS

Column (6) presents the percentage of the general U.S. population experiencing "severe" or "very severe" pain at each level of the PCS. At the bottom two levels of the PCS, 21% and 48% of the general U.S. population experienced severe or very severe bodily pain, whereas pain was more rare at the top levels of the PCS.

The percentages of the general U.S. population reporting "a lot of energy" and "feeling tired" all or most of the time at each level of the PCS are presented in the pairs of columns labeled (7) and (8). These results are most useful in interpreting the top and bottom of the PCS scale range, respectively.

Health Evaluations And PCS

Results in columns (9) and (10) show the percentage of the general U.S. population that evaluated their health as "excellent" versus "fair or poor" at each level of the PCS. "Excellent" evaluations are very rare except at the very top of the scale range. Evaluations of "fair" or "poor" increase progressively from the top to the bottom of the PCS scale range, reaching very high percentages at the bottom two levels of the PCS scale.

Table 9.3 presents data for eight SF-36 items used in content-based interpretations of nine levels of MCS scores. This table follows the same format as described above for the PCS (see How to Use These Tables, p. 67).

Downhearted/Blue And MCS

Column (1) of Table 9.3 presents the percentage of the general U.S. population feeling "downhearted or blue" all or most of the time at nine levels of the MCS scores. As illustrated, the downhearted or blue item clearly defines the bottom of the MCS scale: it is only at the lowest level of the MCS that a large percentage (44%) of respondents endorsed this item.

Feeling Happy And MCS

As shown in column (2) of Table 9.3, there is a more consistent increase in the percentage reporting being happy from the lower to the higher MCS scale levels (from 96.4% to 5.7%, lowest to highest).

Role Disability And MCS

Columns (3), (4), and (5) show the percentages of the general U.S. population reporting limitations of various kinds in everyday role activities *due to emotional problems*. For each of the items, there is a progressive increase in the percentage reporting limitations from the higher to the lower levels of the MCS scores. As the rate of increase diminishes at the higher levels, the Δ/Δ columns become smaller again, as would be expected.

Social Disability And MCS

Column (6) (Social) presents the percentage of the general U.S. population who report interference in usual social activities all or most of the time. At the bottom five levels of the MCS scale, 14.0% to 38.5% reported such limitations.

Feeling Tired/Having Energy And MCS

The last two pairs of columns in Table 9.3, (7) and (8), present percentages of the general U.S. population "feeling tired" and "having a lot of energy" all or most of the time at each level of the MCS. As with the role disability items, a systematic relationship between MCS scores and reports of tiredness and energy are apparent, with large percentages of individuals reporting tiredness at the lower MCS levels and large percentages of individuals reporting energy at the higher MCS levels.

TABLE 9.3 PERCENTAGE OF ADULTS ENDORSING SELECTED SF-36 ITEMS AT NINE LEVELS OF MCS SCORES: GENERAL U.S. POPULATION

MCS SCORES				DISTRESS/WELL-BEING				ROLE DISABILITY						SOCIAL		VITALITY			
				1 Downhearted Blue		2 Happy Person		3 Cut Down Worktime		4 Accomplished Less at Work		5 Worked Less Carefully		6 Activity Limitation		7 Tired		8 Lot of Energy	
LEVELS	RANGE	MEAN	(N)	%	Δ/Δ	%	Δ/Δ	%	Δ/Δ	%	Δ/Δ	%	Δ/Δ	%	Δ/Δ	%	Δ/Δ	%	Δ/Δ
1	65 - 74	67	28	0.0	0.0	96.4	-0.2	0.0	0.1	0.0	0.3	0.0	0.1	0.0	0.3	7.1	-0.6	64.3	-0.8
2	60 - 64	61.5	269	0.0	0.0	97.4	1.7	0.7	-0.1	1.5	0.1	0.4	0.1	1.5	0.2	3.7	-0.1	68.8	1.4
3	55 - 59	57.1	729	0.1	0.2	89.8	5.4	0.4	0.7	1.9	2.0	1.0	0.9	2.5	1.2	3.3	0.9	62.4	5.4
4	50 - 54	52.3	512	1.0	0.1	63.7	5.0	3.7	1.7	11.5	3.8	5.3	3.0	8.2	1.1	7.8	1.3	36.3	3.0
5	45 - 49	47.2	287	1.4	0.2	38.3	1.1	12.2	3.8	31.0	4.9	20.6	3.0	14.0	0.1	14.3	2.2	21.0	1.1
6	40 - 44	41.9	190	2.7	1.2	32.6	0.9	32.6	5.7	57.1	5.1	36.5	5.6	14.3	0.8	25.8	0.8	15.3	0.3
7	35 - 39	37.2	153	8.6	0.4	28.1	4.3	59.5	3.3	81.0	2.2	62.7	3.3	18.3	0.3	29.4	2.9	13.8	1.5
8	30 - 34	32.1	102	10.8	4.0	5.9	0.0	76.5	1.1	92.2	0.2	79.4	0.8	19.8	2.2	44.1	1.2	5.9	0.0
9	9 - 29	23.8	123	43.9		5.7		85.4		94.3		86.2		38.5		53.7		5.7	

NOTE: All table entries are percentages

KEY TO COLUMN DEFINITIONS

1 % Report being downhearted or blue all or most of the time (MH4)
2 % reporting being happy all or most of the time (MH5)
3 % cut down amount of time spent at work due to emotional problems (RE1)
4 % accomplished less than would like due to emotional problems (RE2)
5 % didn't do work as carefully due to emotional problems (RE3)
6 % physical or emotional problems interfere with social activities (SF2)
7 % reporting feeling tiered all or most of the time (VT4)
8 % reporting having a lot of energy all or most of the time (VT2)

Criterion-Based Interpretation

Criterion-based tests of validity are based on analyses of relationships between the measures in question and other variables, referred to as "criteria," measured either concurrently or after some period of time. Criteria relied upon here were chosen to be conceptually related to the PCS and MCS and, in the absence of a "gold standard," to provide the most useful interpretation guidelines. Specifically, these criteria include variables that: (1) were important both clinically and socially (e.g., clinical diagnosis and job loss, respectively); (2) represented plausible outcomes of the variations in physical and mental health; and (3) were measured independently of the PCS and MCS scales.

Current Work Status And PCS

An important social consequence of poor physical health status is that it may prevent one from working at a paying job. For each of four levels of PCS scores, Table 9.4 presents the percentage of MOS participants who were working at a paying job when the MOS began (N = 2,069). Work status was determined concurrently with the PCS scale. The percentage of MOS patients who were eligible to work and could not work ranged from a high of 57.6% for PCS scores below 35 (level 4) to a low of 5.2% for PCS scores greater than or equal to 55 (level 1). For each one-point difference in PCS scale scores below 45, a two-point increase was observed in the percentage unable to work. Much less difference in the percentage reporting inability to work was observed between the two top scale levels (levels 1-2).

TABLE 9.4 PERCENTAGE OF MOS PATIENTS[1] UNABLE TO WORK AT FOUR LEVELS OF THE PCS

PCS SCORES				CANNOT WORK	
LEVELS	RANGE	MEAN	(N)	%	Δ/Δ
1	55-72	57.5	326	5.2	
					0.1
2	45-54	49.9	715	6.3	
					2.1
3	35-44	39.8	502	27.1	
					2.2
4	8-34	26.2	526	57.6	

[1] MOS baseline sample eligible to work with complete SF-36 data (N = 2,069).

Subsequent Job Loss And PCS

Table 9.5 presents estimates of the percentages of MOS patients (working initially) who had lost their jobs one or two years later because of their health, at four levels of baseline PCS scores. Only patients who reported that they were working at a paying job at "baseline" and who were available at one- and two-year follow-ups were included in the analyses. There is a perfect ordering (from the top to the bottom PCS score levels) of the percentage reporting job loss at follow-up. The change was substantial, approximately a 10-fold increase in job loss, from the top to the bottom PCS levels. As shown in the Δ/Δ columns, approximately a one percentage point change in the probability of job loss is apparent (at one and two years) for each one-point change in PCS scores.

TABLE 9.5 PERCENTAGE OF WORKING MOS PATIENTS[1] WHO REPORTED JOB LOSS AT THE ONE AND TWO-YEAR FOLLOW-UP, FOUR LEVELS OF THE PCS

PCS SCORES				FOLLOW-UP (%)			
				ONE YEAR		TWO YEAR	
LEVELS	RANGE	MEAN	(N)	%	Δ/Δ	%	Δ/Δ
1	55-72	57.6	130	3.1		3.8	
					0.9		0.9
2	45-54	49.9	321	10.0		11.0	
					0.8		1.1
3	35-44	40.4	184	17.9		21.7	
					1.1		1.1
4	8-34	27.2	115	32.2		35.8	

1 MOS sample working at baseline and who reported not being able to work due to health at one year (N = 750) and two year (N = 735) follow-up assessment

Hospital Stays And PCS

Table 9.6 presents the percentage of MOS patients reporting one or more overnight stays in a hospital during the six-month period following completion of the SF-36. Percentages were estimated for four levels of PCS scores. The percent hospitalized overnight increases with lower PCS scale scores. From the top PCS level to the bottom, the percentage of patients hospitalized overnight nearly tripled. In the 8-44 point range on the PCS, each one-point difference was associated with approximately a 0.4 percentage-point difference in hospitalization rates.

Doctor Visits And PCS

Table 9.7 presents results for two criteria: the percentage of the general U.S. population reporting a doctor visit in the past month and the percentage with one or more chronic conditions across eight levels of the PCS scale (rates of chronic conditions are discussed below). Information about doctor visits was collected by self-report concurrently with the SF-36. The percentage of the general U.S. population reporting one or more doctor visits in the past month increases gradually from a low of 12% at the highest PCS level to a high of 53% at the lowest PCS level, more than a four-fold increase.

TABLE 9.6 PERCENTAGE OF MOS PATIENTS[1] WHO WERE HOSPITALIZED OVERNIGHT WITHIN SIX MONTHS, FOUR LEVELS OF THE PCS

PCS SCORES				HOSPITALIZED OVERNIGHT	
LEVELS	RANGE	MEAN	(N)	%	Δ/Δ
1	55-72	57.8	271	4.4	
					0.1
2	45-54	50.1	584	5.3	
					0.3
3	35-44	40.1	364	8.0	
					0.4
4	8-34	26.7	302	12.9	

1 MOS longitudinal sample with data at baseline and six-month follow-up assessments, (N = 1,521).

TABLE 9.7 PERCENTAGE OF THE GENERAL U.S. POPULATION REPORTING A RECENT VISIT TO THE DOCTOR AND ONE OR MORE PHYSICAL CONDITIONS, EIGHT LEVELS OF THE PCS

PCS SCORES				RECENT DR. VISIT[1]		1+ PHYSICAL CONDITIONS[2]	
LEVELS	RANGE	MEAN	(N)	%	Δ/Δ	%	Δ/Δ
1	60-73	61.9	157	12.0		26.1	
					0.6		1.4
2	55-59	56.8	691	15.0		33.1	
					1.1		4.9
3	50-54	52.3	565	20.0		55.2	
					1.2		4.0
4	45-49	47.3	304	26.0		75.3	
					1.4		1.3
5	40-44	42.2	194	33.0		81.9	
					1.6		1.1
6	35-39	37.1	161	41.0		78.6	
					1.4		1.4
7	30-34	32.0	131	48.0		94.7	
					0.6		0.2
8	8-29	23.3	190	53.0		96.8	

1 Percentage reporting visit to a medical doctor within the past month (N=637)
2 Percentage reporting one or more of the following conditions: hypertension, congestive heart failure, myocardial infarction, diabetes, angina, chronic lung disease, arthritis, back/sciatica, or weakness/limitations in arms or legs (N=1,419)

Probability Of A Chronic Condition And PCS

Table 9.7 also presents the percentage of the general U.S. population reporting one or more chronic conditions across the eight levels of PCS scores. The percentage reporting one or more chronic conditions ranged from 26.1% at the top of the scale to 96.8% at the bottom of the scale, a 3.7-fold increase.

Five-Year Survival And PCS

An important test of the validity of the PCS scale scores is their usefulness in predicting five-year mortality. Ongoing MOS studies of the PCS scale scores and five-year mortality rates suggest that differences in scores have substantial implications for survival. As illustrated in Figure 7.1, findings-to-date indicate that the percentage who died within five years increased from only 1.8% at the top of the PCS scale to 21.5% at the bottom scale level, nearly a 12-fold increase (see Table 7.8). Predictions based on logistic regression yielded very large differences in odds-ratios of dying across PCS score levels, with and without statistical adjustment for differences in age. As illustrated in Table 7.8, patients scoring at the bottom scale level were nearly seven times more likely to die within the following five years than patients scoring at the top scale level, with adjustment for differences in age. Patients at scale levels two and three were twice as likely to die as patients scoring at the top level.

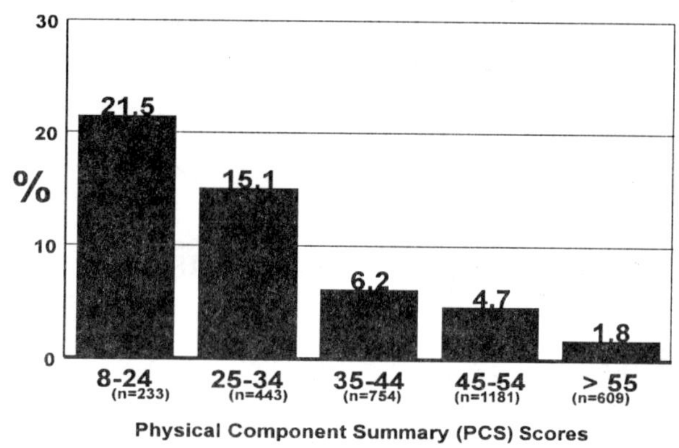

TABLE 9.8 FIVE-YEAR MORTALITY RATES FOR MOS PATIENTS[1] AT FIVE LEVELS OF THE PCS

	PCS Scores			Died		Odds-Ratio of Dying	
Levels	Range	Mean	(N)	%	Δ/Δ	Unadjusted	Age Adjusted[2]
1	55-72	57.8	609	1.8		1	1
					0.4		
2	45-54	50.0	1181	4.7		2.7**	2.0*
					0.1		
3	35-44	39.9	754	6.2		3.6**	2.2*
					0.9		
4	25-34	29.9	443	15.1		9.7**	4.8**
					0.7		
5	8-24	20.4	233	21.5		14.8**	6.8**

1 MOS longitudinal sample with complete SF-36 data at baseline assessment (N = 3,220).
2 Results from a logistic regression model predicting death and controlling for age at baseline assessment.
** $p < .001$ * $p < .05$

Depression Screener and MCS

Results useful in interpreting MCS scores are presented in Table 7.9, including rates of positive screening for likelihood of depression, substantial life stress, and life satisfaction observed across the MCS levels measured concurrently in the general U.S. population. Definitions for these "criteria" are documented in Appendix A. Table 9.9 first presents the percentage of the general U.S. population who screened positive for likelihood of depression at each of nine levels of the MCS scale. These percentages increased consistently from a low of 10.7% at the highest MCS scale level to a high of 93.5% at the lowest scale level, an 8.7-fold increase. These results underscore the clinical relevance of differences in MCS scores in the general U.S. population and offer guidelines for interpreting specific score differences in clinical terms throughout the scale range. The implications of these results for using the MCS as a screening tool are addressed in Chapter 12 on clinical applications.

TABLE 9.9 RATES OF POSSIBLE DEPRESSION, STRESS, AND LIFE SATISFACTION IN THE GENERAL U.S. POPULATION, NINE LEVELS OF THE MCS

MCS Scores				Screen for Depression[1]		Stress[2]		Life Satisfaction[3]	
Levels	Range	Mean	(N)	%	Δ/Δ	%	Δ/Δ	%	Δ/Δ
1	65-74	67	28	10.7		0.0		78.6	
					0.3		1.2		0.9
2	60-64	61.5	269	12.3		6.7		73.4	
					1.4		1.1		1.6
3	55-59	57.1	729	18.4		11.5		66.3	
					2.2		1.4		3.9
4	50-54	52.3	512	29.1		18.4		47.5	
					3.2		2.4		3.1
5	45-49	47.2	287	45.6		30.5		31.9	
					2.5		1.3		-0.1
6	40-44	41.9	190	58.9		37.6		32.4	
					3.2		1.0		3.0
7	35-39	37.2	153	73.9		42.5		18.4	
					3.0		2.4		2.2
8	30-34	32.1	102	89.2		54.9		7.0	
					0.5		2.9		0.2
9	9-29	23.8	123	93.5		78.9		5.7	

1 Respondents who answered YES to one or more of the following: two or more weeks in the last year feeling sad, blue, or depressed; two or more years in your life you felt depressed most days; felt depressed much of the time in the last year.

2 Quite a bit or a great deal of stress experienced in your daily living in the past four weeks.

3 How happy, satisfied, pleased with your personal life (% extremely happy or very happy).

Life Stress And MCS

The second of the three "criteria" presented in Table 9.9 is the percentage of the general U.S. population experiencing a great deal of stress in daily living across nine levels of the MCS scale. None reported such stress at the highest MCS level and the percentages ranged from a low of 6.7% at the second MCS level to a high of 78.9% at the lowest level. A perfect ordering of these percentages is apparent across the nine MCS levels.

Life Satisfaction And MCS

The third "criteria" analyzed in Table 9.9 is a widely-used measure of "quality of life," specifically the percentage of the general U.S. population who are happy, satisfied, or pleased with their life all or most of the time. These percentages are reported for nine levels of the MCS scale. A 13.8-fold increase in the percent satisfied or pleased with their life is apparent at the top level of the MCS (78.6%) relative to the bottom level (only 5.7%). The percentages decline nearly consistently with an aberration observed only between levels 5 and 6. Not surprisingly, the MCS correlates substantially with evaluations of quality of life in both the general U.S. population ($r = 0.57$, $p < 0.001$) as shown here, and among MOS patients ($r = 0.68$, $p < 0.001$) as documented further in Chapter 8 (see Table 8.6).

Diagnosis Of Clinical Depression And MCS

Table 9.10 presents results for two clinical "criteria" — a clinical diagnosis of clinical depression and the percentage receiving mental health specialty care — at nine levels of the MCS scale. A perfect ordering of the percentage of patients with a diagnosis of clinical depression is apparent across levels of the MCS scale, from a low of 0.0% at the top level to a high of 59.4% at lowest level. As indicated in the Δ/Δ column, these percentages tend to increase at an increasing rate (from less than 1% to more than 2% per MCS point) from the top to bottom. These results are very similar to results reported above for the general U.S. population, although a much lower prevalence was observed in the MOS, as would be expected for more stringent diagnostic criteria (e.g., a three-item self-report screener in the general population study versus a diagnostic interview schedule in the MOS).

Mental Health Treatment And MCS

Table 9.10 also presents estimates of the percentage of MOS patients receiving mental health treatment from a formally trained mental health specialist during the six-month period after administration of the SF-36. These percentages are reported for eight levels of the MCS. At the top two MCS levels (collapsed) the percentage receiving mental health specialty treatment from a mental health specialist was only 2.9% compared with 69.3% at the bottom MCS scale levels. The percentages increased consistently across scale levels and the largest differences in the percentage treated were observed at the lower three levels of the MCS (2.0 - 3.2 percentage-point difference in treatment rate per MCS point).

TABLE 9.10 PERCENTAGE OF MOS PATIENTS DIAGNOSED WITH DEPRESSIVE DISORDER AND MENTAL HEALTH SPECIALTY CARE, NINE LEVELS OF THE MCS

MCS SCORES				CLINICAL DEPRESSION[1]		RECEIVING MENTAL HEALTH SPECIALITY CARE[2]	
Levels	**Range**	**Mean**	**(N)**	**%**	**Δ/Δ**	**%**	**Δ/Δ**
1	65-72	66.2	78	0.0		--[a]	
					0.4		--
2	60-64	61.4	421	1.9		2.9	
					0.3		0.7
3	55-59	57.1	861	3.0		5.8	
					0.9		1.5
4	50-54	52.2	519	7.3		13.0	
					0.8		0.6
5	45-49	47.1	348	11.2		16.2	
					1.0		1.3
6	40-44	42.1	259	16.2		22.7	
					2.5		2.5
7	35-39	37.2	234	28.6		35.1	
					2.2		3.2
8	30-34	32.1	209	39.7		51.4	
					2.2		2.0
9	3-29	23.2	291	59.4		69.3	

1 MOS baseline sample with complete SF-36 data (N = 3,220)
2 MOS longitudinal sample with SF-36 data at baseline and six-month follow-up (N = 1,739)
a Level 9 (65-72) was collapsed with level 8 due to insufficient sample size.

Burden Of Chronic Conditions

Estimates of the health burden associated with clinically-defined groups known to differ in physical and mental health have proven very useful in interpreting health status scores and changes in scores over time (Brook, Ware, Rogers, et al., 1984; Ware, Brook, Rogers, et al., 1986). Because many adults with a clinical condition have more than one (Stewart, Greenfield, Hays, et al., 1989), it is necessary to take "co-morbidity" into account along with other confounding factors (e.g., age differences) in making estimates of the health burden associated with a specific condition.

Statistical Method

To estimate the impact of each of the five MOS tracer conditions alone on PCS and MCS scores and the added effects of 16 comorbid conditions, we used multivariate statistical methods. These methods insure that the formula used to estimate the impact of each condition adjusts as much as possible for differences in demographic and socioeconomic characteristics, and for other conditions.

Overall F-tests confirmed that the set of variables defining the five tracer conditions and 16 comorbid conditions in the MOS differed significantly from zero (see Table footnotes). An independent regression model was estimated for the PCS and MCS scales. The same statistical approach was followed in estimating the impact of self-reported conditions in the general U.S. population.

Sixteen of the 27 comorbid conditions were each common enough to estimate their unique effects on the PCS and MCS. The other 12 were "controlled for" in the model, but results are not reported. Results to date support an additive model; the unique impact of each did not vary much across other conditions as observed in previous MOS analyses (Stewart, Greenfield, Hays, et al., 1989).

Disease Impact: MOS

Table 9.11 presents estimates of the burden of chronic conditions for use in interpreting differences in PCS and MCS scores. These are estimates of the unique effects of the five "tracer" conditions studied in the MOS along with 16 comorbid conditions, adjusting for socio-demographic variables (as described above).

As shown in Table 9.11, the largest effects on PCS scores in the MOS were observed for rheumatoid arthritis (-7.61, ± 1.9), hip impairment (-6.09, ± 1.4), congestive heart failure (-5.43, ± 1.2), osteoarthritis (-5.19, ± 1.2), and ulcers (-5.01, ± 2.1). All of these effects exceeded five points, which is one-half of a standard deviation, and all involve physical conditions. Other significant effects are documented in Table 9.11, including differences for all five "tracer" conditions and for 10 of 16 comorbid conditions, for which differences were estimated.

Only two conditions were associated with significant effects on the MCS scores. The largest difference was observed for clinical depression (-12.72, ± 1.1), a difference of more than a standard deviation. The only other significant difference in the MCS scores was observed for asthma (-6.20, ± 2.0).

Disease Impact: General Population

In the general U.S. population, the largest effects observed on the PCS, which were in the 6 - 8 point range, were observed for limitations in the use of an arm or leg (-7.15, ± 0.9) and for congestive heart failure (-6.72, ± 1.3) (see Table 9.12). Other substantial differences were observed for (in decreasing order of impact): back pain/sciatica (-3.75, ± 0.5), angina (-3.67, ± 1.2) diabetes/low blood sugar (-3.44, ± 0.8), chronic lung disease (-3.12, ± 0.9), myocardial infarction in the past year (-2.75, ± 1.2), and arthritis or rheumatism (-2.77, ± 0.5). Differences for hypertension and allergies were smaller, but statistically significant.

TABLE 9.11 ESTIMATES OF THE UNIQUE EFFECTS OF CHRONIC CONDITIONS ON THE PCS AND MCS, MOS PATIENTS (N = 1,790)

		PCS		MCS	
Comparison Group Means	**N**	**53.27[a]**	**(1.2)**	**48.95[a]**	**(1.2)**
Tracer Conditions					
Clinical Depression	262	-2.34[c]	(1.0)	-12.72[a]	(1.1)
Congestive Heart Failure (CHF)	218	-5.43[a]	(1.2)	-.98	(0.9)
Diabetes Type II	442	-3.48[a]	(0.7)	.58	(0.6)
Hypertension	1293	-1.85[c]	(0.8)	.61	(0.7)
Recent Myocardial Infarction (MI)	107	-3.24[b]	(1.0)	-.87	(1.0)
Comorbid Conditions					
Anemia	76	-3.05[c]	(1.5)	.62	(1.2)
Angina (No MI)	288	-4.02[a]	(0.8)	-.39	(0.7)
Asthma	50	-.86	(1.7)	-6.20[b]	(2.0)
Back Pain/Sciatica	502	-4.38[a]	(0.7)	-.83	(0.7)
COPD	117	-3.14[c]	(1.3)	-1.15	(1.0)
Dermatitis	356	-.85	(0.8)	-.71	(0.8)
Hip Impairment	75	-6.09[a]	(1.4)	-2.28	(1.5)
Irritable Bowel Disease	81	-2.92	(1.6)	-1.25	(1.2)
Kidney Disease	24	-1.89	(2.7)	-1.23	(3.0)
Musculoskeletal Complaints	341	-2.10[b]	(0.7)	-.16	(0.7)
Osteoarthritis	164	-5.19[a]	(1.2)	1.26	(1.0)
Other Lung Disease	26	2.04	(1.9)	-.16	(2.0)
Past MI	165	-3.08[b]	(1.0)	-.92	(1.2)
Rheumatoid Arthritis	39	-7.61[a]	(1.9)	3.01	(1.6)
Ulcer	53	-5.01[c]	(2.1)	-1.05	(1.6)
Urinary Tract Infection	127	-.89	(0.9)	-.75	(1.1)
Adjusted R2		0.3365		0.2858	
F (model)		19.53[a]		15.62[a]	

[a] $p < 0.001$
[b] $p < 0.01$
[c] $p < 0.05$
Comparison group is a hypothetical MOS female patient age 18-44 years, with 12 years education and no chronic conditions.
Numbers in parentheses are standard errors.
Note: These models are adjusted for main effects of age, sex, race, and education.

The largest effect on the MCS in the general U.S. population was observed for those who screened positive for likelihood of depression using three screening items from the MOS screener (Burnam, Wells, Leake, et al., 1988). Those with depression scored nearly one standard deviation (-9.30, ± 0.5) lower on the MCS. Six other conditions impacted the MCS a statistically significant amount, including: chronic lung disease (-3.03, ± 0.9), visual impairments (-2.92, ± 0.7), and dermatitis (-2.00, ± 0.8); significant differences in the 1 - 2 point range were back pain/sciatica, hearing impairments, and dermatitis. A noteworthy difference in MCS scores (-2.36, ± 1.2) for MI was not statistically significant at conventional levels due to a small sample size.

TABLE 9.12 ESTIMATES OF THE UNIQUE EFFECTS OF CHRONIC CONDITIONS ON THE PCS AND MCS, GENERAL U.S. POPULATION (N = 2,393)

		PCS		MCS	
Comparison Group Means	**N**	54.45[a]	(0.5)	52.46[a]	(0.5)
Chronic Conditions					
Allergy	842	-.82[c]	(0.4)	.04	(0.4)
Angina	112	-3.67[b]	(1.2)	.18	(1.0)
Arthritis	862	-2.77[a]	(0.5)	-.92	(0.5)
Back Pain/Sciatica	531	-3.75[a]	(0.5)	-1.58[b]	(0.5)
Cancer	108	-.83	(0.9)	-.31	(1.1)
Chronic Lung Disease	194	-3.12[a]	(0.9)	-3.03[b]	(0.9)
Congestive Heart Failure (CHF)	93	-6.72[a]	(1.3)	-1.36	(1.2)
Depression Screen	700	-.42	(0.4)	-9.30[a]	(0.5)
Dermatitis	224	-.41	(0.6)	-2.00[c]	(0.8)
Diabetes	156	-3.44[a]	(0.8)	.30	(0.9)
Hearing Impairment	405	-.94	(0.6)	-1.16[c]	(0.6)
Hypertension	701	-1.53[a]	(0.4)	-.10	(0.5)
Limitation in use of Arm(s)/Leg(s)	274	-7.15[a]	(0.9)	-.16	(0.8)
Myocardial Infarction (MI)	69	-2.75[c]	(1.2)	-2.36	(1.2)
Vision Impairment	280	-1.11	(0.7)	-2.92[a]	(0.7)
Adjusted R^2		0.4679		0.3039	
F (model)		73.54[a]		37.00[a]	

a $p < 0.001$
b $p < 0.01$
c $p < 0.05$
Comparison group is white females, age 18-44 years, with 12 years education. Results adjust for age, sex, race, and education. Numbers in parentheses are standard errors.
Note: These models are adjusted for main effects of age, sex, race, and education.

Comparison Of Estimates

Although different methods were used to determine "tracer" conditions (physician report) and comorbid conditions (physician and patient reports) in the MOS, in comparison with the general U.S. population (self-report), estimates for most conditions included in both investigations showed considerable agreement. Of those significant in both studies, hypertension showed the smallest effect on the PCS in both the MOS and U.S. studies (-1.85 and -1.53, respectively). Congestive heart failure had one of the largest effects on PCS among conditions common to both studies (-5.43 and -6.72, respectively). Diabetes estimates fell in the middle range (-3.48 and -3.44, respectively) in both studies.

Among the largest discrepancies in results for the PCS were estimates for rheumatoid arthritis and osteoarthritis in the MOS in comparison with "arthritis" in the general population survey (-7.61 and -5.19 versus -2.77, respectively). Both studies showed the largest effects on the MCS for depression, although the impact of depression on the MCS was about one-third larger in the MOS, which used more extensive clinical criteria. Visual impairment and hearing impairment, which were not studied in the MOS, showed significant negative effects on the MCS in the general U.S. population survey.

Effects Of Aging

Given the substantial differences in PCS scores observed across age groups for both men and women in cross-sectional analyses (see Chapter 8), it is reasonable to expect change scores for the PCS scale to favor younger adults. If confirmed in longitudinal analyses, age-related differences in the impact of a year of aging might offer another basis for interpreting changes in PCS scores.

Changes in PCS scores were estimated for three age groups among MOS patients with only uncomplicated hypertension. This group of patients was selected for purposes of estimating age effects because they were the most "well" of those followed longitudinally in the MOS; thus age differences in health transitions were least likely to be confounded with medical comorbidity.

As shown in Table 9.13, the average change in PCS scores over a two-year follow-up differed significantly across the three age groups ($F = 4.5$, $p < 0.01$). This significant result was accounted for by the significant average decline in PCS scores ($\Delta = -2.0$, $p < 0.001$) among those 65 years of age and older (mean age = 71.4). The decline of two PCS points during the two-year follow-up period amounts to one PCS point per year. Thus, for example, it is reasonable to explain that each one-point decline in PCS scores observed in a clinical trial of alternative treatments is equal to the age-related decline in physical health among those 65 and older.

TABLE 9.13 ESTIMATES OF THE EFFECTS OF AGING TWO YEARS ON PCS SCORES, MOS PATIENTS WITH UNCOMPLICATED HYPERTENSION (N = 581)

Age Groups	Mean Age	(N)	Difference Score (Δ)		Δ/year
18-44	38.4	93	1.1	(0.8)	0.5
45-64	56.7	225	-0.8	(0.6)	-0.4
65+	71.4	263	-2.0*	(0.6)	-1.0*
F for Effect of Age			4.5[a]		

Significance of mean change in PCS scores for each age group: * $p < .001$
Significance test for the difference in mean change scores across age groups: [a] $p < .01$
Note: Uncomplicated hypertension defined as documented for the "minor medical" group in McHorney, Ware, & Raczek, 1993. Numbers in parentheses are standard errors.

Summary Of Effect Sizes

Among the results discussed in Chapter 9 are those from numerous cross-sectional and longitudinal group-level comparisons of average PCS and MCS scores. Because these comparisons involve groups known to differ in meaningful ways, results from these comparisons should be useful in: (a) interpreting score differences in future studies; (b) explaining results to others; and (c) planning future studies. To facilitate their use for these and other purposes, differences observed from group comparisons are summarized below.

PCS Scores

Tables 9.14 and 9.15 summarize results from cross-sectional and longitudinal comparisons, respectively, of average PCS scores for groups presented in this and other chapters. Each table orders average differences from the largest to the smallest "effect size." Because the PCS (and MCS) have a standard deviation (SD) of 10 in the general U.S. population, table entries can be easily interpreted in SD units by dividing each difference by 10 (moving the decimal one place to the left). Thus, the first entry in Table 9.14, which is 14.41, represents a difference of 1.44 SD units between groups with and without serious physical morbidity. Table 9.14 presents results from 62 cross-sectional comparisons of PCS scores. Differences that were significant statistically under the conditions of the study are indicated using three conventional levels for two-tailed tests. However, because sample sizes and other unique features of study designs and analytic methods influence statistical conclusions, they should be interpreted cautiously. For each comparison, the definition of the groups or the intervention that occurred between repeated measurements is defined very briefly, under the column headed "comparison," and the table notes where in this manual results are displayed and/or a reference if results have been published.

TABLE 9.14 RANK ORDER OF AVERAGE GROUP DIFFERENCES IN PCS SCORES OBSERVED IN CROSS-SECTIONAL STUDIES

Difference	Comparison	Sample	Source
14.41[a]	Patients with and w/out Serious Physical Morbidity	MOS Depressed Patients	Table 8.4
12.83[a]	Serious Physical and Mental (vs) Minor Physical	MOS Patients	Table 8.3
11.68[a]	Serious Mental (vs) Serious Physical	MOS Patients	Table 8.3
10.10[a]	Serious Physical (vs) Minor Physical	MOS Patients	Table 8.3
8.29[a]	CHF Severity 2 (vs) Severity 1	MOS CHF Patients	Ware, et al., 1995, Appendix Table B2
7.65[a]	CHF (vs) Hypertension	MOS Patients	Ware, et al., 1995, Appendix Table B1
7.61[a]	Rheumatoid Arthritis, Unique Effect	MOS Patients	Table 9.13
7.60[a]	Age 18-44 (vs) Age 65+, Uncomplicated Hypertension	MOS Hypertension Patients	Ware, et al., 1995, Table 7.15
7.15[a]	Limitations in Use of Arm/Leg, Unique Effect	General U.S. Population	Table 9.12
6.72[a]	CHF, Unique Effect	General U.S. Population	Table 9.12
6.09[a]	Hip Impairment, Unique Effect	MOS Patients	Table 9.11
5.57[a]	CHF (vs) Diabetes	MOS Patients	Ware, et al., 1995, Appendix Table B1
5.43[a]	CHF, Unique Effect	MOS Patients	Table 9.11
5.22[b]	CHF (vs) MI	MOS Patients	Ware, et al., 1995, Appendix Table B1
5.20[c]	Diabetes Severity 4 (vs) Severity 2	MOS Diabetic Patients	Ware, et al., 1995, Appendix Table B2
5.19[a]	Osteoarthritis, Unique Effect	MOS Patients	Table 9.11
5.01[c]	Ulcers, Unique Effect	MOS Patients	Table 9.11
4.80[c]	Diabetes Severity 4 (vs) Severity 1	MOS Patients	Ware, et al., 1995, Appendix Table B2
4.38[a]	Back Pain/Sciatica, Unique Effect	MOS Patients	Table 9.11
4.02[a]	Angina, Unique Effect	MOS Patients	Table 9.11
4.00[c]	Age 45-64 (vs) Age 65+, Uncomplicated Hypertension	MOS Hypertension Patients	Ware, et al., 1995, Table 7.15
3.75[a]	Back Pain/Sciatica, Unique Effect	General U.S. Population	Table 9.12
3.67[b]	Angina, Unique Effect	General U.S. Population	Table 9.12
3.60[c]	Age 18-44 (vs) Age 45-64, Uncomplicated Hypertension	MOS Hypertension Patients	Ware, et al., 1995, Table 7.15
3.48[a]	Diabetes, Unique Effect	MOS Patients	Table 9.11
3.44[a]	Diabetes, Unique Effect	General U.S. Population	Table 9.12
3.24[b]	MI, Unique Effect	MOS Patients	Table 9.11
3.14[c]	COPD, Unique Effect	MOS Patients	Table 9.11
3.12[a]	Chronic Lung Disease, Unique Effect	General U.S. Population	Table 9.12
3.08[b]	Past MI, Unique Effect	MOS Patients	Table 9.11

TABLE 9.14 RANK ORDER OF AVERAGE GROUP DIFFERENCES IN PCS SCORES OBSERVED IN CROSS-SECTIONAL STUDIES (CONTINUED)

Difference	Comparison	Sample	Source
3.05[c]	Anemia, Unique Effect	MOS Patients	Table 9.11
2.97	Diabetes Severity 4 (vs) Severity 3	MOS Diabetic Patients	Ware, et al., 1995, Appendix Table B2
2.92	Irritable Bowel Disease, Unique Effect	MOS Patients	Table 9.11
2.77[a]	Arthritis, Unique Effect	General U.S. Population	Table 9.12
2.75[c]	MI, Unique Effect	General U.S. Population	Table 9.12
2.73	Patients with and w/out Serious Mental	MOS Serious Physical Patients	Table 8.4
2.43[c]	Hypertension (vs) MI	MOS Patients	Ware, et al., 1995, Appendix Table B1
2.34[c]	Clinical Depression, Unique Effect	MOS Patients	Table 9.11
2.23	Diabetes Severity 3 (vs) Severity 2	MOS Patients	Ware, et al., 1995, Appendix Table B2
2.10[b]	Musculoskeletal Complaints, Unique Effect	MOS Patients	Table 9.11
2.08[c]	Diabetes (vs) Hypertension	MOS Patients	Ware, et al., 1995, Appendix Table B1
2.04	Other Lung Disease, Unique Effect	MOS Patients	Table 9.11
1.89	Kidney Disease, Unique Effect	MOS Patients	Table 9.11
1.85[c]	Hypertension, Unique Effect	MOS Patients	Table 9.11
1.83	Diabetes Severity 3 (vs) Severity 1	MOS Patients	Ware, et al., 1995, Appendix Table B2
1.80	Depression (vs) Minor Physical	MOS Patients	Ware, et al., 1995, Appendix Table B8
1.58[c]	Depression (vs) Minor Physical	MOS Patients	Table 8.3
1.53[a]	Hypertension, Unique Effect	General U.S. Population	Table 9.12
1.11	Vision Impairment, Unique Effect	General U.S. Population	Table 9.12
1.03	Hypertension Severity 2 (vs) Severity 1	MOS Patients	Ware, et al., 1995, Appendix Table B2
.94	Hearing Impairment, Unique Effect	General U.S. Population	Table 9.12
.89	UTI, Unique Effect	MOS Patients	Table 9.11
.86	Asthma, Unique Effect	MOS Patients	Table 9.11
.85	Dermatitis, Unique Effect	MOS Patients	Table 9.11
.83	Cancer, Unique Effect	General U.S. Population	Table 9.12
.82[c]	Allergies, Unique Effect	General U.S. Population	Table 9.12
.50	Ulcer Treatment — Maintenance (vs) Intermittent Therapy	Duodenal Ulcer Patients	Rampal, et al., 1994 (Figure 9.4)
.42	Depression, Unique Effect	General U.S. Population	Table 9.12
.41	Dermatitis, Unique Effect	General U.S. Population	Table 9.12
.40	Diabetes Severity 2 (vs) Severity 1	MOS Patients	Ware, et al., 1995, Appendix Table B2
.35	Diabetes (vs) MI	MOS Patients	Ware, et al., 1995, Appendix Table B1

[a] $p < .001$ [b] $p < .01$ [c] $p < .05$

PCS Cross-Sectional Differences

The largest differences in PCS scores observed to date were observed in comparisons between groups with serious physical conditions relative to patients without serious physical conditions.

The largest cross-sectional difference in PCS scores (-14.41, $p < 0.001$) was observed between depressed patients with and without serious physical comorbidity, as defined above (e.g., CHF). Cross-sectional differences greater than 10 points on the PCS summary scale (i.e., more than one SD unit) were also observed for three other comparisons involving groups of patients known to differ in the seriousness of their *physical* morbidity as clinically defined (see Table 9.14).

PCS Longitudinal Differences

Table 9.15 presents 27 average changes in PCS scores observed in longitudinal comparisons. Another finding that may be useful in interpreting changes in PCS scores is the decline (Δ = -2.0) associated with two years of aging among patients with uncomplicated hypertension who were 65 and older (mean age = 71.4). Each year of aging for this group was associated with a one-point decline in PCS scores, on average.

Many ongoing studies will contribute to the understanding of the PCS and MCS scores that should be considered clinical and socially relevant. Guidelines for judging the clinical and social relevance of differences in such differences must await the result of those studies.

Although these are very large differences in terms of SD units (Cohen, 1988), even larger differences between groups would be expected, for example, in analyses of groups at even more severe levels of either physical or mental (emotional) morbidity. The differences reported above and any difference of 0.8 SD units or larger would be considered large according to conventional statistical standards (Cohen, 1988). Results from many ongoing studies will further contribute to the understanding of the PCS and MCS scores and the sizes of differences that should be considered clinically and socially relevant. Chapter 9 documents a wide range of differences that should be useful in interpreting the PCS and MCS scores and in explaining those differences to others. More definitive guidelines for establishing the importance of differences must await the results of future studies.

The three largest average changes in PCS scores were estimated from studies comparing scores before and after treatment for physical conditions. The treatment included hip replacement (Δ = 9.55), therapy for low back pain (Δ = 7.66), and heart valve replacement (Δ = 7.64). These three studies are discussed further in Chapter 11 (Applications: Outcomes Research) and in the articles referenced. Another study of treatment effects yielded significant average changes in PCS scores, including maintenance drug therapy for ulcers (Δ = 4.60) and intermittent drug therapy for ulcers (Δ = 3.20) (see Rampal, Martin, Marquis, et al., 1994)

TABLE 9.15 RANK ORDER OF AVERAGE CHANGE IN PCS SCORES OBSERVED IN LONGITUDINAL STUDIES

Average Change	Comparison	Sample	Source
9.55[a]	Hip Replacement, Before and After	Hip Replacement Patients	Katz, et al., 1992 (Figure 9.2)
7.66[a]	Low Back Pain Therapy, Before and After	Spine Center Patients	Lansky, et al., 1992 (Figure 9.3)
7.64[a]	Heart Valve Replacement, Before and After	AVR and MVR Patients	Phillips & Lansky, 1992 (Figure 9.1)
-6.60[b]	Average Change in 1 Year for Patients Reporting "Lot More Limited"	MOS Patients	Appendix Table B7
4.60[c]	Ulcer, Before and After Maintenance Treatment, 1 Year	Duodenal Ulcer Patients	Rampal, et al., 1994 (Figure 9.4)
-3.90[c]	Average Change in 1 Year for Patients Reporting "Somewhat More Limited"	MOS Patients	Appendix Table B7
3.80[c]	Average Change in 1 Year for Patients Reporting "Less Limited"	MOS Patients	Appendix Table B7
-3.30[b]	COPD, 1 Year Change	MOS Patients	Table 14.45
3.20[c]	Ulcer, Before and After Intermittent Treatment, 1 Year	Duodenal Ulcer Patients	Rampal, et al., 1994 (Figure 9.4)
-2.09[c]	Osteoarthritis, 1 Year Change	MOS Patients	Table 14.48
-2.00[c]	Aging 2 Years, Age Group 65+ — Uncomplicated Hypertension	MOS Patients	Table 9.15
-1.96	Musculoskeletal Complaints, 1 Year Change	MOS Patients	Table 14.47
-1.69	CHF, 1 Year Change	MOS Patients	Table 14.39
1.40	Average Change in 1 Year for Patients Reporting "Less Limited"	MOS Patients	Appendix Table B7
-1.24	Angina, 1 Year Change	MOS Patients	Table 14.49
-1.23	Recovery from Depression	MOS Patients	Ware, et al., 1995 Appendix Table B9
1.10	Aging 2 Years, Age Group 18-44 — Uncomplicated Hypertension	MOS Patients	Table 9.15
-.80	Aging 2 Years, Age Group 45-64 — Uncomplicated Hypertension	MOS Patients	Table 9.15
-.70	Varicosities, 1 Year Change	MOS Patients	Table 14.50
-.70	BPH, 1 Year Change	MOS Patients	Table 14.44
-.64	Clinical Depression, 1 Year Change	MOS Patients	Table 14.38
.44	MI, 1 Year Change	MOS Patients	Table 14.41
-.40	Hypertension, 1 Year Change	MOS Patients	Table 14.40
-.33	Back Pain/Sciatica, 1 Year Change	MOS Patients	Table 14.43
.22	Diabetes, 1 Year Change	MOS Patients	Table 14.42
-.20	Dermatitis, 1 Year Change	MOS Patients	Table 14.46
-.10	Average Change in 1 Year for patients Reporting "Stayed the Same"	MOS Patients	Appendix Table B7

[a] $p < .001$ [b] $p < .01$ [c] $p < .05$

TABLE 9.16 RANK ORDER OF AVERAGE GROUP DIFFERENCES IN MCS SCORES OBSERVED IN CROSS-SECTIONAL ANALYSES

Difference	Comparison	Sample	Source
16.67[a]	Serious Mental (vs) Minor Physical	MOS Patients	Table 8.3
14.61[a]	Serious Mental (vs) Serious Physical	MOS Patients	Table 8.3
12.72[a]	Depression, Unique Effect	MOS Patients	Table 9.11
12.60[a]	Serious Physical + Mental (vs) Mental + Minor Physical	MOS Patients	Table 8.4
10.54[a]	Mental + Serious Physical (vs) Serious Physical	MOS Patients	Table 8.4
9.30[a]	Depression, Unique Effect	General U.S. Population	Table 9.12
6.20[b]	Asthma, Unique Effect	MOS Patients	Table 9.11
4.67[c]	CHF Severity 2 (vs) Severity 1	MOS Patients	Ware, et al., 1995 Appendix B2
4.08[c]	Mental (vs) Mental + Serious Physical	MOS Patients	Table 8.4
3.03[b]	Chronic Lung Disease, Unique Effect	General U.S. Population	Table 9.12
3.01	Rheumatoid Arthritis, Unique Effect	MOS Patients	Table 9.11
2.92[a]	Vision Impairment, Unique Effect	General U.S. Population	Table 9.12
2.57	Diabetes Severity 2 (vs) Severity 3	MOS Patients	Ware, et al., 1995 Appendix B2
2.36	MI, Unique Effect	General U.S. Population	Table 9.12
2.28	Hip Impairment, Unique Effect	MOS Patients	Table 9.11
2.10	Diabetes Severity 4 (vs) Severity 3	MOS Patients	Ware, et al., 1995 Appendix B2
2.06[b]	Serious Physical (vs) Minor Physical	MOS Patients	Table 8.3
2.00[c]	Dermatitis, Unique Effect	General U.S. Population	Table 9.12
1.97	CHF (vs) Hypertension	MOS Patients	Ware, et al., 1995 Appendix B1
1.71	MI (vs) Hypertension	MOS Patients	Ware, et al., 1995 Appendix B1
1.61	CHF (vs) Diabetes	MOS Patients	Ware, et al., 1995 Appendix B1
1.58[b]	Back Pain/Sciatica, Unique Effect	General U.S. Population	Table 9.12
1.36	CHF, Unique Effect	General U.S. Population	Table 9.12
1.35	MI (vs) Diabetes	MOS Patients	Ware, et al., 1995 Appendix B1
1.33	Diabetes Severity 2 (vs) Severity 1	MOS Patients	Ware, et al., 1995 Appendix B2
1.26	Osteoarthritis, Unique Effect	MOS Patients	Table 9.11
1.25	Irritable Bowel Disease, Unique Effect	MOS Patients	Table 9.11
1.24	Diabetes Severity 3 (vs) Severity 1	MOS Patients	Ware, et al., 1995 Appendix B2

TABLE 9.16 RANK ORDER OF AVERAGE GROUP DIFFERENCES IN MCS SCORES OBSERVED IN CROSS-SECTIONAL ANALYSES (CONTINUED)

Difference	Comparison	Sample	Source
1.23	Kidney Disease, Unique Effect	MOS Patients	Table 9.11
1.16[c]	Hearing Impairment, Unique Effect	General U.S. Population	Table 9.12
1.16	Hypertension Severity 1 (vs) Severity 2	MOS Patients	Ware, et al., 1995 Appendix B2
1.15	COPD, Unique Effect	MOS Patients	Table 9.11
1.05	Ulcers, Unique Effect	MOS Patients	Table 9.11
.98	CHF, Unique Effect	MOS Patients	Table 9.11
.92	Arthritis, Unique Effect	General U.S. Population	Table 9.12
.92	Past MI, Unique Effect	MOS Patients	Table 9.12
.90	Ulcer Treatment — Intermittent (vs) Maintenance	Duodenal Ulcer Patients	Rampal, et al., 1994 (Figure 9.4)
.87	MI, Unique Effect	MOS Patients	Table 9.11
.86	Diabetes Severity 4 (vs) Severity 1	MOS Patients	Ware, et al., 1995 Appendix B2
.83	Back Pain/Sciatica, Unique Effect	MOS Patients	Table 9.11
.75	UTI, Unique Effect	MOS Patients	Table 9.11
.71	Dermatitis, Unique Effect	MOS Patients	Table 9.11
.62	Anemia, Unique Effect	MOS Patients	Table 9.11
.61	Hypertension, Unique Effect	MOS Patients	Table 9.11
.58	Diabetes, Unique Effect	MOS Patients	Table 9.11
.47	Diabetes Severity 4 (vs) Severity 2	MOS Patients	Ware, et al., 1995 Appendix B2
.39	Angina, Unique Effect	MOS Patients	Table 9.11
.36	Diabetes (vs) Hypertension	MOS Patients	Ware, et al., 1995 Appendix B1
.31	Cancer, Unique Effect	General U.S. Population	Table 9.12
.30	Diabetes, Unique Effect	General U.S. Population	Table 9.12
.26	CHF (vs) MI	MOS Patients	Ware, et al., 1995 Appendix B1
.18	Angina, Unique Effect	General U.S. Population	Table 9.12
.16	Other Lung Disease, Unique Effect	MOS Patients	Table 9.11
.16	Limitations in Use of Arm/Leg, Unique Effect	General U.S. Population	Table 9.12
.16	Musculoskeletal Complaints, Unique Effect	MOS Patients	Table 9.11
.10	Hypertension, Unique Effect	General U.S. Population	Table 9.12
.04	Allergies, Unique Effect	General U.S. Population	Table 9.12

[a] $p < .001$ [b] $p < .01$ [c] $p < .05$

TABLE 9.17 RANK ORDER OF AVERAGE CHANGES IN MCS SCORES OBSERVED IN LONGITUDINAL STUDIES

Average Change	Comparison	Sample	Source
10.93[a]	Recovery From Depression	MOS Depression Patients	Ware, et al., 1995 Appendix B9
-7.30[b]	Average Change in 1 Year for Patients Reporting "A Lot More Limited"	MOS Patients	Appendix B7
7.20[b]	Average Change in 1 Year for Patients Reporting "A Lot Less Limited"	MOS Patients	Appendix B7
6.40[c]	Ulcer — Before and After Maintenance Treatment, 1 Year	Duodenal Ulcer Patients	Rampal, et al., 1994 (Figure 9.4)
5.40[c]	Ulcer — Before and After Intermittent Treatment, 1 Year	Duodenal Ulcer Patients	Rampal, et al., 1994 (Figure 9.4)
4.78[c]	COPD, 1 Year Change	MOS Patients	Appendix E45
-4.00[c]	Average Change in 1 Year for Patients Reporting "Somewhat More Limited"	MOS Patients	Appendix B7
3.86[a]	Clinical Depression, 1 Year Change	MOS Patients	Appendix E38
3.73[b]	Hip Replacement, Before and After	Hip Replacement Patients	Katz, et al., 1992 (Figure 9.2)
3.18[c]	Heart Valve Replacement, Before and After	AVR and MVR Patients	Phillips & Lansky, 1992 (Figure 9.1)
2.50[c]	Average Change in 1 Year for Patients Reporting "Somewhat Less Limited"	MOS Patients	Appendix B7
1.57	MI, 1 Year Change	MOS Patients	Appendix E41
1.31	Low Back Pain Therapy, Before and After	Spine Center Patients	Lansky, et al., 1992 (Figure 9.3)
-1.24	Musculoskeletal Complaints, 1 Year Change	MOS Patients	Appendix E47
-1.00	Varicosities, 1 Year Change	MOS Patients	Appendix E50
.91	CHF, 1 Year Change	MOS Patients	Appendix E39
.56	Back Pain/Sciatica, 1 Year Change	MOS Patients	Appendix E43
-.21	Osteoarthritis, 1 Year Change	MOS Patients	Appendix E48
.20	Hypertension, 1 Year Change	MOS Patients	Appendix E40
.18	Diabetes, 1 Year Change	MOS Patients	Appendix E42
-.17	Dermatitis, 1 Year Change	MOS Patients	Appendix E46
-.13	BPH, 1 Year Change	MOS Patients	Appendix E44
.10	Average Change in 1 Year for Patients Reporting "Stayed the Same"	MOS Patients	Appendix B7
.10	Angina, 1 Year Change	MOS Patients	Appendix E49

[a] $p < .001$ [b] $p < .01$ [c] $p < .05$

MCS Scores

The largest differences in MCS scores from cross-sectional studies involved comparisons between groups differing in seriousness of mental disorder (see Table 9.16). Other large differences include the effects of asthma (-6.20), congestive heart failure (-4.67), and chronic lung disease (-3.03). Interestingly, the estimate of the unique effect of vision impairment on MCS scores (-2.92) is large and significant in the general U.S. population. Table 9.16 also includes significant and unique negative effects of dermatitis and back pain/sciatica on MCS scores.

Changes in MCS scores summarized in Table 9.17 were statistically significant for all differences greater than two points. The largest average change (Δ = 10.93) was observed for the MOS patients who (according to clinical criteria) recovered from clinical depression. Patients who reported being "more distressed" at one-year follow-up also had large average declines in their MCS scores, as would be expected (Δ = 7.30).

Significant changes in MCS scores were also reported in response to drug therapy for ulcers (Δ = 6.40 or 5.40, depending on regimen) and following hip replacement (Δ = 3.73) and heart valve replacement (Δ = 3.18).

Evaluation of Changes In PCS And MCS Scores

The scoring and interpretation of changes in PCS and MCS scores assumes much about how those changes are evaluated by those who experience them. Analyses of personal evaluations of actual changes in PCS and MCS scores over a one-year period tend to support these assumptions (Ware, Kosinski, Bayliss, et al., 1995; see also Chapter 8 and Appendix A). To address this issue further and to expand the SF-36 interpretation guidelines to include the values of patients, self-evaluated changes over a one-year interval were used as "criteria" for interpreting measured changes in PCS and MCS scores among MOS patients. MOS patients were asked two questions about physical functioning and mental health during their first year follow-up survey: "Compared to one year ago, are you more or less limited now in your everyday physical activities because of your health?" with five response choices ranging from "a lot more limited now" to "a lot less limited now." A similar question was asked for changes in mental health.

Table 9.18 presents the percentages evaluating their physical status as "more" to "less" limited (five categories of evaluation) at each of nine levels of measured change in PCS scores over the one-year period. Trends in results are also illustrated in Figures 9.2-9.4, which charts the percentages giving favorable evaluations of change (Figure 9.2), about the same (Figure 9.3), and unfavorable evaluations (Figure 9.4) at different levels of change in PCS scale scores. Overall, the figures and Table 7.18 support the hypothesized interpretation of changes in PCS scores. Specifically, measured declines (change levels 6-9) are most likely to be evaluated unfavorably (more limited or somewhat more limited) and measured improvements (change levels 1-4) are most likely to be evaluated favorably. Those scoring the same at both assessments (level 5) are most likely to evaluate their status as the same (73.7%). The percentage evaluating their health as the same declines with the magnitude of improvement or worsening in PCS scores over time, to slightly more than one-third at the highest and lowest PCS levels.

TABLE 9.18 PERCENTAGE OF MOS PATIENTS REPORTING MORE OR LESS PHYSICAL LIMITATIONS AFTER ONE YEAR, NINE CATEGORIES OF PCS CHANGE SCORES (N = 1,539)

Measured PCS Changes				Self-Evaluated Physical Transition[1]				
Level of Change	Range	Mean Change	(N)	A lot more limited	Some-what more limited	About the same	Some-what less limited	A lot less limited
1	16 to 34	20.5	55	1.8	7.3	38.2	21.8	30.9
2	11 to 15	12.6	80	2.5	11.2	50.0	15.0	21.3
3	6 to 10	7.6	166	4.2	10.8	57.2	13.2	14.6
4	1 to 5	2.8	381	4.5	7.3	63.8	10.8	13.6
5	0	0.0	95	5.2	4.2	73.7	9.5	7.4
6	-5 to -1	-2.6	405	5.4	13.5	64.9	8.1	8.1
7	-10 to -6	-7.7	193	6.8	21.2	53.9	11.4	6.7
8	-15 to -11	-12.8	83	12.0	27.8	43.4	12.0	4.8
9	-43 to -16	-21.2	72	29.2	26.4	34.7	6.9	2.8

1 Self-evaluated transition: Compared to a year ago, are you more or less limited now in your everyday physical activities because of your health?

FIGURE 9.2 PLOT OF SELF-EVALUATED PHYSICAL HEALTH TRANSITIONS AND CHANGES IN PCS SCORES OVER ONE YEAR (N=1539)

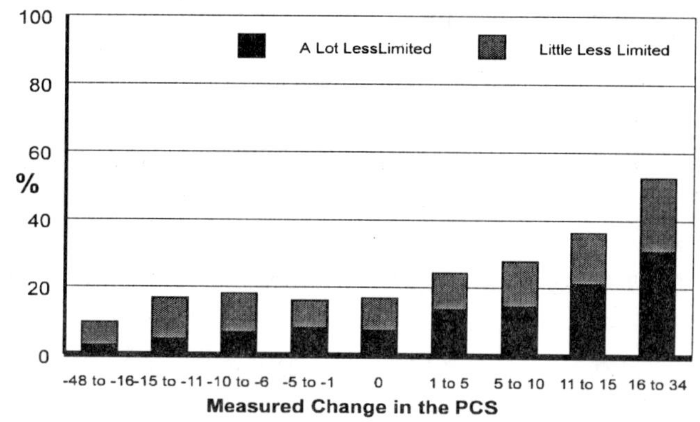

FIGURE 9.3 PLOT OF SELF-EVALUATED PHYSICAL HEALTH TRANSITIONS AND CHANGES IN PCS SCORES OVER ONE YEAR (N=1539)

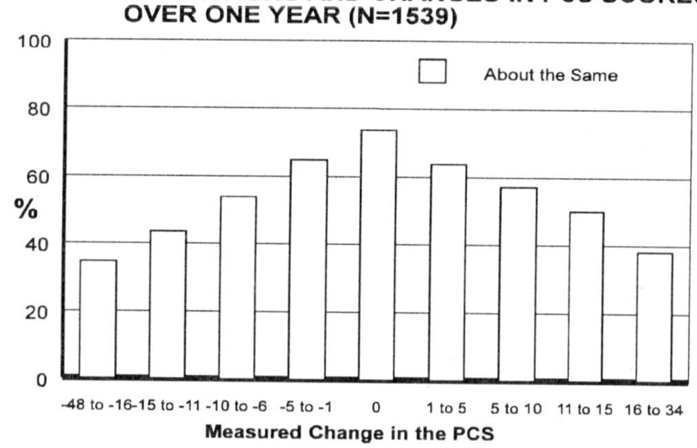

FIGURE 9.4 PLOT OF SELF-EVALUATED PHYSICAL HEALTH TRANSITIONS AND CHANGES IN PCS SCORES OVER ONE YEAR (N=1539)

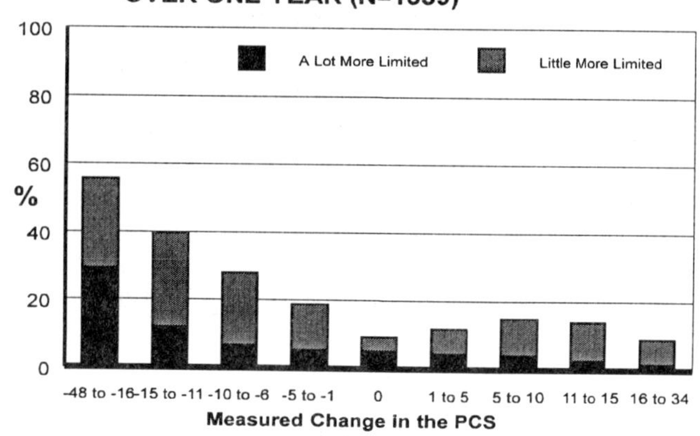

TABLE 9.19 PERCENTAGE OF MOS PATIENTS REPORTING MORE OR LESS EMOTIONAL PROBLEMS AFTER ONE YEAR, NINE CATEGORIES OF MCS CHANGE SCORES (N = 1,539)

Measured MCS Changes				Self-Evaluated Mental Transition[1]				
Level of Change	Range	Mean Change	(N)	A lot more often	Some-what more often	About the same	Some-what less often	A lot less often
1	16 to 45	22.5	111	0.0	2.7	19.8	22.5	55.0
2	11 to 15	12.7	89	2.2	6.7	36.0	20.3	34.8
3	6 to 10	7.6	158	3.2	6.3	41.8	24.0	24.7
4	1 to 5	2.6	358	2.2	7.3	58.1	16.8	15.6
5	0	0.0	109	0.0	9.2	65.2	12.8	12.8
6	-5 to –1	-2.7	384	2.1	9.9	59.9	15.1	13.0
7	-10 to –6	-7.7	131	7.7	16.0	51.1	17.6	7.6
8	-15 to –11	-13.0	61	11.5	22.9	42.6	11.5	11.5
9	-37 to -16	-21.0	58	19.0	34.5	29.3	13.8	3.4

[1] Self-evaluated transition: Compared to one year ago, how often do you feel bothered by emotional problems, such as feeling anxious, depressed, or irritable now?

As shown in Table 9.19 (and Figure 9.3), patients who worsened in MCS scores were much more likely to evaluate their current mental health unfavorably in comparison with one year ago. Likewise, those whose MCS scores improved were much more likely to evaluate their current mental health favorably in comparison to one year ago.

Final Comment

Generally, smaller average changes were less likely to be significant, as would be expected. All average *changes* greater than two points on the PCS were statistically significant and none below two points were significant in the 27 longitudinal studies summarized here in Table 9.15. With only two exceptions out of 62 studies, the same pattern held true for cross-sectional studies involving the PCS, as summarized in Table 9.15. However, statistical significance should not be equated with clinical and social relevance, which are addressed earlier in this chapter.

FIGURE 9.5 PLOT OF SELF-EVALUATED MENTAL HEALTH TRANSITIONS AND CHANGES IN THE MCS SCORES OVER ONE YEAR (N=1539)

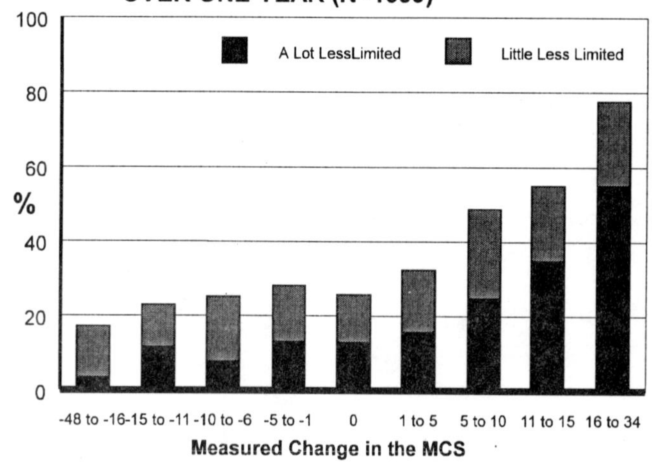

FIGURE 9.6 PLOT OF SELF-EVALUATED MENTAL HEALTH TRANSITIONS AND CHANGES IN THE MCS SCORES OVER ONE YEAR (N=1539)

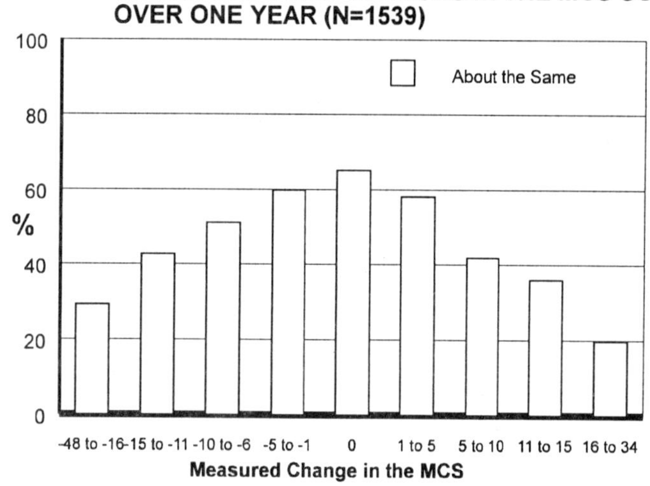

FIGURE 9.7 PLOT OF SELF-EVALUATED MENTAL HEALTH TRANSITIONS AND CHANGES IN THE MCS SCORES OVER ONE YEAR (N=1539)

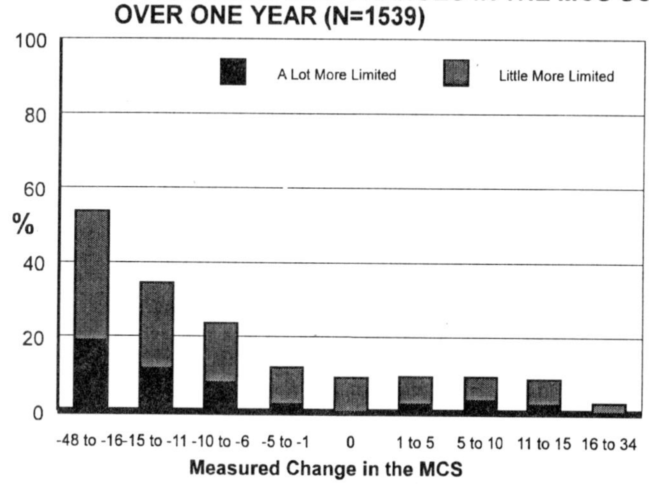

Chapter 10: Norms: 1998 General U.S. Population

This chapter presents norms for SF-36 scales and summary measures from both standard and acute forms in the 1998 general U.S. population. The chapter is divided into three sections. The first section explains norm-based interpretations and provides background information. The remaining two major sections present: (1) 1998 general U.S. population norms for the standard form (4-week recall scales and summary measures; and (2) 1998 general U.S. population norms for the acute form (1-week recall) scales and summary measures.

Background

Normative data makes it possible to interpret SF-36 scale and summary measure scores for an individual respondent or the average for a group of respondents by comparing them with the distribution of scores for other individuals. Scores can be understood as departures from expected or typical scores; these expected or typical scores are called norms. Norms can be computed at the individual or group level. At the individual level, norms are scores that are typical of the individual under stable conditions. At the group level, norms are average values for a group and can be calculated based on a sample from the general population. Norm-based interpretation answers the questions of whether or not an observed score is typical: Is the score one would expect to find for this individual or group of individuals?

Because estimates of scores for the scales and summary measures of the SF-36 are "norm-based", they have the advantage of a direct interpretation in this regard. For example, it is useful to know that scores above and below 50 are above and below the mean, respectively, in the general U.S. population for all SF-36 scales and summary measures. However, because health status varies with age, gender and with the presence of diseases, specific norms for subgroups of the general U.S. population are presented in this chapter to facilitate the interpretation of SF-36 scale scores and summary measure scores for these subgroups.

Norm-based comparisons require valid norms for a well-defined and representative sample of the population of interest. This chapter presents such data for the SF-36 standard and acute forms. Some view the publication of such norms as more than just a convenience. Accepted guidelines for the standardization, scoring, and the documentation of widely used psychological tests emphasize the publication of norms prior to their widespread use (APA, 1985).

This chapter presents SF-36 scale and summary measure norms for representative samples of the 1998 non-institutionalized general U.S. population. Norms are presented separately for standard (N=1,982) and acute (N=1,646) forms. Because health status scores for some concepts differ significantly across age groups and for men and women, norms are presented for the total population and separately for seven age groupings and for males and females. In addition, norms are presented for individuals with various chronic conditions (self-reported) using data from the 1998 general U.S. population.

Figure 10.1 Guide to Tables Presenting Normative Data (Standard Form)

Norms for SF-36 Scales and Summary Measures

SF-36 Norms for the General U.S. Population

Figure 10.2 Guide to Tables Presenting Normative Data (Acute Form)

Norms for SF-36 Scales and Summary Measures

How The SF-36 Was Normed

U.S. general population norms were estimated from responses to the 1998 National Survey of Functional Health Status, which included the SF-36 Health Survey. Sampling and data collection methods are described below.

Sampling

Households were drawn from the sampling frames, maintained by National Family Opinion (NFO) Research. The NFO panel includes 550,000 households representative of the non-institutionalized adult U.S. population and is matched to the U.S. Census data on geographical region, market size, age, income (SES) and household size. Panel households are balanced demographically to the four Census regions and the nine Census divisions and are also in the correct proportion by state within each of the nine divisions. Households are identified by frequently used geographical classifications to provide complete sampling and identification flexibility including 1) Metropolitan Statistical Areas (MSA), county or groups of counties with at least one city of 50,000 of more inhabitants, with the exception of New England MSA's which consist of towns or cities rather than counties. NFO Panel members are located in more than 300 MSA's; 2) Consolidated Metropolitan Statistical Areas (CMSA), a group of two or more adjacent primary metropolitan statistical areas with combined populations of more than one million. NFO households are located in all 20 CMSA's; 3) Counties, NFO households are located in 99.4% of the more than 3,000 counties located in contiguous states; 4) Federal Information Processing Standards (FIP Place Codes) used to designate all cities and towns; and 5) Census tracts, geographical areas of approximately 4,000 people each used for statistical analysis of Census data. The NFO panel is managed to maintain current demographic information about household members.

The NFO used a two-stage area probability sample design. In the first stage, quota sampling was used based on age, sex, and income. The primary sampling units (PSUs) used were Standard Metropolitan Statistical Areas or non-metropolitan counties. These PSUs were stratified by region, market size, age, income and household size before selection. The units of selection at the second stage were households stratified according to age, sex, and race.

To better represent the demographic characteristic's of the US population in 1998, weights based on the 1998 census were applied to equate the ages and gender of respondents, in comparison with that census.

Data Collection

Data were collected by the National Research Corporation (NRC) using a single wave of questionnaires mailed to randomly selected members of the NFO panel. Pre-notification announcements, replacement surveys, reminders and follow-up postcards, were not utilized. Data were collected for 12 weeks between October and December 1998. At the end of the data collection period, the un-locatable rate was 8% for respondents consistent with previous NFO surveys using this strategy, and the overall response rate for the survey was 67.8%.

A total of 1,982 completed the Standard form and 1,646 completed the Acute form. The mean age of respondents was 50.7 years (18-96) and 23% were elderly (65 and older). More than half of the respondents were female (59.6%) and the majority were white (84.2%), with at least 12 years of education (79.8%). Sampling weights were applied to adjust the sample to match the age, gender, and age by gender distribution of the 1998 census.

U.S. NORMS FOR SF-36 SCALES AND SUMMARY MEASURES: STANDARD (4-WEEK RECALL) AND ACUTE FORMS (1-WEEK RECALL)

Normative data for SF-36 scales and summary measures for standard and acute forms are presented separately in this chapter. Tables 10.1 through 10.21 present descriptive statistics for each SF-36 scale and summary measure for the standard form. Tables 10.22 through 10.42 present descriptive statistics for each SF-36 scale and summary measure for the acute form.

Tables presenting normative data include descriptive statistics for each SF-36 scale and summary measure in the 1998 general U.S. population. These include the mean, median (50th percentile), 25th and 75th percentiles, standard deviation, and observed range of scores.

NORMS FOR THE SF-36 SCALES AND SUMMARY MEASURES

Tables 10.2 (standard form) and 10.23 (acute form) present descriptive statistics for each SF-36 scale and summary measure in the total general U.S. population (males and females combined and separately). The mean and standard deviations for the total sample are 50 and 10, respectively, for all scales and summary measures because of the scoring method used in their standardization (see chapters 5 and 6). The medians (50 percentile score) for each scale are generally higher than the mean scores.

This reflects some skewness of the score distributions in the 1998 general US population, with more respondents scoring above the mean.

To determine whether the score for an individual or the average (mean) for a particular group is above or below the average for the U.S. general population, look at the first row of Table 10.1 (standard form) or Table 10.22 (acute form). For example, the mean Physical Functioning (PF) scale score in the general U.S. population is 50.00 (see the upper left-hand corner of Table 10.1). Scores above and below 50.00 are above and below average, respectively.

SCALE AND SUMMARY MEASURE NORMS FOR MALES AND FEMALES

Tables 10.3- 10.4 (standard form) and Tables 10.24-10.25 (1-week recall) present SF-36 scale and summary measure norms separately for males and females in the 1998 U.S. general population. These tables are useful in determining whether a score for males or females is above or below the average score for males and females in the 1998 general U.S. population.

SCALE AND SUMMARY MEASURE NORMS FOR AGE GROUPS

Tables 10.5 (standard form) and 10.26 (acute form) present SF-36 scale and summary measure norms for six different age groups among males and females combined. These age groupings were selected (1) to be large enough to satisfy minimum standards for precision; (2) to correspond with standard practices for defining age-specific groups; and (3) to correspond with age groupings used by others in reporting norms for the SF-36 (Brazier et al., 1992; Jenkinson et al., 1993, Ware et al., 1993, Ware et al., 1994) and that are forthcoming from other countries. Comparing results across age groups clearly shows that health status, in particular physical health, is related to age. Generally, the scores for all physical health scales and summary measures decline with age. For example, whereas the mean PF score for the total sample is 50.00, the mean for the 18 to 34 group is higher (54.07) and the mean for the 75 and older group is lower (41.77) (Table 10.5).

SCALE AND SUMMARY MEASURE NORMS FOR MALES AND FEMALES BY AGE GROUP

Tables 10.6-10.7 (standard form) and Tables 10.26-10.27 (1-week recall) present SF-36 scale and summary measure norms by age group separately for males and females in the 1998 U.S. general population. These tables are useful in determining whether a score for males or females is above or below the average score for males and females in a particular age group in the 1998 general U.S. population.

SCALE AND SUMMARY MEASURE NORMS FOR CHRONIC CONDITIONS

The 1998 general U.S. population survey included a checklist of 13 chronic conditions. This checklist asked respondents if their doctor had ever told them they had any of the following conditions or if they now had any of the following conditions: heart disease, hypertension, lung disease, diabetes, ulcers, kidney disease, liver disease, anemia, cancer, depression, osteoarthritis, rheumatoid arthritis, or low back pain or sciatica. Tables

10.8-10.21 (standard form) and Tables 10.29-10.42 (1-week recall) present SF-36 scale and summary measure norms for individuals with these various chronic conditions (self reported) and for a "well" group of respondents who did not report any of the chronic conditions on the chronic condition checklist. The norms in these tables are not adjusted for differences in socio-demographic characteristics and comorbid conditions. It is important to keep this in mind when making comparisons. For example, in interpreting general population norms for those who self-reported heart disease (Table 10.14 and 10.35), note that the majority also suffered from other conditions on the checklist and that the average age was generally higher than that of the total general population.

STANDARD FORM

TABLE 10.1 Frequency Distribution for PCS and MCS Scale Scores (4-Week Recall): 1998 General U.S. Population (N=1,982)

PCS Scale

Score	f	%	Cum. %
69	1	0.05	100.00
68	1	0.05	99.95
67	2	0.10	99.9
66	5	0.25	99.8
65	7	0.35	99.55
64	6	0.30	99.19
63	15	0.76	98.89
62	13	0.66	98.13
61	36	1.82	97.48
60	87	4.39	95.66
59	105	5.30	91.27
58	104	5.25	85.97
57	144	7.27	80.73
56	123	6.21	73.46
55	116	5.85	67.26
54	97	4.89	61.40
53	103	5.20	56.51
52	80	4.04	51.31
51	77	3.88	47.28
50	79	3.99	43.39
49	62	3.13	39.40
48	37	1.87	36.28
47	53	2.67	34.41
46	48	2.42	31.74
45	38	1.92	29.31
44	39	1.97	27.40
43	33	1.66	25.43
42	30	1.51	23.76
41	36	1.82	22.25
40	22	1.11	20.43
39	23	1.16	19.32
38	26	1.31	18.16
37	33	1.66	16.85
36	20	1.01	15.19
35	29	1.46	14.18
34	19	0.96	12.71
33	33	1.66	11.76
32	25	1.26	10.09
31	19	0.96	8.83
30	19	0.96	7.87
29	20	1.01	6.91
28	15	0.76	5.90
27	9	0.45	5.15
26	11	0.55	4.69
25	10	0.50	4.14
24	9	0.45	3.63
23	6	0.30	3.18
22	13	0.66	2.88
21	17	0.86	2.22
20	10	0.50	1.36
19	5	0.25	0.86
18	1	0.05	0.61
17	1	0.05	0.55
16	2	0.10	0.50
15	5	0.25	0.40
14	2	0.10	0.15
13	1	0.05	0.05
Total	1982		

MCS Scale

Score	f	%	Cum. %
73	1	0.05	100.00
71	1	0.05	99.95
68	3	0.15	99.90
67	2	0.10	99.75
66	7	0.35	99.65
65	11	0.55	99.29
64	9	0.45	98.74
63	23	1.16	98.28
62	37	1.87	97.12
61	47	2.37	95.26
60	105	5.30	92.89
59	119	6.00	87.59
58	151	7.62	81.58
57	123	6.21	73.97
56	111	5.60	67.76
55	115	5.80	62.16
54	115	5.80	56.36
53	106	5.35	50.55
52	68	3.43	45.21
51	71	3.58	41.78
50	75	3.78	38.19
49	63	3.18	34.41
48	45	2.27	31.23
47	42	2.12	28.96
46	43	2.17	26.84
45	36	1.82	24.67
44	44	2.22	22.86
43	36	1.82	20.64
42	35	1.77	18.82
41	21	1.06	17.05
40	26	1.31	15.99
39	25	1.26	14.68
38	17	0.86	13.42
37	21	1.06	12.56
36	27	1.36	11.50
35	23	1.16	10.14
34	17	0.86	8.98
33	16	0.81	8.12
32	19	0.96	7.32
31	12	0.61	6.36
30	13	0.66	5.75
29	14	0.71	5.10
28	13	0.66	4.39
27	10	0.50	3.73
26	12	0.61	3.23
25	7	0.35	2.62
24	7	0.35	2.27
23	6	0.30	1.92
22	5	0.25	1.61
21	6	0.30	1.36
20	4	0.20	1.06
19	2	0.10	0.86
18	2	0.10	0.76
17	2	0.10	0.66
16	2	0.10	0.55
15	3	0.15	0.45
9-13	6	0.30	0.30
Total	1982		

Norms For The General U.S. Population: (4-Week Recall)

TABLE 10.2 NORMS FOR THE GENERAL U.S. POPULATION, TOTAL SAMPLE

Total Sample (N=1,982)	PF	RP	BP	GH	VT	SF	RE	MH	PCS	MCS
Mean	50.00	50.00	50.00	50.00	50.00	50.00	50.00	50.00	50.00	50.00
25th Percentile	46.65	49.18	42.19	43.87	44.32	46.28	44.81	44.19	45.46	45.07
50th Percentile (median)	55.05	56.24	51.61	50.89	51.42	57.14	55.34	52.71	53.17	52.89
75th Percentile	57.14	56.24	55.90	57.91	58.52	57.14	55.34	57.26	57.05	57.19
Standard Deviation	10.00	10.00	10.00	10.00	10.00	10.00	10.00	10.00	10.00	10.00
Range	15-58	27-57	19-63	17-64	20-71	13-58	23-56	7-65	12-69	8-73

TABLE 10.3 NORMS FOR THE GENERAL U.S. POPULATION, MALE SAMPLE

Males (N=784)	PF	RP	BP	GH	VT	SF	RE	MH	PCS	MCS
Mean	51.50	50.85	50.63	50.19	50.69	50.79	50.37	50.96	50.92	50.49
25th Percentile	50.85	49.17	46.04	46.21	44.32	46.28	55.34	45.90	47.53	46.06
50th Percentile (median)	55.04	56.24	51.61	52.29	51.42	57.14	55.34	52.71	53.54	53.32
75th Percentile	57.14	56.24	55.90	57.91	58.52	57.14	55.34	57.26	57.16	57.14
Standard Deviation	8.91	9.58	9.65	9.76	9.54	9.48	9.86	9.41	9.28	9.25
Range	12-58	27-57	19-63	17-64	23-71	13-58	23-56	7-65	15-69	8-68

TABLE 10.4 NORMS FOR THE GENERAL U.S. POPULATION, FEMALE SAMPLE

Females (N=1,198)	PF	RP	BP	GH	VT	SF	RE	MH	PCS	MCS
Mean	48.61	49.21	49.41	49.82	49.35	49.27	49.66	49.11	49.15	49.54
25th Percentile	44.56	42.09	41.77	43.87	41.95	40.85	44.80	43.63	43.46	44.01
50th Percentile (median)	52.94	56.24	50.76	50.89	49.05	57.13	55.34	50.44	52.56	52.29
75th Percentile	57.14	56.24	55.89	57.91	56.15	57.13	55.34	57.25	56.92	57.22
Standard Deviation	10.73	10.32	10.28	10.22	10.37	10.40	10.12	10.43	10.60	10.40
Range	15-58	27-57	19-63	17-64	23-71	13-58	23-56	7-65	12-69	12-73

Norms For The General U.S. Population: (4-Week Recall)

TABLE 10.5 NORMS FOR FIVE AGE GROUPS, MALES AND FEMALES COMBINED: THE GENERAL U.S. POPULATION

Ages 18-34 (N=366)	PF	RP	BP	GH	VT	SF	RE	MH	PCS	MCS
Mean	54.07	52.45	52.05	51.36	49.14	50.45	50.02	49.05	53.76	48.00
25th Percentile	52.95	56.24	46.47	47.61	41.95	46.28	44.80	43.62	51.14	43.08
50th Percentile (median)	57.14	56.24	51.61	53.23	49.05	57.13	55.34	50.44	55.76	50.84
75th Percentile	57.14	56.24	57.60	57.91	56.15	57.13	55.34	54.98	58.06	55.37
Standard Deviation	6.09	7.85	8.94	8.95	9.75	9.09	9.54	9.66	7.04	9.57
Range	15-58	27-57	19-63	17-64	23-66	19-58	23-56	14-65	20-67	12-68

Ages 35-44 (N=435)	PF	RP	BP	GH	VT	SF	RE	MH	PCS	MCS
Mean	52.06	51.50	50.73	50.85	50.29	50.76	50.94	49.33	51.81	49.61
25th Percentile	50.85	49.17	46.04	46.20	44.32	46.28	55.34	43.63	49.21	45.54
50th Percentile (median)	55.04	56.24	51.61	53.23	51.42	57.13	55.34	52.71	54.29	52.67
75th Percentile	57.14	56.24	55.90	57.91	58.52	57.13	55.34	57.25	57.59	56.71
Standard Deviation	7.95	9.01	9.46	9.75	9.74	9.10	9.10	10.47	8.54	9.88
Range	17-58	27-57	19-63	17-64	23-70	13-58	23-56	7-65	14-69	8-66

Ages 45-54 (N=417)	PF	RP	BP	GH	VT	SF	RE	MH	PCS	MCS
Mean	49.40	50.10	49.19	49.31	50.40	50.07	50.60	49.44	49.37	50.32
25th Percentile	46.65	49.17	41.76	43.86	44.32	46.28	55.34	43.62	44.40	45.76
50th Percentile (median)	52.94	56.24	50.75	50.88	51.42	57.13	55.34	52.71	52.23	53.91
75th Percentile	57.14	56.24	55.89	57.91	58.52	57.13	55.34	57.25	56.68	57.24
Standard Deviation	10.01	9.94	10.19	10.70	10.49	10.09	9.53	10.71	10.37	10.27
Range	15-58	27-57	19-63	17-64	23-71	13-58	23-56	14-65	12-69	9-73

Norms For The General U.S. Population: (4-Week Recall)

TABLE 10.5 (CONTINUED)

Ages 55-64 (N=310)	PF	RP	BP	GH	VT	SF	RE	MH	PCS	MCS
Mean	47.80	48.98	48.69	49.66	51.30	50.68	50.06	52.08	47.77	52.29
25th Percentile	42.46	42.09	41.76	43.86	44.32	46.28	55.34	48.17	41.76	48.50
50th Percentile (median)	52.94	56.24	50.75	50.88	53.78	57.13	55.34	54.98	51.07	55.43
75th Percentile	55.04	56.24	55.89	56.97	58.52	57.13	55.34	59.53	55.50	58.35
Standard Deviation	10.30	10.65	10.80	10.17	10.25	10.13	10.63	9.35	10.34	9.39
Range	15-58	27-57	19-63	19-64	23-71	13-58	23-56	9-65	14-64	17-67

Ages 65+ (N=454)	PF	RP	BP	GH	VT	SF	RE	MH	PCS	MCS
Mean	41.77	44.04	46.89	47.26	49.95	47.63	48.08	51.83	42.72	52.38
25th Percentile	31.97	27.95	37.48	39.18	44.32	40.85	44.80	45.89	33.40	47.62
50th Percentile (median)	44.55	49.17	46.47	48.54	51.42	51.70	55.34	54.98	44.61	55.24
75th Percentile	52.94	56.24	55.89	55.57	56.15	57.13	55.34	59.53	52.40	59.62
Standard Deviation	12.40	11.78	10.82	10.72	10.04	12.02	11.64	9.25	11.55	9.55
Range	15-58	27-57	19-63	17-64	23-71	13-58	23-56	14-65	14-65	15-69

Norms For The General U.S. Population: (4-Week Recall)

TABLE 10.6 NORMS FOR MALES BY AGE GROUPS: THE GENERAL U.S. POPULATION

Ages 18-34 (N=132)	PF	RP	BP	GH	VT	SF	RE	MH	PCS	MCS
Mean	55.36	53.17	52.65	52.01	50.32	51.66	50.63	50.91	54.40	49.32
25th Percentile	55.04	56.24	46.47	48.54	44.32	46.28	55.34	47.60	52.39	44.72
50th Percentile (median)	57.14	56.24	51.61	53.23	51.42	57.13	55.34	52.71	56.13	51.54
75th Percentile	57.14	56.24	59.32	57.91	58.12	57.13	55.34	57.25	57.97	55.46
Standard Deviation	4.38	7.22	8.33	7.97	8.84	7.74	9.32	8.21	6.13	8.16
Range	17-58	27-57	19-63	26-64	23-66	24-58	23-56	18-65	25-66	13-61

Ages 35-44 (N=203)	PF	RP	BP	GH	VT	SF	RE	MH	PCS	MCS
Mean	52.78	52.02	51.07	50.91	51.06	51.65	51.81	50.68	51.97	50.80
25th Percentile	52.48	56.24	46.47	46.20	44.32	46.28	55.34	45.89	49.92	48.06
50th Percentile (median)	55.04	56.24	51.61	53.23	51.42	57.13	55.34	54.98	53.75	53.31
75th Percentile	57.14	56.24	55.89	57.91	58.52	57.13	55.34	57.25	57.43	56.88
Standard Deviation	6.76	8.83	9.28	9.83	9.26	8.82	8.36	9.87	7.99	8.92
Range	19-58	27-57	19-63	17-64	23-71	13-58	23-56	7-65	23-66	8-64

Ages 45-54 (N=167)	PF	RP	BP	GH	VT	SF	RE	MH	PCS	MCS
Mean	51.00	50.99	50.45	49.62	51.29	50.44	50.48	49.37	50.90	49.93
25th Percentile	48.75	49.17	46.04	43.86	44.32	46.28	55.34	41.35	46.95	45.37
50th Percentile (median)	55.04	56.24	51.61	50.88	53.78	57.13	55.34	54.98	53.89	54.31
75th Percentile	57.17	56.24	55.89	57.91	60.88	57.13	55.34	59.53	57.10	57.58
Standard Deviation	8.74	9.37	9.95	10.45	10.81	10.38	9.65	11.42	9.67	11.05
Range	17-58	27-57	19-63	19-64	23-71	13-58	23-56	14-65	15-69	9-68

Norms For The General U.S. Population: (4-Week Recall)
TABLE 10.6 (CONTINUED)

Ages 55-64 (N=106)		PF	RP	BP	GH	VT	SF	RE	MH	PCS	MCS
	Mean	49.16	49.03	49.13	49.02	51.57	51.40	50.17	53.32	48.05	52.48
	25th Percentile	44.55	42.09	42.19	43.86	46.68	46.28	55.34	50.44	42.36	50.13
	50th Percentile (median)	52.94	56.24	51.18	50.88	53.78	57.13	55.34	57.25	51.48	55.99
	75th Percentile	55.04	56.24	55.89	55.57	58.52	57.13	55.34	59.53	54.71	58.40
	Standard Deviation	9.04	10.86	10.19	10.22	9.77	9.44	11.00	8.31	9.73	8.98
	Range	21-58	27-57	25-63	19-64	23-71	19-58	23-56	20-65	24-64	20-66

Ages 65+ (N=176)		PF	RP	BP	GH	VT	SF	RE	MH	PCS	MCS
	Mean	43.11	44.96	46.71	46.49	49.59	47.37	47.54	51.59	43.51	51.48
	25th Percentile	34.07	35.02	37.48	39.18	44.32	40.85	44.80	45.89	33.88	46.19
	50th Percentile (median)	46.65	49.17	46.47	48.54	51.42	51.70	55.34	54.98	46.32	54.41
	75th Percentile	52.94	56.24	55.89	55.57	56.15	57.13	55.34	59.53	52.47	58.48
	Standard Deviation	12.65	11.78	10.89	10.96	9.73	11.98	11.88	9.11	11.28	9.61
	Range	15-58	27-57	19-63	19-64	23-70	13-58	23-56	23-65	18-65	15-67

Norms For The General U.S. Population: (4-Week Recall)

TABLE 10.7 NORMS FOR FEMALES BY AGE GROUPS: THE GENERAL U.S. POPULATION

Ages 18-34 (N=234)	PF	RP	BP	GH	VT	SF	RE	MH	PCS	MCS
Mean	52.76	51.72	51.44	50.69	47.96	49.22	49.39	47.15	53.10	46.66
25th Percentile	50.85	49.17	46.47	46.20	41.95	40.85	44.80	41.35	49.35	39.76
50th Percentile (median)	55.04	56.24	54.18	53.23	49.05	54.42	55.34	49.02	55.05	49.96
75th Percentile	57.14	56.24	57.60	57.91	56.15	57.13	55.34	54.98	58.26	55.29
Standard Deviation	7.19	8.38	9.50	9.82	10.48	10.15	9.73	10.61	7.81	10.65
Range	15-58	27-57	29-63	17-64	23-66	19-58	23-56	14-65	20-67	12-68

Ages 35-44 (N=232)	PF	RP	BP	GH	VT	SF	RE	MH	PCS	MCS
	51.36	50.97	50.38	50.79	49.52	49.88	50.09	47.99	51.65	48.44
25th Percentile	50.85	49.17	46.04	46.20	44.32	46.28	44.80	41.35	47.44	42.23
50th Percentile (median)	55.04	56.24	51.61	53.23	49.05	51.70	55.34	49.30	54.42	51.43
75th Percentile	57.14	56.24	55.89	57.91	56.15	57.13	55.34	57.25	58.09	56.57
Standard Deviation	8.93	9.17	9.654	9.68	10.14	9.31	9.72	10.90	9.07	10.63
Range	17-58	27-57	19-63	17-64	23-71	13-58	23-56	7-65	14-69	13-66

Ages 45-54 (N=250)	PF	RP	BP	GH	VT	SF	RE	MH	PCS	MCS
Mean	47.87	49.25	47.98	49.01	49.55	49.73	50.72	49.50	47.90	50.69
25th Percentile	43.16	42.09	41.76	42.93	41.95	46.28	55.34	43.62	41.66	46.23
50th Percentile (median)	52.94	56.24	46.47	50.88	51.42	57.13	55.34	52.71	50.63	53.30
75th Percentile	57.14	56.24	55.89	57.91	56.15	57.13	55.34	57.25	56.36	57.06
Standard Deviation	10.89	10.40	10.29	10.95	10.13	9.81	9.44	10.00	10.82	9.47
Range	15-58	27-57	19-63	17-64	23-71	19-58	23-56	16-65	12-65	18-73

Norms For The General U.S. Population: (4-Week Recall)

TABLE 10.7 (CONTINUED)

Ages 55-64 (N=204)		PF	RP	BP	GH	VT	SF	RE	MH	PCS	MCS
	Mean	46.56	48.93	48.29	50.25	51.05	50.03	49.96	50.95	47.51	51.79
	25th Percentile	41.93	42.09	41.76	43.86	44.32	46.28	50.07	45.89	41.47	47.99
	50th Percentile (median)	50.85	56.24	50.75	53.23	51.42	57.13	55.34	52.71	50.86	55.16
	75th Percentile	55.04	56.24	55.89	57.91	60.88	57.13	55.34	59.53	56.06	58.04
	Standard Deviation	11.21	10.50	11.34	10.12	10.69	10.71	10.32	10.10	10.90	9.75
	Range	15-58	27-57	19-63	19-64	25-71	13-58	23-56	9-65	14-62	17-66

Ages 65+ (N=278)		PF	RP	BP	GH	VT	SF	RE	MH	PCS	MCS
	Mean	40.82	43.39	47.02	47.81	50.20	47.82	48.46	52.00	42.17	53.02
	25th Percentile	29.87	27.95	37.48	39.18	41.95	40.85	44.80	48.17	33.27	48.68
	50th Percentile (median)	44.55	42.09	46.47	48.54	51.42	51.70	55.34	52.71	42.68	55.78
	75th Percentile	50.85	56.24	55.89	55.57	58.52	57.13	55.34	59.53	51.87	59.85
	Standard Deviation	12.15	11.77	10.79	10.54	10.27	12.08	11.47	9.35	11.72	9.48
	Range	15-58	27-57	19-63	17-64	23-71	13-58	23-56	14-65	14-63	20-69

Norms For The General U.S. Population: (4-Week Recall)

TABLE 10.8 NORMS FOR "HEALTHY" GROUP WITH NO CHRONIC CONDITIONS: GENERAL U.S. POPULATION

Healthy (N=571)	PF	RP	BP	GH	VT	SF	RE	MH	PCS	MCS
Mean	54.67	54.68	56.27	55.37	54.36	54.06	52.85	53.04	55.83	52.48
25th Percentile	55.04	56.24	51.61	50.88	49.05	51.70	55.34	50.44	53.75	49.90
50th Percentile (median)	57.14	56.24	55.89	56.97	56.15	57.13	55.34	54.98	56.86	54.26
75th Percentile	57.14	56.24	62.74	60.25	60.88	57.13	55.34	59.53	59.21	57.57
Standard Deviation	5.61	4.98	6.89	7.05	8.05	6.10	7.11	7.56	5.34	7.25
Range	15-58	27-57	24-63	28-64	25-71	13-58	23-56	18-65	27-67	22-68

TABLE 10.9 NORMS FOR ANEMIA: GENERAL U.S. POPULATION

Anemia (N=82)	PF	RP	BP	GH	VT	SF	RE	MH	PCS	MCS
Mean	47.09	45.47	44.99	45.75	44.22	45.11	44.74	46.75	46.12	45.24
25th Percentile	43.16	35.02	37.48	36.84	37.22	35.42	34.27	39.08	37.54	38.77
50th Percentile (median)	52.94	49.17	42.19	48.54	46.68	46.28	44.80	48.17	48.69	47.11
75th Percentile	57.14	56.24	51.61	53.23	51.42	57.13	55.34	54.98	56.26	52.94
Standard Deviation	11.94	11.30	10.35	10.78	9.10	12.25	11.92	10.34	11.70	10.37
Range	15-58	27-57	19-63	19-64	23-66	13-58	23-56	25-65	14-66	18-65

TABLE 10.10 NORMS FOR BACK PAIN, SCIATICA: GENERAL U.S. POPULATION

Back Pain (N=766)	PF	RP	BP	GH	VT	SF	RE	MH	PCS	MCS
Mean	46.60	46.44	44.55	46.46	46.52	46.87	47.60	47.63	45.60	47.95
25th Percentile	40.36	35.02	37.48	39.18	39.58	40.85	44.80	41.35	37.99	41.82
50th Percentile (median)	50.85	49.17	46.47	48.54	46.68	51.70	55.34	50.44	48.56	50.86
75th Percentile	55.04	56.24	51.61	53.23	53.78	57.13	55.34	57.25	54.43	56.16
Standard Deviation	11.31	11.43	9.28	10.55	10.21	11.16	11.25	10.88	10.84	10.97
Range	15-58	27-57	19-63	17-64	23-71	13-58	23-56	7-65	14-65	8-73

Norms For The General U.S. Population: (4-Week Recall)

TABLE 10.11 NORMS FOR CANCER (EXCEPT SKIN): GENERAL U.S. POPULATION

Cancer (N=70)	PF	RP	BP	GH	VT	SF	RE	MH	PCS	MCS
Mean	41.01	43.25	43.32	43.40	46.86	43.23	44.17	49.95	41.14	48.54
25th Percentile	29.87	27.95	33.63	36.84	39.58	35.42	34.27	43.62	32.14	41.36
50th Percentile (median)	42.46	49.17	41.76	43.86	46.68	46.28	55.34	52.71	41.49	51.32
75th Percentile	52.94	56.24	51.61	50.88	53.78	57.13	55.34	57.25	49.41	59.27
Standard Deviation	13.34	12.09	10.64	10.94	10.96	12.60	13.15	10.17	11.52	11.24
Range	15-58	27-57	19-63	19-64	23-68	13-58	23-56	20-65	17-61	20-67

TABLE 10.12 NORMS FOR DEPRESSION: GENERAL U.S. POPULATION

Depression (N=256)	PF	RP	BP	GH	VT	SF	RE	MH	PCS	MCS
Mean	43.54	43.04	42.93	40.86	40.51	39.01	39.27	36.51	45.13	36.78
25th Percentile	34.07	27.95	33.63	31.22	32.48	29.99	23.73	27.72	34.46	28.30
50th Percentile (median)	48.75	42.09	41.76	41.52	41.95	40.85	34.27	36.81	47.26	36.53
75th Percentile	55.04	56.24	51.61	50.88	46.68	46.28	55.34	45.89	56.07	45.47
Standard Deviation	12.72	11.91	10.74	11.41	9.99	11.95	12.37	11.28	12.54	11.60
Range	15-58	27-57	19-63	17-63	23-68	13-58	23-56	7-62	12-69	8-66

TABLE 10.13 NORMS FOR DIABETES: GENERAL U.S. POPULATION

Diabetes (N=169)	PF	RP	BP	GH	VT	SF	RE	MH	PCS	MCS
Mean	42.26	44.60	44.89	41.19	45.90	44.93	46.33	48.10	42.05	48.24
25th Percentile	29.87	27.95	37.48	33.56	37.22	35.42	34.27	41.35	31.76	43.22
50th Percentile (median)	46.65	49.17	46.47	41.52	46.68	46.28	55.34	50.44	45.02	50.86
75th Percentile	55.04	56.24	55.89	50.88	56.15	57.13	55.34	57.25	51.94	57.90
Standard Deviation	13.30	12.00	10.61	10.91	11.68	12.30	12.83	11.99	11.49	12.00
Range	15-58	27-57	19-63	17-62	23-66	13-58	23-56	7-65	14-60	8-67

Norms For The General U.S. Population: (4-Week Recall)

TABLE 10.14 NORMS FOR HEART DISEASE: GENERAL U.S. POPULATION

Heart Dis. (N=184)	PF	RP	BP	GH	VT	SF	RE	MH	PCS	MCS
Mean	39.39	42.23	43.18	40.47	45.63	43.95	45.88	48.10	39.36	48.84
25th Percentile	29.87	27.95	37.48	31.81	39.58	35.42	34.27	41.35	30.22	41.62
50th Percentile (median)	42.46	42.09	41.76	41.52	46.68	46.28	55.34	50.44	39.57	51.49
75th Percentile	50.85	56.24	51.61	48.54	53.78	57.13	55.34	57.25	49.02	58.23
Standard Deviation	12.80	12.04	10.42	10.98	10.28	12.29	12.80	11.62	11.31	11.44
Range	15-58	27-57	19-63	19-64	23-66	13-58	23-56	14-65	14-62	17-67

TABLE 10.15 NORMS FOR HYPERTENSION: GENERAL U.S. POPULATION

Hypertension (N=503)	PF	RP	BP	GH	VT	SF	RE	MH	PCS	MCS
Mean	43.80	46.07	46.50	45.68	48.34	47.75	48.84	49.60	44.08	50.63
25th Percentile	36.16	35.02	37.48	38.24	41.95	40.85	44.80	43.62	35.91	44.79
50th Percentile (median)	46.65	49.17	46.47	47.61	49.05	51.70	55.34	52.71	46.47	53.42
75th Percentile	55.04	56.24	55.89	53.23	56.15	57.13	55.34	57.25	53.54	58.05
Standard Deviation	11.93	11.75	10.49	10.43	10.28	11.32	11.12	10.41	11.56	10.00
Range	15-58	27-57	19-63	17-64	23-71	13-58	23-56	9-65	12-65	14-73

TABLE 10.16 NORMS FOR KIDNEY DISEASE: GENERAL U.S. POPULATION

Kidney Dis. (N=45)	PF	RP	BP	GH	VT	SF	RE	MH	PCS	MCS
Mean	37.35	40.19	40.38	36.56	42.22	40.52	45.11	44.48	36.79	46.08
25th Percentile	24.51	27.95	33.20	24.98	37.22	35.42	34.27	39.08	26.40	38.49
50th Percentile (median)	36.16	35.02	37.91	36.84	41.95	40.85	55.34	41.35	37.00	45.00
75th Percentile	52.94	56.24	46.04	43.86	51.42	51.70	55.34	54.98	48.58	55.89
Standard Deviation	14.61	12.27	8.28	10.30	8.69	12.20	12.66	10.39	11.43	11.29
Range	15-58	27-57	25-56	19-54	23-52	19-58	23-56	24-60	21-58	25-67

Norms For The General U.S. Population: (4-Week Recall)

TABLE 10.17 NORMS FOR LIVER DISEASE: GENERAL U.S. POPULATION

Liver Dis. (N=35)		PF	RP	BP	GH	VT	SF	RE	MH	PCS	MCS
	Mean	45.65	42.01	41.63	38.36	45.27	40.49	40.93	44.59	42.65	42.75
	25th Percentile	38.26	27.95	33.20	28.88	39.58	24.56	23.73	36.81	33.40	37.03
	50th Percentile (median)	50.85	42.09	41.76	39.18	49.05	46.28	44.80	50.44	41.39	43.66
	75th Percentile	52.94	56.24	55.89	48.54	53.78	57.13	55.34	57.25	55.42	56.26
	Standard Deviation	12.16	13.55	13.28	12.29	11.49	16.30	15.32	15.40	13.96	15.20
	Range	19-58	27-57	19-63	17-63	23-61	13-58	23-56	7-65	19-60	8-62

TABLE 10.18 NORMS FOR LUNG DISEASE: GENERAL U.S. POPULATION

Lung Dis. (N=100)		PF	RP	BP	GH	VT	SF	RE	MH	PCS	MCS
	Mean	37.82	39.29	42.70	38.60	41.84	40.58	42.95	44.74	38.26	44.94
	25th Percentile	27.77	27.95	33.63	28.88	37.22	29.99	23.73	34.54	30.53	33.92
	50th Percentile (median)	38.26	35.02	41.76	38.24	41.95	40.85	44.80	48.17	37.00	47.36
	75th Percentile	46.65	49.17	50.78	50.88	46.68	51.70	55.34	54.98	47.35	55.18
	Standard Deviation	12.35	11.68	10.71	12.34	9.40	12.47	13.90	12.20	11.09	12.54
	Range	15-58	27-57	19-63	17-64	23-64	13-58	23-56	14-65	18-62	15-67

TABLE 10.19 NORMS FOR OSTEOARTHRITIS: GENERAL U.S. POPULATION

OA (N=286)		PF	RP	BP	GH	VT	SF	RE	MH	PCS	MCS
	Mean	38.97	41.20	40.77	42.99	45.31	43.69	45.57	47.56	38.85	48.72
	25th Percentile	27.77	27.95	33.20	35.90	39.58	35.42	34.27	41.35	29.19	41.24
	50th Percentile (median)	40.36	42.09	41.76	43.86	46.68	46.28	55.34	48.17	39.01	51.27
	75th Percentile	50.85	56.24	46.47	50.88	51.42	57.13	55.34	57.25	48.64	57.77
	Standard Deviation	12.75	11.96	9.86	10.70	10.07	12.54	12.72	10.64	11.81	10.98
	Range	15-58	27-57	19-63	17-64	23-71	13-58	23-56	7-65	14-62	13-73

Norms For The General U.S. Population: (4-Week Recall)

TABLE 10.20 NORMS FOR RHEUMATOID ARTHRITIS: GENERAL U.S. POPULATION

RA (N=133)	PF	RP	BP	GH	VT	SF	RE	MH	PCS	MCS
Mean	42.52	43.17	42.19	43.24	47.11	44.75	45.40	47.46	41.66	48.11
25th Percentile	34.07	27.95	33.20	33.56	39.58	35.42	34.27	41.35	33.05	41.36
50th Percentile (median)	46.65	49.17	41.76	46.20	46.68	46.28	55.34	48.17	42.68	50.14
75th Percentile	52.94	56.24	50.75	53.23	56.15	57.13	55.34	57.25	51.04	56.56
Standard Deviation	12.65	12.37	10.25	11.97	10.67	12.28	13.15	11.25	11.37	11.22
Range	15-58	27-57	19-63	17-64	23-71	13-58	23-56	7-65	14-58	8-65

TABLE 10.21 NORMS FOR ULCERS: GENERAL U.S. POPULATION

Ulcers (N=145)	PF	RP	BP	GH	VT	SF	RE	MH	PCS	MCS
Mean	43.40	43.33	42.77	41.62	43.93	43.84	44.81	44.21	42.62	45.03
25th Percentile	34.07	27.95	33.63	33.56	34.85	35.42	34.27	34.54	33.88	36.29
50th Percentile (median)	46.65	49.17	41.76	41.52	44.32	46.28	55.34	48.17	44.16	47.92
75th Percentile	55.04	56.24	51.61	50.88	53.78	57.13	55.34	54.98	52.84	55.30
Standard Deviation	12.87	12.05	10.53	11.44	11.22	12.28	12.79	12.97	11.68	12.71
Range	15-58	27-57	19-63	17-64	23-64	13-58	23-56	7-65	14-65	8-66

ACUTE FORM

TABLE 10.22 Frequency Distribution for PCS and MCS Scale Scores (1-Week Recall): 1998 General U.S. Population (N=1,646)

PCS Scale				MCS Scale			
Score	F	%	Cum. %	Score	F	%	Cum. %
70	1	0.06	100.00	73	1	0.06	100.00
69	2	0.12	99.94	71	1	0.06	99.94
68	1	0.06	99.82	70	1	0.06	99.88
67	7	0.43	99.76	67	4	0.24	99.82
66	2	0.12	99.33	66	6	0.36	99.57
65	4	0.24	99.21	65	6	0.36	99.21
64	1	0.06	98.97	64	13	0.79	98.85
63	8	0.49	98.91	63	16	0.97	98.06
62	8	0.49	98.42	62	32	1.94	97.08
61	32	1.94	97.93	61	28	1.70	95.14
60	53	3.22	95.99	60	58	3.52	93.44
59	78	4.74	92.77	59	97	5.89	89.91
58	114	6.93	88.03	58	113	6.87	84.02
57	109	6.62	81.11	57	114	6.93	77.16
56	104	6.32	74.48	56	106	6.44	70.23
55	102	6.20	68.17	55	101	6.14	63.79
54	103	6.26	61.97	54	104	6.32	57.65
53	75	4.56	55.71	53	94	5.71	51.34
52	73	4.43	51.15	52	66	4.01	45.63
51	60	3.65	46.72	51	61	3.71	41.62
50	69	4.19	43.07	50	63	3.83	37.91
49	48	2.92	38.88	49	48	2.92	34.08
48	34	2.07	35.97	48	49	2.98	31.17
47	34	2.07	33.90	47	42	2.55	28.19
46	30	1.82	31.83	46	22	1.34	25.64
45	30	1.82	30.01	45	23	1.40	24.30
44	29	1.76	28.19	44	34	2.07	22.90
43	25	1.52	26.43	43	22	1.34	20.84
42	29	1.76	24.91	42	21	1.28	19.5
41	23	1.40	23.15	41	32	1.94	18.23
40	24	1.46	21.75	40	23	1.40	16.28
39	30	1.82	20.29	39	16	0.97	14.88
38	22	1.34	18.47	38	24	1.46	13.91
37	12	0.73	17.13	37	26	1.58	12.45
36	26	1.58	16.4	36	14	0.85	10.87
35	24	1.46	14.82	35	19	1.15	10.02
34	22	1.34	13.37	34	12	0.73	8.87
33	25	1.52	12.03	33	17	1.03	8.14
32	17	1.03	10.51	32	15	0.91	7.11
31	16	0.97	9.48	31	10	0.61	6.20
30	11	0.67	8.51	30	13	0.79	5.59
29	14	0.85	7.84	29	6	0.36	4.80
28	20	1.22	6.99	28	5	0.30	4.43
27	21	1.28	5.77	27	8	0.49	4.13
26	10	0.61	4.50	26	6	0.36	3.65
25	7	0.43	3.89	25	10	0.61	3.28
24	12	0.73	3.46	24	5	0.30	2.67
23	13	0.79	2.73	23	7	0.43	2.37
22	10	0.61	1.94	22	3	0.18	1.94
21	3	0.18	1.34	21	5	0.30	1.76
20	3	0.18	1.15	20	5	0.30	1.46
19	9	0.55	0.97	19	6	0.36	1.15
18	2	0.12	0.43	18	3	0.18	0.79
17	1	0.06	0.30	16	2	0.12	0.61
16	1	0.06	0.24	14	3	0.18	0.49
15	1	0.06	0.18	13	1	0.06	0.30
12	1	0.06	0.12	12	1	0.06	0.24
11	1	0.06	0.06	3-11	3	0.18	0.18
Total	1646	100		Total	1646	100	

Norms For The General U.S. Population: Acute Form

TABLE 10.23 NORMS FOR THE GENERAL U.S. POPULATION, TOTAL SAMPLE

Total Sample (N=1646)	PF	RP	BP	GH	VT	SF	RE	MH	PCS	MCS
Mean	50	50	50	50	50	50	50	50	50	50
25th Percentile	47.01	49.04	44.86	43.66	44.20	45.35	45.15	45.23	45.40	45.80
50th Percentile (median)	55.15	56.13	50.26	52.92	51.08	56.30	55.40	52.18	53.48	53.06
75th Percentile	57.19	56.13	61.05	57.55	57.95	56.30	55.40	56.82	57.21	57.00
Standard Deviation	10	10	10	10	10	10	10	10	10	10
Range	16-58	27-57	19-62	17-64	23-70	12-57	24-56	5-64	11-71	3-74

TABLE 10.24 NORMS FOR THE GENERAL U.S. POPULATION, MALE SAMPLE

Males (N=659)	PF	RP	BP	GH	VT	SF	RE	MH	PCS	MCS
Mean	51.71	51.45	51.42	51.17	51.43	51.28	51.41	51.26	51.46	51.17
25th Percentile	51.08	49.04	45.28	45.97	46.49	50.82	55.40	47.55	48.62	48.04
50th Percentile (median)	55.15	56.13	54.41	52.92	53.37	56.30	55.40	54.50	54.24	53.66
75th Percentile	57.19	56.13	61.05	57.55	60.24	56.30	55.40	59.14	57.67	57.25
Standard Deviation	8.65	9.07	9.21	9.54	9.65	9.13	8.77	9.03	8.86	8.59
Range	16-58	27-57	19-62	17-64	23-70	12-57	24-56	5-64	16-67	11-72

TABLE 10.25 NORMS FOR THE GENERAL U.S. POPULATION, FEMALE SAMPLE

Females (N=987)	PF	RP	BP	GH	VT	SF	RE	MH	PCS	MCS
Mean	48.42	48.66	48.69	48.92	48.67	48.82	48.70	48.84	48.65	48.91
25th Percentile	42.93	41.95	40.71	43.66	41.91	45.35	45.15	42.91	41.91	43.50
50th Percentile (median)	53.12	56.13	50.26	50.60	48.79	56.30	55.40	52.18	52.16	52.47
75th Percentile	57.19	56.13	61.05	56.62	57.95	56.30	55.40	56.82	56.72	56.69
Standard Deviation	10.87	10.62	10.52	10.30	10.14	10.61	10.86	10.69	10.86	10.88
Range	16-58	27-57	19-62	17-64	23-70	12-57	24-56	5-64	11-71	3-74

Norms For The General U.S. Population: Acute Form

TABLE 10.26 NORMS FOR FIVE AGE GROUPS, MALES AND FEMALES COMBINED: THE GENERAL U.S. POPULATION

Ages 18-34 (N=293)	PF	RP	BP	GH	VT	SF	RE	MH	PCS	MCS
Mean	53.47	51.69	51.70	51.83	49.71	50.57	49.81	48.98	53.31	48.30
25th Percentile	53.12	49.04	45.28	48.29	41.91	45.35	45.15	42.91	50.23	43.87
50th Percentile (median)	57.19	56.13	54.41	54.30	51.08	56.30	55.40	52.18	55.97	51.73
75th Percentile	57.19	56.13	61.05	58.93	57.95	56.30	55.40	56.82	58.39	55.60
Standard Deviation	7.21	8.85	9.49	9.47	9.74	9.40	10.21	9.81	8.10	10.08
Range	18-58	27-57	19-62	17-64	23-70	12-57	24-56	5-64	24-71	3-63

Ages 35-44 (N=371)	PF	RP	BP	GH	VT	SF	RE	MH	PCS	MCS
Mean	52.89	51.85	51.11	50.66	50.19	50.86	51.74	50.07	52.04	50.05
25th Percentile	51.08	49.04	45.28	45.97	44.20	45.35	55.40	45.22	49.63	47.31
50th Percentile (median)	55.15	56.13	54.41	52.92	51.08	56.30	55.40	52.18	54.46	53.41
75th Percentile	57.19	56.13	61.05	57.55	57.95	56.30	55.40	56.82	57.25	56.53
Standard Deviation	7.28	8.41	9.19	9.32	9.68	8.98	8.49	10.52	7.99	9.80
Range	16-58	27-57	19-62	17-64	23-68	17-57	24-56	5-64	16-68	11-67

Ages 45-54 (N=332)	PF	RP	BP	GH	VT	SF	RE	MH	PCS	MCS
Mean	50.41	50.75	49.63	48.91	49.97	49.82	50.56	49.97	49.95	50.03
25th Percentile	49.04	49.04	41.13	43.66	44.20	45.35	45.15	45.23	46.20	45.74
50th Percentile (median)	55.15	56.13	50.26	50.60	51.08	56.30	55.39	52.18	52.92	53.29
75th Percentile	57.19	56.13	61.05	55.23	57.95	56.30	55.39	57.98	56.59	57.13
Standard Deviation	9.53	9.49	9.78	10.29	10.47	10.53	9.38	10.23	9.69	9.83
Range	16-58	27-57	19-62	17-64	23-70	12-57	24-56	8-64	12-70	6-65

Norms For The General U.S. Population: Acute Form

TABLE 10.26 (CONTINUED)

Ages 55-64 (N=248)		PF	RP	BP	GH	VT	SF	RE	MH	PCS	MCS
	Mean	47.04	49.58	48.21	49.43	50.67	49.95	49.69	50.30	47.90	51.07
	25th Percentile	42.93	41.95	40.71	41.34	44.20	45.35	45.15	45.23	42.88	47.42
	50th Percentile (median)	51.08	56.13	49.43	51.99	51.08	56.30	55.40	52.18	51.55	54.67
	75th Percentile	55.15	56.13	54.41	57.55	60.24	56.30	55.40	59.14	55.29	57.72
	Standard Deviation	10.98	10.15	10.51	10.13	10.34	10.39	9.99	10.36	10.71	9.90
	Range	16-58	27-57	19-62	19-64	23-70	12-57	24-56	15-64	15-67	15-67

Ages 65+ (N=402)		PF	RP	BP	GH	VT	SF	RE	MH	PCS	MCS
	Mean	41.32	43.97	46.94	47.19	49.90	48.04	47.74	51.66	42.61	52.36
	25th Percentile	32.30	27.77	36.56	39.03	41.91	39.88	40.03	47.55	33.19	47.69
	50th Percentile (median)	42.93	49.04	49.43	48.29	48.79	56.30	55.40	54.50	43.67	54.48
	75th Percentile	51.08	56.13	54.41	55.23	57.95	56.30	55.40	59.14	53.35	58.86
	Standard Deviation	11.51	11.85	10.91	10.67	10.21	11.25	11.50	8.96	11.42	9.24
	Range	16-58	27-57	19-62	17-64	23-70	12-57	24-56	17-64	11-62	17-74

Norms For The General U.S. Population: Acute Form

TABLE 10.27 NORMS FOR MALES BY AGE GROUPS: THE GENERAL U.S. POPULATION

Ages 18-34 (N=106)		PF	RP	BP	GH	VT	SF	RE	MH	PCS	MCS
	Mean	54.63	52.59	52.91	54.19	52.02	52.06	51.34	50.92	54.42	50.32
	25th Percentile	55.15	56.13	45.28	50.60	46.49	50.82	55.40	47.55	53.24	47.37
	50th Percentile (median)	57.19	56.13	54.41	57.08	53.37	56.30	55.40	54.50	56.45	53.40
	75th Percentile	57.19	56.13	61.05	59.86	60.24	56.30	55.40	56.82	58.65	56.18
	Standard Deviation	5.91	8.38	8.49	7.93	8.89	8.62	9.24	8.03	6.82	8.09
	Range	18-58	27-57	28-62	26-64	28-70	23-57	24-56	28-62	29-67	23-60

Ages 35-44 (N=178)		PF	RP	BP	GH	VT	SF	RE	MH	PCS	MCS
	Mean	53.14	52.75	51.65	50.79	50.71	51.44	52.72	50.79	52.33	50.89
	25th Percentile	53.12	56.13	45.28	45.97	44.20	50.82	55.40	45.23	50.10	47.69
	50th Percentile (median)	57.19	56.13	54.41	52.92	52.22	56.30	55.40	52.18	54.73	53.18
	75th Percentile	57.19	56.13	61.05	57.55	57.95	56.30	55.40	59.14	57.59	57.25
	Standard Deviation	7.26	7.62	9.10	9.13	9.45	8.59	7.19	10.03	7.69	8.97
	Range	16-58	27-57	19-62	24-64	23-68	17-57	24-56	5-64	16-63	11-67

Ages 45-54 (N=130)		PF	RP	BP	GH	VT	SF	RE	MH	PCS	MCS
	Mean	53.17	52.91	51.79	49.70	51.55	51.83	52.13	51.57	52.14	51.29
	25th Percentile	52.10	56.13	49.43	43.66	46.49	50.82	55.40	47.55	49.79	48.11
	50th Percentile (median)	55.15	56.13	54.41	52.92	53.37	56.30	55.40	54.50	53.76	53.67
	75th Percentile	57.19	56.13	61.05	56.62	60.24	56.30	55.40	59.14	56.94	57.16
	Standard Deviation	5.92	7.23	8.34	9.22	9.92	8.34	7.39	8.92	6.97	8.19
	Range	26-58	27-57	19-62	21-64	23-70	12-57	24-56	15-64	18-64	14-65

Norms For The General U.S. Population: Acute Form

TABLE 10.27 (CONTINUED)

Ages 55-64 (N=82)		PF	RP	BP	GH	VT	SF	RE	MH	PCS	MCS
	Mean	48.12	50.94	49.46	50.30	51.44	50.69	50.27	51.79	49.02	51.88
	25th Percentile	44.97	49.04	44.86	43.66	44.20	50.82	45.15	47.55	45.61	49.27
	50th Percentile (median)	51.08	56.13	54.41	52.92	53.37	56.30	55.40	54.50	51.85	55.20
	75th Percentile	55.15	56.13	54.41	57.55	60.24	56.30	55.40	59.14	56.16	58.32
	Standard Deviation	10.11	9.46	10.51	9.75	10.29	10.18	9.56	9.97	10.13	9.71
	Range	18-58	27-57	19-62	26-64	23-70	17-57	24-56	22-64	19-67	19-67

Ages 65+ (N=163)		PF	RP	BP	GH	VT	SF	RE	MH	PCS	MCS
	Mean	43.82	45.51	48.70	47.32	51.08	49.05	49.51	51.94	44.42	52.87
	25th Percentile	34.78	34.85	40.71	40.41	44.20	45.35	45.15	47.54	35.47	48.77
	50th Percentile (median)	47.00	49.04	50.25	49.67	53.36	56.29	55.39	54.50	46.39	54.40
	75th Percentile	53.11	56.13	54.40	56.61	60.24	56.29	55.39	59.13	54.51	58.75
	Standard Deviation	11.48	11.71	10.17	11.63	10.85	10.80	10.40	9.04	11.22	8.53
	Range	16-58	27-57	24-62	17-64	23-70	12-57	24-56	17-64	19-62	17-72

Norms For The General U.S. Population: Acute Form

TABLE 10.28 NORMS FOR FEMALES BY AGE GROUPS: THE GENERAL U.S. POPULATION

Ages 18-34 (N=187)	PF	RP	BP	GH	VT	SF	RE	MH	PCS	MCS
Mean	52.30	50.78	50.48	49.44	47.36	49.06	48.27	47.01	52.18	46.26
25th Percentile	51.07	49.04	41.12	43.65	39.61	45.35	45.15	40.59	49.08	40.82
50th Percentile (median)	55.15	56.13	54.40	50.60	48.78	56.29	55.39	49.86	55.18	50.11
75th Percentile	57.18	56.13	61.04	57.54	55.66	56.29	55.39	56.81	58.08	54.47
Standard Deviation	8.17	9.23	10.29	10.29	10.03	9.93	10.93	11.08	9.10	11.42
Range	20-58	27-57	19-62	17-64	23-65	12-57	24-56	5-64	24-71	3-63

Ages 35-44 (N=193)	PF	RP	BP	GH	VT	SF	RE	MH	PCS	MCS
Mean	52.63	50.96	50.58	50.54	49.67	50.28	50.77	49.35	51.75	49.23
25th Percentile	51.07	49.04	45.27	45.97	44.20	45.35	55.39	45.22	48.43	47.04
50th Percentile (median)	55.15	56.13	50.25	52.91	51.07	56.29	55.39	52.18	54.38	53.46
75th Percentile	57.18	56.13	61.04	57.54	57.95	56.29	55.39	56.81	57.17	56.20
Standard Deviation	7.31	9.06	9.26	9.53	9.90	9.34	9.52	10.96	8.29	10.51
Range	24-58	27-57	28-62	17-64	23-65	17-57	24-56	10-64	23-68	13-61

Ages 45-54 (N=202)	PF	RP	BP	GH	VT	SF	RE	MH	PCS	MCS
Mean	47.77	48.69	47.57	48.15	48.45	47.89	49.05	48.43	47.86	48.83
25th Percentile	42.93	41.94	40.71	41.34	41.91	39.87	45.15	40.59	40.28	40.84
50th Percentile (median)	53.11	56.13	49.42	50.60	48.78	56.29	55.39	52.18	51.51	52.79
75th Percentile	57.18	56.13	54.40	55.23	57.95	56.29	55.39	56.81	56.19	56.92
Standard Deviation	11.41	10.86	10.60	11.19	10.79	11.97	10.76	11.14	11.33	11.06
Range	16-58	27-57	19-62	17-64	23-70	12-57	24-56	8-64	12-70	6-64

Norms For The General U.S. Population: Acute Form

TABLE 10.28 (CONTINUED)

Ages 55-64 (N=166)	PF	RP	BP	GH	VT	SF	RE	MH	PCS	MCS
Mean	46.06	48.34	47.07	48.64	49.95	49.27	49.16	48.93	46.88	50.32
25th Percentile	38.86	41.94	40.71	41.34	44.20	45.35	45.15	42.90	41.01	44.78
50th Percentile (median)	51.07	56.13	49.42	50.60	51.07	56.29	55.39	52.18	50.39	53.67
75th Percentile	55.15	56.13	54.40	57.54	57.95	56.29	55.39	56.81	55.14	57.19
Standard Deviation	11.67	10.63	10.42	10.45	10.37	10.57	10.38	10.57	11.15	10.06
Range	16-58	27-57	19-62	19-64	23-68	12-57	24-56	15-64	15-66	15-66

Ages 65+ (N=239)	PF	RP	BP	GH	VT	SF	RE	MH	PCS	MCS
Mean	39.55	42.88	45.69	47.10	49.06	47.31	46.49	51.45	41.32	51.98
25th Percentile	30.71	27.76	36.56	38.10	41.91	39.87	34.90	47.54	31.43	46.45
50th Percentile (median)	39.37	41.94	45.27	48.28	48.78	56.29	55.39	52.18	41.50	54.47
75th Percentile	49.04	56.13	54.40	55.23	57.95	56.29	55.39	59.13	51.84	58.94
Standard Deviation	11.22	11.85	11.24	9.95	9.66	11.51	12.06	8.92	11.40	9.71
Range	16-58	27-57	19-62	19-64	23-70	12-57	24-56	22-64	11-62	23-74

TABLE 10.29 NORMS FOR "HEALTHY" GROUP WITH NO CHRONIC CONDITIONS: GENERAL U.S. POPULATION

Healthy (N=480)	PF	RP	BP	GH	VT	SF	RE	MH	PCS	MCS
Mean	54.63	54.43	55.60	55.21	53.98	53.78	53.19	53.16	55.37	52.64
25th Percentile	55.15	56.13	54.40	50.60	48.78	56.29	55.39	49.86	53.75	49.79
50th Percentile (median)	57.18	56.13	54.40	56.61	55.66	56.29	55.39	54.50	56.70	54.51
75th Percentile	57.18	56.13	61.04	59.85	60.24	56.29	55.39	59.13	58.69	57.35
Standard Deviation	5.38	5.42	6.71	6.59	8.43	6.03	6.40	7.44	5.49	7.00
Range	18-58	27-57	28-62	28-64	28-70	17-57	24-56	19-64	26-67	16-67

Norms For The General U.S. Population: Acute Form

TABLE 10.30 NORMS FOR ANEMIA: GENERAL U.S. POPULATION

Anemia (N=63)	PF	RP	BP	GH	VT	SF	RE	MH	PCS	MCS
Mean	45.89	44.30	44.45	43.09	45.19	42.19	41.61	44.43	45.53	42.72
25th Percentile	36.82	27.76	36.56	34.40	37.32	34.40	24.65	35.95	38.33	32.06
50th Percentile (median)	51.07	49.04	45.27	45.97	44.20	39.87	45.15	47.54	48.61	47.91
75th Percentile	57.18	56.13	50.25	52.91	55.66	56.29	55.39	56.81	54.90	55.26
Standard Deviation	12.08	11.75	10.49	11.83	11.56	12.94	13.90	13.51	11.25	13.92
Range	16-58	27-57	19-62	17-64	23-65	12-57	24-56	15-64	21-66	14-63

TABLE 10.31 NORMS FOR BACK PAIN, SCIATICA: GENERAL U.S. POPULATION

Back Pain (N=615)	PF	RP	BP	GH	VT	SF	RE	MH	PCS	MCS
Mean	46.83	46.51	44.46	46.39	46.53	47.03	47.49	46.98	45.84	47.58
25th Percentile	38.86	34.58	36.56	39.03	39.61	39.87	34.90	40.59	38.13	40.40
50th Percentile (median)	51.07	49.04	45.27	48.28	46.49	50.82	55.39	49.86	49.41	51.03
75th Percentile	55.15	56.13	50.25	55.23	55.66	56.29	55.39	54.50	54.55	55.86
Standard Deviation	11.50	11.31	9.92	10.83	10.31	11.60	11.53	11.14	11.09	11.25
Range	16-58	27-57	19-62	17-64	23-70	12-57	24-56	5-64	12-70	6-74

TABLE 10.32 NORMS FOR CANCER (EXCEPT SKIN): GENERAL U.S. POPULATION

Cancer (N=49)	PF	RP	BP	GH	VT	SF	RE	MH	PCS	MCS
Mean	43.86	46.89	46.16	42.77	48.01	47.69	48.62	48.66	43.80	49.94
25th Percentile	34.78	34.85	36.56	36.75	39.61	39.87	45.15	40.59	38.08	41.32
50th Percentile (median)	49.04	56.13	49.42	43.65	51.07	56.29	55.39	52.18	44.76	52.25
75th Percentile	53.11	56.13	54.40	50.60	57.95	56.29	55.39	59.13	52.13	57.46
Standard Deviation	11.73	11.44	10.96	11.06	11.33	12.16	11.27	10.54	10.76	10.78
Range	16-58	27-57	19-62	17-63	23-65	12-57	24-56	17-64	18-59	17-74

Norms For The General U.S. Population: Acute Form

TABLE 10.33 NORMS FOR DEPRESSION: GENERAL U.S. POPULATION

Depression (N=206)	PF	RP	BP	GH	VT	SF	RE	MH	PCS	MCS
Mean	43.46	42.68	43.28	40.46	39.95	39.04	38.23	35.87	45.31	35.93
25th Percentile	32.75	27.76	36.56	32.08	30.45	28.92	24.65	28.99	34.59	27.25
50th Percentile (median)	47.00	41.94	40.71	39.03	39.61	39.87	34.90	35.95	46.83	35.83
75th Percentile	55.15	56.13	54.40	50.60	46.49	50.82	55.39	45.22	55.19	43.95
Standard Deviation	12.52	12.03	11.67	11.69	10.29	12.75	12.55	11.99	12.53	11.99
Range	16-58	27-57	19-62	17-64	23-65	12-57	24-56	5-60	18-71	3-65

TABLE 10.34 NORMS FOR DIABETES: GENERAL U.S. POPULATION

Diabetes (N=145)	PF	RP	BP	GH	VT	SF	RE	MH	PCS	MCS
Mean	43.97	45.36	45.87	40.94	45.20	46.01	47.18	47.88	43.14	48.05
25th Percentile	34.78	34.85	36.97	33.47	37.32	39.87	45.15	40.59	34.59	41.49
50th Percentile (median)	45.87	49.04	45.27	40.41	46.49	50.82	55.39	49.86	43.83	50.71
75th Percentile	53.11	56.13	54.40	50.60	53.36	56.29	55.39	56.81	53.23	56.46
Standard Deviation	11.05	11.48	10.62	10.88	10.33	12.08	11.83	11.34	10.86	10.98
Range	16-58	27-57	19-62	19-63	23-70	12-57	24-56	5-64	15-67	11-65

TABLE 10.35 NORMS FOR HEART DISEASE: GENERAL U.S. POPULATION

Heart Dis. (N=146)	PF	RP	BP	GH	VT	SF	RE	MH	PCS	MCS
Mean	39.26	40.93	44.12	41.15	44.97	44.28	45.86	48.29	39.26	48.95
25th Percentile	30.71	27.76	36.56	33.47	37.32	34.40	34.90	42.90	31.50	41.61
50th Percentile (median)	38.86	41.94	41.12	41.34	44.20	45.35	55.39	52.18	38.72	51.26
75th Percentile	49.04	56.13	52.72	49.67	51.07	56.29	55.39	56.81	48.18	57.76
Standard Deviation	11.32	11.66	10.59	10.07	10.19	12.43	12.37	10.71	10.62	10.95
Range	16-58	27-57	19-62	17-64	23-70	12-57	24-56	15-64	15-59	14-67

Norms For The General U.S. Population: Acute Form

TABLE 10.36 NORMS FOR HYPERTENSION: GENERAL U.S. POPULATION

Hypertension (N=414)	PF	RP	BP	GH	VT	SF	RE	MH	PCS	MCS
Mean	44.63	46.09	46.76	45.15	47.36	47.63	48.35	48.94	44.60	49.62
25th Percentile	34.78	34.85	36.55	38.10	39.61	39.87	45.15	42.90	36.46	43.62
50th Percentile (median)	48.13	49.04	45.27	45.97	48.02	56.29	55.39	49.86	47.80	52.70
75th Percentile	55.15	56.13	54.40	52.91	55.66	56.29	55.39	56.81	53.35	57.16
Standard Deviation	11.38	11.42	10.59	10.44	10.38	11.25	11.02	10.43	10.95	10.20
Range	16-58	27-57	19-62	17-64	23-70	12-57	24-56	10-64	12-67	14-67

TABLE 10.37 NORMS FOR KIDNEY DISEASE: GENERAL U.S. POPULATION

Kidney Dis. (N=42)	PF	RP	BP	GH	VT	SF	RE	MH	PCS	MCS
Mean	44.64	42.15	44.05	40.86	48.38	42.71	45.40	47.82	42.16	47.53
25th Percentile	36.82	27.76	36.56	33.47	41.91	34.40	34.90	38.27	33.92	36.65
50th Percentile (median)	44.97	41.94	40.71	38.10	44.20	45.35	55.39	47.54	44.10	48.38
75th Percentile	55.15	56.13	50.25	50.60	57.95	56.29	55.39	59.13	54.40	57.93
Standard Deviation	11.28	12.11	10.72	11.91	10.42	13.48	12.43	13.19	12.12	12.92
Range	18-58	27-57	24-62	17-63	30-68	17-57	24-56	19-64	21-59	24-74

TABLE 10.38 NORMS FOR LIVER DISEASE: GENERAL U.S. POPULATION

Liver Dis. (N=39)	PF	RP	BP	GH	VT	SF	RE	MH	PCS	MCS
Mean	39.43	42.00	42.20	41.32	47.27	46.19	46.83	49.53	38.73	51.03
25th Percentile	31.73	27.76	32.82	36.71	44.20	34.40	34.90	45.22	27.83	47.76
50th Percentile (median)	36.82	41.94	36.56	43.65	48.78	50.82	55.39	49.86	38.88	54.30
75th Percentile	47.00	56.13	61.04	48.28	55.66	56.29	55.39	59.13	51.83	59.35
Standard Deviation	11.29	12.90	12.80	9.87	10.10	12.34	11.97	11.77	12.78	12.44
Range	24-58	27-57	28-62	17-53	30-65	23-57	24-56	26-64	21-58	24-74

Norms For The General U.S. Population: Acute Form

TABLE 10.39 NORMS FOR LUNG DISEASE: GENERAL U.S. POPULATION

Lung Dis. (N=64)	PF	RP	BP	GH	VT	SF	RE	MH	PCS	MCS
Mean	38.82	40.48	43.31	38.71	43.11	42.20	46.13	46.31	38.40	47.38
25th Percentile	28.67	27.76	36.56	31.16	37.32	34.40	34.90	38.27	28.51	41.06
50th Percentile (median)	38.86	34.85	44.86	36.71	44.20	45.35	55.39	47.54	38.63	52.06
75th Percentile	51.07	56.13	50.25	48.28	51.07	56.29	55.39	56.81	46.17	56.01
Standard Deviation	11.75	11.71	10.03	9.77	9.76	12.62	12.24	11.91	10.93	11.94
Range	16-58	27-57	19-62	17-63	23-61	12-57	24-56	19-64	19-61	19-66

TABLE 10.40 NORMS FOR OSTEOARTHRITIS: GENERAL U.S. POPULATION

OA (N=246)	PF	RP	BP	GH	VT	SF	RE	MH	PCS	MCS
Mean	39.14	41.36	39.67	40.99	44.09	42.78	43.50	45.46	38.97	46.35
25th Percentile	28.67	27.76	32.41	31.16	35.80	34.40	34.90	35.95	30.98	35.47
50th Percentile (median)	38.86	41.94	36.97	41.34	44.20	45.35	45.15	47.54	39.15	48.74
75th Percentile	49.04	56.13	45.27	50.60	51.07	56.29	55.39	54.50	48.18	56.34
Standard Deviation	11.82	11.87	9.91	11.51	10.56	12.75	12.85	11.68	11.24	12.27
Range	16-58	27-57	19-62	17-64	23-70	12-57	24-56	10-64	11-65	13-74

TABLE 10.41 NORMS FOR RHEUMATOID ARTHRITIS: GENERAL U.S. POPULATION

RA (N=147)	PF	RP	BP	GH	VT	SF	RE	MH	PCS	MCS
Mean	39.85	41.64	40.29	41.68	43.98	43.13	45.51	46.52	39.11	47.54
25th Percentile	28.67	27.76	32.82	33.47	37.32	34.40	34.90	40.59	28.80	38.95
50th Percentile (median)	40.89	41.94	40.29	43.65	44.20	45.35	55.39	57.54	40.28	50.23
75th Percentile	51.07	56.13	45.27	50.60	51.07	56.29	55.39	54.50	49.15	55.74
Standard Deviation	12.85	12.13	10.62	11.53	10.01	12.94	12.52	10.29	12.23	10.83
Range	16-58	27-57	19-62	17-64	23-65	12-57	24-56	15-64	11-61	14-74

Norms For The General U.S. Population: Acute Form

TABLE 10.42 NORMS FOR ULCERS: GENERAL U.S. POPULATION

Ulcers (N=125)		PF	RP	BP	GH	VT	SF	RE	MH	PCS	MCS
	Mean	44.85	44.04	42.59	43.53	44.44	43.88	44.98	43.23	44.10	44.32
	25th Percentile	36.82	27.76	36.56	35.79	37.32	34.40	34.90	35.95	37.24	37.22
	50th Percentile (median)	49.04	49.04	41.12	43.65	44.20	50.82	55.39	45.22	45.28	47.31
	75th Percentile	55.15	56.13	50.25	52.91	53.36	56.29	55.39	52.18	53.81	53.13
	Standard Deviation	12.40	11.50	10.52	11.61	10.44	13.04	12.09	11.88	11.35	11.55
	Range	16-58	27-57	19-62	17-64	23-65	12-57	24-56	5-64	11-62	10-67

Chapter 11: Applications: Outcomes Research

Background

Alternative treatments and health care in general should be judged in terms of "how closely the result approaches the fundamental objectives of prolonging life, relieving distress, restoring function, and preventing disability" (Lembcke, 1952). Accordingly, outcomes research broadens the definition of outcome beyond traditional clinical endpoints to represent the implications of disease and treatment in terms of what people are able to do and how they feel. As reviewed elsewhere (Ware, 1995), substantial advances have been made in the validity and practicality of patient-based methods for assessing these outcomes. The reason for using these methods is that much is known about the dollar costs of health care and little is known about the health benefits. It is becoming increasingly accepted that patients are the best source of information about health benefits.

Results summarized in Chapter 6 illustrate advantages of both the SF-36 profile of eight scales and the PCS and MCS summary scales. Other surveys that offer both kinds of scaling options include the Sickness Impact Profile (Bergner, Bobbitt, Carter, et al., 1981) and the Duke Health Profile (Parkerson, Broadhead, & Tse, 1990). Measures that yield a single score without the option of analyzing individual dimensions include the Index of Well-Being (Kaplan & Anderson, 1988) and the EuroQOL (EuroQol Group, 1990).

This chapter summarizes results from re-analyses of four published studies that compared SF-36 health profiles to estimate health outcomes following: a) heart valve replacement surgery (Phillips & Lansky, 1992); b) hip replacement surgery (Katz, Larson, Phillips, et al., 1992); c) treatment for low back pain (Lansky, Butler, & Waller, 1992); and d) drug therapy for duodenal ulcers (Rampal, Martin, Marquis, et al., 1994). The first two of these studies were also discussed in the original *SF-36® User's Manual* (Ware, Snow, Kosinski, et al., 1993). Numerous other studies -- 85 at last count -- are cited in the references.

Published results from these four longitudinal studies were used to estimate the PCS and MCS scores and to compare findings and conclusions with those for the eight-scale SF-36 profile. These comparisons were made with two objectives: a) to address the issue of what is gained and what is lost with reliance on the SF-36 summary measures; and b) to illustrate the use of the interpretation guidelines presented in Chapters 7 and 8 to interpret results published by others. Are interpretation guidelines useful in understanding the implications and consequences of differences in outcomes for patients measured using the PCS and MCS?

For each study, mean scores for the eight SF-36 scales were aggregated using the formulas for the PCS and MCS scales in Chapter 4. The resulting estimates represent the mean scores that would have been observed for the PCS and MCS, if those summaries had been computed at the time of the original analyses. In the place of variance estimates, which cannot be estimated for the PCS and MCS from published descriptive statistics for SF-36 scales, estimates of standard deviations from the general U.S. population were relied upon. (From the published variance estimates for the SF-36 scales across the four studies, it appears that the general population standard deviations used here provide good approximations for purposes of significance testing for differences in PCS and MCS scores.)

In the examples presented below, we use interpolation to estimate the "criterion" value associated with different PCS and MCS scores, based on data provided in the tables in Chapter 9 and 14. A detailed explanation of how this was done is presented at the end of the chapter.

Heart Valve Replacement

Phillips & Lansky (1992) reported SF-36 profiles for 62 patients before and after heart valve replacement. Among the conclusions from their study were: a) substantial decrements in all eight SF-36 health status scales before surgery, particularly for five of the scales, (PF, RP, VT, SF, and RE); and b) significant improvements in all eight SF-36 scales after surgery.

Figure 11.1 compares SF-36 profiles before surgery with those at six-month follow-up. (The "normative" profile originally published is not reproduced.) The estimates for the PCS and MCS, which we have added to Figure 11.1, are consistent with results for the profile of eight scores. The average score of 35.1 for the PCS before surgery is well below the mean of 50 for the general U.S. population, and is below the mean observed for the PCS in norms for nearly all chronic conditions studied in the MOS and general population (Appendix E). These results indicate that the summaries would have led to very similar conclusions about the physical and mental health burden of these patients just prior to heart surgery.

The improvements in the eight SF-36 scales observed at the six-month follow-up after surgery were also captured by the PCS and MCS. Because the two summary scales take into account the correlations among the eight scales, they help to clarify that the burden of heart valve disease is concentrated in the physical dimension of health and that, although improvements in both the PCS and MCS were significant, improvement following heart valve replacement was concentrated in the physical dimension ($\Delta = 7.6$ for the PCS and 3.2 for the MCS).

The average improvement of 7.6 points in the PCS following surgery (from 35.1 to 42.7) can be interpreted using the norms in Chapter 14, as well as the content- and criterion-based guidelines presented in Chapter 9. Both the initial score of 35.1 and the amount of change observed must be taken into account because the interpretation guidelines depend on both, as explained in Chapter 9. Examples of results useful in interpreting an improvement of 7.6 from a pre-treatment PCS score of 35.1 are listed below (source tables from Chapters 9 and 14 are given in parentheses):

FIGURE 11.1 MEAN SF-36 SCORES BEFORE AND AFTER HEART VALVE REPLACEMENT SURGERY (N=62)

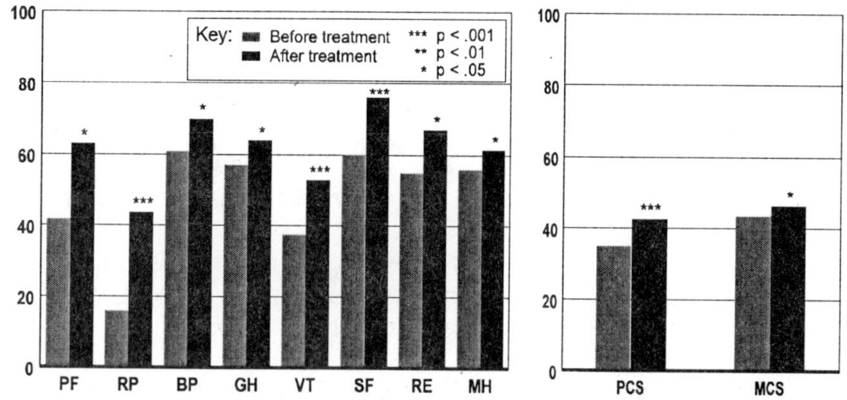

Source: Phillips & Lansky, 1992 (SF-36 data); PCS and MCS estimated from published data.

Norm-based interpretations using tables in Chapter 8 reveal that:

A. The average PCS score of 35.1 before surgery is 1.5 SD units below the mean (Table 8.1) and specifically just below the 11th percentile.

B. The change in the PCS scale from 35.1 to 42.7 represents an improvement from the 11th to the 20th percentile (Table 8.2).

C. Changes in the MCS, an average of 43.3 to 46.5 ($\Delta = +3.2$), represents an improvement from approximately the 22nd to the 28th percentile in the general U.S. population (Table 8.2).

Content-based interpretations include specific estimates of percentage-point reductions in the likelihood of limitations in:

D. Walking one block (reduced from 37.3% to 19.1%) (Table 9.2).

E. Climbing one flight of stairs (reduced from 56.1% to 28.7%) (Table 9.2).

Criterion-based interpretation guidelines include:

F. Lowered probability of overnight hospitalization (reduced from 9.0% to 6.5%) (Table 7.6).

One-third decrease in the predicted probability of death within five years (from approximately 12.4% to 8.5%) (Table 7.8 with interpolation).

Although the average improvement in the MCS scores from 43.3 to 46.5 ($\Delta = +3.2$) might seem numerically small, the clinical and social implications appear noteworthy from results presented in Chapter 7, including:

H. A 21% reduction (from 15.0% to 11.8%) in the likelihood of clinical depression (Table 9.10).

I. A 20% reduction (from 21.1% to 16.9%) in the likelihood of mental health treatment (Table 9.10).

J. A 12% reduction in the probability of reporting substantial life stress (from 35.8% to 31.4%) (Table 9.9).

Numerous other norm-based and criterion-based interpretations of these results are possible using the tables presented in Chapters 8 and 7, respectively.

Hip Replacement

The top and bottom panels in figure 11.2 compare un-standardized (0-100 scoring) and standardized (SD units) estimates of changes in the eight SF-36 scales with average changes in PCS and MCS scores for 54 adults following total hip arthroplasty (from Katz, Larson, Phillips, et al., 1992). Note that the PCS and MCS change scores maintain the same relationship across panels because both are scored in SD units. Because the standardization of change scores following treatments is a linear transformation, standardization does not change conclusions from statistical tests for significance. However, standardization does change some conclusions about which SF-36 scales changed most. The top panel (un-standardized) suggests that RP improved substantially more than GH; however, as shown in the second panel (standardized scores), they changed nearly the same amount in SD units and GH is more significant, statistically. Likewise, the top panel suggests that re improved more than MH; however, as shown in the bottom panel, the reverse is true when change scores are expressed in SD units.

Although all eight SF-36 scales improved a statistically significant amount following total hip arthroplasty, comparison of the estimates of changes in the PCS and MCS scales indicates that improvement was much greater in physical health. The PCS improved more than twice as much as the MCS.

Examples of norm-based interpretation using the tables presented in Chapter 8 include:

A. An average improvement of 9.5 in the PCS (from 39.0 to 48.5) represents an improvement in physical health large enough to move from about the 15th to the 33rd percentile of the distribution of scores in the general U.S. population (Table 8.2).

B. An average improvement in MCS scores of 3.8 (from 39.7 to 43.5) represents an improvement in mental health large enough to move from about the 17th percentile to the 22nd percentile (Table 8.2).

FIGURE 11.2 COMPARISON OF UNSTANDARDIZED AND STANDARDIZED CHANGES IN SF-36 SCALE SCORES AND SUMMARY MEASURES FOLLOWING HIP REPLACEMENT (N=54)

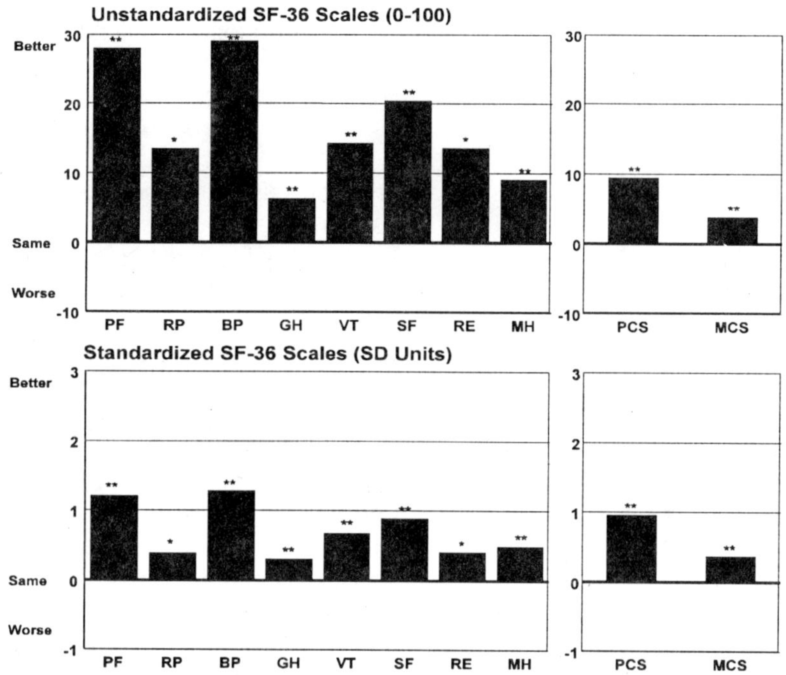

Source: Adapted from Katz, Larson, Phillips, et al., 1992.

* $p < .05$
** $p < .001$

The tables presented in Chapter 9 can be used to interpret the average improvement in the PCS and MCS based on item content. Content-based interpretations indicate that the observed improvement in the PCS score reflects reductions in the percentage of people likely to report on the SF-36:

C. That they had to cut down on work time (87% fewer people had to cut down on work time three months after hip replacement; percent cutting down work time dropped from 42.3 before the operation to 5.25 three months after the operation) (Table 9.2).

D. That they had severe pain (90% reduction in those reporting severe pain from 10.5% before the operation to 1% three months after the operation) (Table 9.2).

Criterion-based interpretations express improvement in the PCS scores in terms of reductions in the percentage of people likely to:

E. Be unable to work (75% reduction in probability of reporting inability to work from 28.8% to 7.1%) (Table 9.5).

F. Have a doctor visit in the past month (38% reduction in the probability of visiting the doctor in the past month from 38.3% to 23.6%) (Table 9.7).

Content-based interpretations associated with the 3.8 point improvement on the MCS scores observed for hip replacement include:

G. A 44% reduction in percentage that worked less carefully due to emotional problems (from 48.7% to 27.4%) (Table 11.3).

H. A 28% reduction in the percentage that accomplish less at work due to emotional problems (from 68.3% to 48.9%) (Table 11.3).

Criterion-based interpretation guidelines include:

I. A 46% increase in the percentage being extremely or very happy with their personal life (from 25.9% to 37.3%) (Table 9.9).

J. A 32% reduction in the likelihood of mental health treatment (from 28.9% to 19.4%) (Table 11.10).

Treatment For Low Back Pain

Lansky, Butler, & Waller (1992) reported SF-36 profiles for 113 spine center patients before and after outpatient treatment of low back pain. Conclusions reached from their study included: (a) substantial deficits were observed during initial assessment of two of the eight SF-36 scales, specifically patients' ability to function in their physical roles and pain; (b) patients reported significant improvement in both physical roles and pain at the 90-day follow-up assessment; and (c) SF-36 scales measuring general health perceptions and emotional functioning did not change significantly during the course of treatment.

Figure 11.3 compares mean scores for the SF-36 profile and the PCS and MCS summary scales before treatment for low back pain and at 90-day follow-up after treatment. Significant improvements were reported for five of the eight SF-36 scales (PF, RP, BP, VT, and SF) and for the PCS summary scale. There were no significant declines. In standard deviation units, improvements were largest for the PF, RP, BP, and SF scales, which is consistent with an improvement in the physical component of health. This interpretation is supported by the large and significant improvement in the PCS scale, in the absence of a significant improvement in the MCS scale. Interestingly, despite this substantial improvement in physical functioning, on average, these patients did not evaluate their health status more favorably after surgery, as indicated by the general health scale scores before and after treatment.

Examples of norm-based interpretations of the PCS and MCS using the tables presented in Appendix E include:

A. An average improvement of 7.6 points on the PCS (from 32.3 to 39.9) represents an improvement in physical health large enough to move from about the 8th to the 17th percentile of the distribution of scores in the general U.S. population (Appendix E2).

B. A before treatment score of 32.3 on the PCS represents 1.8 standard deviation units below the mean of the general U.S. population. A post treatment score of 39.9 on the PCS represents 1.0 standard deviation units below the mean of the general U.S. population (Appendix E2).

C. Before and after treatment scores on the MCS, 47.2 and 48.5 represent 0.28 and 0.15 standard deviation units, respectively, below the mean of the general U.S. population (Appendix E2).

Examples of content-based interpretations using the tables presented in Chapter 7 include:

D. A 36% reduction in the percentage having difficulty performing at work due to physical limitations (from 87.6% to 55.7%) (Table 9.2).

E. A 64% reduction in the likelihood of having severe or very severe bodily pain (from 21.0% to 7.4%) (Table 9.2).

FIGURE 11.3 MEAN SF-36 SCORES BEFORE AND AFTER TREATMENT FOR LOW BACK PAIN (N=113)

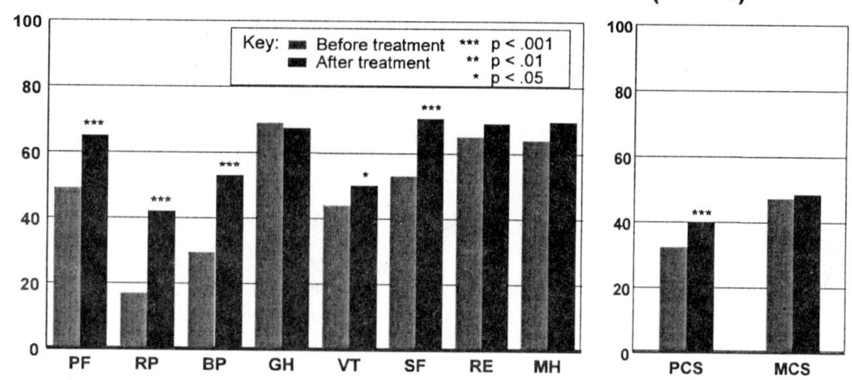

Source: Lansky, Butler, & Waller, 1992 (SF-36 data);
PCS and MCS estimated from published data.

Criterion-based interpretation guidelines include:

F. A 25.7% reduction in job loss over one year (from 26.6% to 18.3%) (Table 9.5).

G. A 22.2% reduction in the likelihood of having seen the doctor in the last month (from 47.6% to 37.0%) (Table 9.7).

The MCS scores after treatment did not differ significantly from those before treatment and, therefore, were not interpreted further.

Duodenal Ulcer Treatment

Rampal, Martin, Marquis, et al. (1994) conducted a study that compared SF-36 profiles over a one-year follow-up period for 581 duodenal ulcer patients, randomized into two drug treatment regimens: maintenance treatment versus intermittent treatment. Among the conclusions from their study were: a) all SF-36 scores improved over time in both treatment regimens; and b) the improvement in SF-36 scores over one year was greater for patients in the maintenance treatment regimen than for patients in the intermittent treatment regimen.

Figure 11.4 compares average *changes* in SF-36 scores and the two summary measures over one year for both treatment regimens. Significant improvements in all eight scales were observed with both treatment regimens, except for the GH scale for those treated intermittently. The estimates for the PCS and MCS, which we have added to Figure 9.4, are consistent with results for the profile of eight scores. Like the SF-36 profile, significant improvements on PCS and MCS scores are observed for both treatment regimens, and the improvement is greater in the maintenance treatment regimen for both summary scales.

Examples of norm-based interpretations for the PCS and MCS using the tables presented in Appendix E include:

A. An average improvement on the PCS from 47.9 to 52.6 for the maintenance treatment regimen represents an improvement in physical health large enough to move from about the 31st to the 46th percentile of the distribution of scores in the general U.S. population (Appendix E2).

B. An average improvement on the MCS from 45.1 to 51.5 for the maintenance treatment regimen represents an improvement large enough to move from nearly one-half a standard deviation (SD) below the general U.S. population mean to 0.15 SD units above that mean.

Examples of content-based interpretations using the tables presented in Chapter 9 include:

C. For those in the maintenance treatment regimen, the improvement in PCS meant a 74% reduction in difficulty performing at work due to physical limitations (from 15.2% to 3.9%) (Table 11.2); and the improvement in MCS meant a 62% reduction in accomplishing less at work due to emotional problems (from 39.0% to 14.7%) (Table 11.3).

D. For those in the intermittent treatment regimen, the improvement in PCS meant a 38% reduction in reports of fair or poor health (from 12.5% to 7.7%) (Table 11.2); and the improvement in MCS meant a 53% reduction in feeling tired all or most of the time (from 21.0% to 9.7%) (Table 11.3).

Examples of criterion-based interpretations using the tables presented in Chapter 9 include:

E. For those in the maintenance treatment regimen, the improvement in PCS meant a 34% reduction in the likelihood of job loss over one year (from 11.5% to 7.5%) (Table 11.5); and the improvement in PCS meant a 38% reduction in the likelihood of clinical depression (from 12.7% to 7.8%) (Table 11.10).

F. For those in the intermittent treatment regimen, the improvement in PCS meant a 15% reduction on the likelihood of having seen the doctor in the last month (from 25.7% to 21.8%) (Table 11.7); and the improvement in MCS meant a 35% reduction in the likelihood of mental health treatment (from 20.0% to 13.0%) (Table 11.10).

Method For Relating PCS And MCS Scale Scores To "Criterion" Scores

Scale scores are interpreted by relating a difference or change in scale score to other specific results as explained in Chapters 7 and 8. Since only ranges and means within ranges for PCS and MCS scale scores and "criteria" are printed in the tables in Chapter 9 and Appendix E, one must calculate ratios of differences and interpolate to estimate the "criterion" value that is associated with a particular score. The numbers presented in the difference ratio column (Δ/Δ) on the tables in Chapter 9 are for difference ratios *between* levels. These can be used to relate differences in scale scores to differences in criterion values for differences that occur *between* the levels on the table. To relate differences in scale scores to differences in criterion values *within* a level, it is necessary to calculate the difference ratio *within* a level. This ratio is then used to associate the scale scores with the "criterion" value. This method is illustrated in an example below in which the death rate associated with scores on the PCS is estimated based on interpolation using data from a portion of Table 9.8.

Death Rate in Five Years Associated with Heart Valve Replacement. Patients had an average PCS score of 35.1 before heart valve replacement and 42.7 after heart valve replacement. How is the change in the PCS score related to predicted differences in the death rate? Portions of Table 9.8 reproduced below in Table 11.1 show the percent of people who died within five years at each of five score ranges on the PCS and the mean PCS score within each of those ranges. The mean scores on PCS before (35.1) and after (42.7) heart valve replacement lie within one level (level 3, Table 9.1). If either of these scores were equivalent to the mean for that level (39.9), the percent that would die in five years (6.2) could be read directly from the table. However, since the percentages associated with these scores are not presented in the table, they must be estimated by interpolation. This requires two steps. First, the appropriate difference ratio (change in criterion per unit change in PCS or MCS) must be calculated. Next, this ratio is used to estimate the criterion value for a particular score. To estimate the predicted change in the percent dying within five years corresponding to the change in PCS scores before and after heart surgery, do the following:

1. *Identify the numbers to use to calculate the change in the criterion (e.g., death rate) per unit change in PCS (i.e., the difference ratio).* This is done by looking at the column of means for each level. Choose those levels whose means are lesser and greater than the lower and higher scores, respectively. On Table 9.1, the scale scores for before (35.1) and after surgery (42.7) fall within the mean PCS scores for levels 4 (29.9) and 2 (50.0).

2. *Calculate the percent change on the criterion (e.g., death rate) per unit change in PCS.* At level 2 (Table 11.1), the mean PCS is 50 and the percent that would die within five years is 4.7. At level 4 (Table 11.1), the mean PCS is 29.9 and the percent that would die within five years is 15.1. To calculate the percent change in death rate per unit change in the PCS, take the difference in the percent who died associated with the mean PCS scores at levels 4 and 2 (15.1%-4.7%=10.4%) and divide it by the difference in the means at levels 2 and 4 (50.0-29.9=20.1). The percent death rate change per unit change in PCS is 0.52 (10.4%/20.1).

TABLE 11.1 PORTION OF TABLE 9.8 USED FOR INTERPRETATION: FIVE-YEAR MORTALITY RATES FOR MOS PATIENTS AT FIVE LEVELS OF THE PCS SCALE

	PCS Scores			Died	
Levels	Range	Mean	(N)	%	Δ/Δ
1	55-72	57.8	609	1.8	
					0.4
2	45-54	50	1181	4.7	
					0.1
3	35-44	39.9	754	6.2	
					0.9
4	25-34	29.9	443	15.1	
					0.7
5	8-24	20.4	233	21.5	

3. *Calculate the percent on the criterion (e.g., the percent who die) at one score value (e.g., the before surgery score).* The percent who die at the before surgery score of 35.1 should be less than those who die at the mean for level 4 (29.9), because the trend in the data is for the death rate to go down as scores go up (higher scores indicate better health). To estimate how many fewer people should die, subtract the mean PCS score at level 2 (29.9) from the before PCS score (35.1) and multiply this result by the percent change in death rate per unit change in PCS [(35.1-29.9)*0.52=2.7%]. Subtract this result (2.7%) from the percentage who die at a score of 29.9 (15.1%) to get the percent who would die at a score of 35.1 (12.4%).

4. *Calculate the percent on the "criterion" (e.g., the percent who die) at the other score value (e.g., the after surgery score).* To get the percent who would die at the average after surgery score of 42.7, multiply the difference between the before (35.1) and after surgery (42.7) PCS scores of 7.6 (42.7-35.1=7.6) by the percent change in death rate per unit change in PCS (0.52). This result (3.95%) should be subtracted from the percent dying at the before surgery score (12.4%-3.95%=8.5%). Thus, the percent who would die at a score of 42.7 is estimated to be 8.5 percent.

It should be understood that the interpretations offered in this chapter are approximations. They are based on data from single studies. Also, simpler rather than more complex calculations are used to promote better understanding. For example, the difference ratios presented in this manual are based on simple averaging and so assume a linear relationship between score levels. When values associated with each score level differ greatly, a more accurate approach would be to put greater weight on the values that are closer to the score of interest. We have calculated simple averages for difference ratios for each of several levels and thereby capture some of the variation in change in criterion associated with change in scores at different levels of scale scores. For example, on Table 9.1, the difference ratio between levels 4 and 3 (0.9) is much larger than that between levels 3 and 2 (0.1). Table 9.2 shows a wide variation in difference ratios for each of the 10 criteria listed.

Final Comment

Outcomes research seeks to inform decision-makers about health benefits in terms of changes in what people are able to do and how they feel. *Generic* measures of these outcomes, such as the PCS and MCS summary scales, provide a common yardstick for purposes of estimating health burden across diseases and for comparing benefits across treatments. The interpretation of group differences detected by these measures can be greatly facilitated using normative data as well as content- and criterion-based interpretation guidelines.

The estimates of changes in PCS and MCS scores discussed above were prepared to illustrate the use of norm-, content-, and criterion-based interpretation guidelines from Chapters 9 and 14. Results for the PCS and MCS were also compared with published results for the eight-scale SF-36 profile to provide preliminary tests of whether the summaries do a good job of reflecting profile changes. The studies re-analyzed here are among the first longitudinal SF-36 studies published. The first three studies reported very large changes following treatment (see Chapter 9, Summary of Effect Sizes). Whether the satisfactory performance of the PCS and MCS in summarizing SF-36 profiles and in detecting hypothesized changes in these studies will generalize to others remains to be determined. In the meantime, documentation of changes in the SF-36 profile along with changes in the PCS and MCS summary scales in the same graph, as illustrated above, facilitates comparisons of results.

Chapter 12: Applications: Clinical Practice

Background

Standardized health surveys have the potential to become the new "laboratory tests" of medical practice (Deyo & Carter, 1992). Without them, it appears that patient functioning and well-being are unlikely to be discussed during a typical medical visit. Two-thirds to three-fourths of U.S. adults reported that physicians rarely or never ask about the extent of their limitations in performing everyday activities, even in the presence of chronic conditions (Schor, Lerner, & Malspeis, 1995). As a result, practicing physicians are unaware of relatively concrete impairment manifested by observable limitations in physical, social, and role functioning (Rubenstein, McCoy, Cope, et al., 1991). Differences in severity of psychological distress also are often not apparent to treating physicians (Wells, Hays, Burnam, et al., 1989). Severely psychologically distressed patients suffering from psychiatric disorders often go unrecognized and untreated even when mental health treatment is generously covered by health insurance (Ware, Manning, Duan, et al., 1984). It has been suggested that more widespread use of standardized health measures may improve clinical practice (American College of Physicians, 1988; Berwick, Murphy, Goldman, et al., 1991).

Standardization of functional status and well-being assessments in everyday medical practice may be useful in: (1) ensuring that all important dimensions of functional status and well-being are considered consistently; (2) detecting, explaining, and tracking changes in functional capacity over time; (3) making it possible to better consider the patient's total functioning when choosing among therapies; (4) guiding the efficient use of community resources and social services; and (5) predicting more accurately the course of chronic disease. Such data also would make it possible for physicians to better inform patients about the clinical and functional tradeoffs involved in alternative treatments (Fowler, Wennberg, Timothy, et al., 1988). Clearly, a great potential exists for standardized measures of functional status and well-being administered routinely as part of the clinical database

Confidence Intervals

As with all health status scales, the interpretation of individual patient scores for the PCS and MCS must take into account the amount of "noise" in the scores that they yield. The "noise level" can be quantified and displayed visually as a confidence interval (CI) around a patient's score. The size of the CI is a function of both the reliability of a score and the standard deviation of the score distribution in the population of interest (see Chapter 7). Because score reliability determines the size of confidence intervals most when *individual* scores are interpreted, psychometricians recommend a much higher standard of score reliability for measures to be interpreted at the individual patient level, as opposed to *average* scores for large groups of patients (Guilford, 1954). For example, lowering the reliability of the PCS from an actual 0.93 to a hypothetical 0.50 would increase the 95% confidence interval for an individual patient PCS score by more than 250% (from ± 5.7 to ± 14.4).

Estimates for the 95% confidence interval for the PCS and MCS are 5.7 and 6.3, respectively, in the general U.S. population. Other estimates for larger intervals are presented in Chapter 7. To the extent that either score reliability or score variability differ in the patient population of interest, relative to those for the general U.S. population used here, confidence intervals should be re-estimated using coefficients of reliability and standard deviations from the population of interest. As documented in Chapter 7 and Appendix E (for reliability and standard deviations, respectively), such differences are sometimes an issue for the patients used as examples here.

Monitoring Individual Patients

Soon after the SF-36 became available, began New England Medical Center (NEMC) testing patient-based systems for monitoring and improving health outcomes in various outpatient clinics. One project included quarterly administrations of the SF-36 to expand the definition of the "adequacy" or "quality" of dialysis beyond traditional laboratory test values among patients with end-stage renal disease (ESRD) (Kurtin, Davies, Meyer, et al., 1992; Meyer, Espindle, DeGiacomo, et al., 1994). Reported results for individual hemodialysis patients illustrate both the feasibility and usefulness of periodic health assessments in managing patients during the progression from advanced renal failure to end-stage renal disease (Meyer, Espindle, DeGiacomo, et al., 1994).

Charts For Longitudinal Data

Figure 12.1 plots the results of 12 quarterly administrations of the SF-36 for one patient over a three-year period that included his seventh and eighth years on dialysis (from Meyer, Espindle, DeGiacomo, et al., 1994). The patient is a middle-aged married male, who is an employed parent. He completed SF-36 forms at the time of regularly scheduled outpatient visits for hemodialysis. Results for each of the eight SF-36 scales for the first two years have been published. Analyses are extended here to include results for the PCS and MCS scales. The solid horizontal line in each panel defines a stable "norm" for a general U.S. population male of the same age. These norms vary considerably across scales, as documented in Appendix E. Visit one scores (1/91) were at or above the norm for six of eight scales (all except VT and PF) and were within the 95% CI for the PCS and MCS. It should be noted that the 95% CIs, which are indicated by the vertical lines above and below the score for each observation, are much narrower for the PCS and MCS (top panel) than for the eight scales (lower panel). As explained and further documented in Chapter 7 and Appendix D, this is an advantage of the two summary measures in monitoring individual patients.

FIGURE 12.1 LONGITUDINAL DATA FOR ESRD PATIENT 1

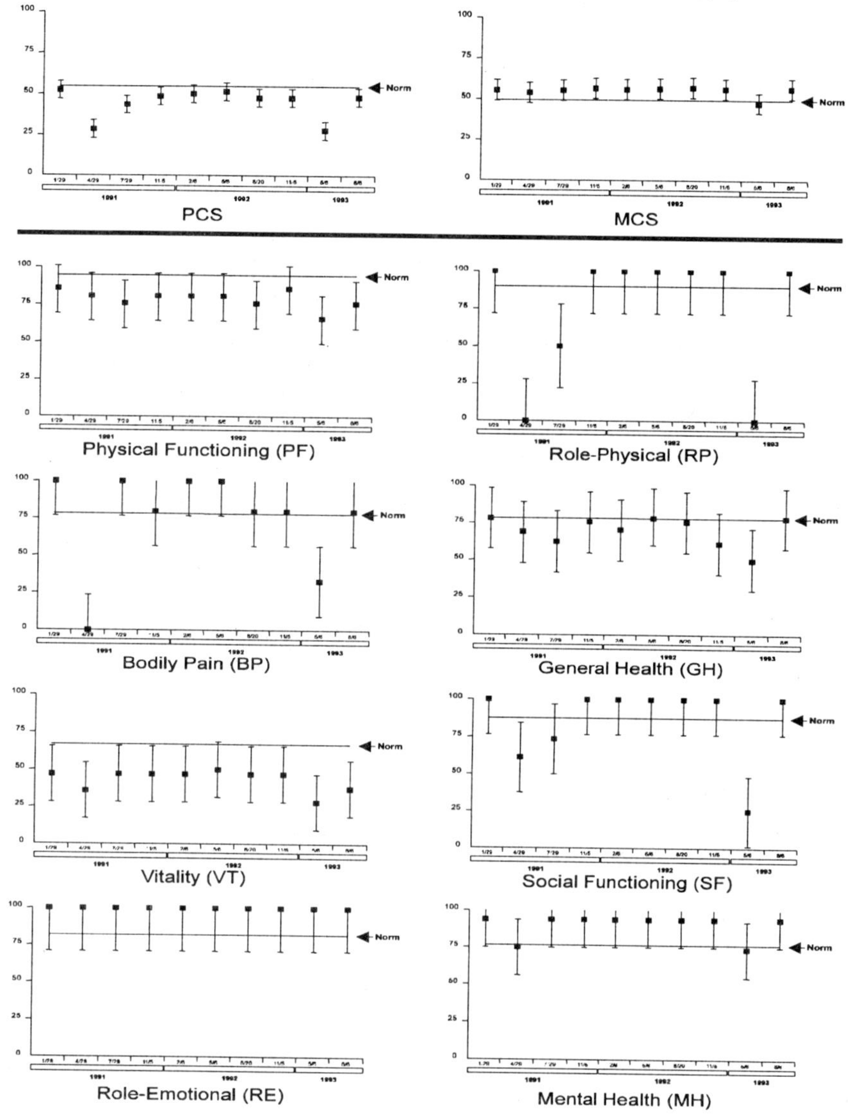

Source: Meyer, Espindle, DeGiacomo, et al., American Journal of Kidney Disease, 1994.

In conjunction with an adverse medical event, this patient's PCS score declined dramatically by visit two (4/91). Underlying the decline in the PCS were drops in the BP, RP, and SF scales. Recovery to levels high enough that the 95% CI included the general population norm were observed for the BP scale by the third observation period (7/91); followed by recovery to the norm for the RP and SF scales by the fourth period (11/91). Improvements in these scales are reflected in the PCS, which came within two standard errors of normal by the fifth and sixth visits. The PCS did not completely reach the norm because of the VT scale score, which remained well below the norm across all visits. This pattern of low VT scores is often observed for patients with chronic renal failure. Longitudinal monitoring revealed that this patient's functional health and well-being remained stable throughout most of the observation period.

Figure 12.1 illustrates a format for displaying longitudinal results for an individual patient that NEMC clinicians have found useful. The figure also illustrates several important lessons. First, the PCS and MCS reflect changes that are observed in specific SF-36 scales. Second, general population norms can be useful in understanding individual patient scores, which were below the norm for physical health, but above the norm for mental health. Third, this example calls attention to the much smaller size of confidence intervals around individual patient scores for the PCS and MCS relative to the eight SF-36 scales. CIs were particularly large for the RP and SF scales relative to the PCS and MCS. These differences are explained in Chapters 4 and 5. Finally, this example illustrates the value of establishing a personal norm for each individual patient. Changes over time for an individual patient may be best judged in relation to what is "normal" for that patient.

The display of longitudinal observations for an individual patient is simplified by the PCS and MCS scales. Because longitudinal results for only one dimension of health can be effectively displayed in the same chart, eight charts were required for a display of longitudinal data for the SF-36 scales (Meyer, Espindle, DeGiacomo, et al., 1994). If the PCS and MCS are used to summarize that information, as illustrated here, only two displays are required. Results for the eight scales provide useful back-up for use in better understanding what is underlying a change in a PCS or MCS summary score.

Profiles For Individual Patients

Along with short forms like the SF-36 and systems that rapidly process survey forms with a high degree of reproducibility, acceptance by clinicians also requires that the display of a profile be user-friendly. Figure 12.2 illustrates another format for displaying SF-36 profiles and the PCS and MCS scales for individual patients that is currently being evaluated.

Figure 12.2 shows the SF-36 profile and the PCS and MCS summary scores for the patient with ESRD, discussed above. "Initial" (I) and "follow-up" (F) visits correspond to the first and second visits discussed above. The bar graphs for the SF-36 profile and for the PCS and MCS, along with the scores printed, reveal that this patient had worsened substantially between SF-36 administrations. Significant declines, which are larger than the 95% confidence interval, are indicated by downward arrows () in Figure 10.2. Significant declines were observed for four of the scales (RP, BP, SF, and MH) and for the PCS. The decline of 24 points (from 52 to 28) in the PCS scores represents a decline from just below the median (50th percentile) to well below the 25th percentile for a 38-year-old male (see norms in Appendix E5).

FIGURE 12.2 INITIAL AND FOLLOW-UP PROFILES FOR ESRD PATIENT 1

SF-36 Health Status Profile

Patient ID: 1 Sex: Male Educ: n/a
Site: 3 Age: 38 Race: n/a
Diagnosis: End-Stage Renal Disease

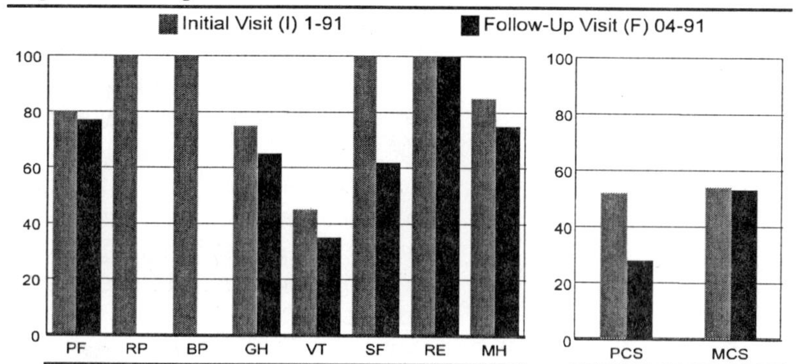

	PF	RP	BP	GH	VT	SF	RE	MH		PCS	MCS
I	80	100	100	75	45	100	100	85	I	52	54
F	77	0	0	65	35	62	100	75	F	28	53
Δ		▼	▼			▼		▼	Δ	▼	

Change in score (Δ) shows improvement (▲) or worsening (▼) beyond 95% CI for individual patient.

Data Quality	Initial	Follow-Up
Version used	Standard	Standard
Overall quality	Excellent	Excellent
Items complete %	100%	100%
Consistency of responses %	100%	100%

Data Quality

The printout shown in Figure 12.2 also summarizes data quality. Specifically, it indicates that the Standard SF-36 form and scoring were used for both initial and follow-up administrations. Thus, it is appropriate to compare them. Further, the overall data quality was "excellent." Specifically, 100% of the items were complete, and the Response Consistency Index (RCI), which is an indicator of the patient's consistency in responding across 15 pairs of SF-36 items, yielded 100% consistency scores for both administrations. In the general population (N = 2,474) and in the MOS (N = 3,434), 90.3% and 94.5% had no inconsistent responses, respectively; 6.1% and 3.4% had one inconsistent response. The RCI and normative data for interpreting the RCI are explained in the original *SF-36® User's Manual* (Ware, Snow, Kosinski, et al., 1993).

Processing Systems

Processing system for the SF-36 have the features discussed above, including the RCI for monitoring data quality, along with other options. With advances in data processing systems, a doctor and patient can monitor the patient's functional health and well-being on a regular basis, inexpensively, without delay, and with highly reproducible results. Such systems remove the practical barriers to monitoring patient health outcomes routinely in everyday clinical practice.

Patient Profiles: More Examples

Figures 12.3 and 12.4 present additional examples of the longitudinal monitoring of PCS and MCS scores for an individual patient. The patients involved were selected from among those followed during the first year of the MOS. The first patient is a 37-year old female who, according to clinical criteria (documented in Appendix A), recovered from a depressive disorder that was diagnosed when the MOS began. As was the case for the great majority of these patients (McHorney, Ware, Lu, et al., 1994), data quality was more than satisfactory for both assessments nearly one year apart. As indicated by the upward arrows (⇧), improvements in her scores were greater than would be expected by chance for six of the eight SF-36 scales. Comparison of scores for the PCS and MCS, which take correlations among the eight scales into account, clearly indicates that this patient's improvement was concentrated in the mental component of health status. Her initial (I) MCS score of 19 was below that of nearly 99% of women her age in the general U.S. population at baseline and improved to a score of 44, which is above the 25th percentile (see norms in Appendix E4). This improvement in the MCS scores of 25 points is about seven times greater than the average improvement observed for depressed patients in the MOS (see norms in Appendix E38). In addition to the decrease in suffering associated with a MCS score change from only 19, which indicates substantial psychological distress, to a score of 44, interpretation guidelines in Chapter 9 suggest that this patient's probability of receiving mental health specialty care (an important cost consideration) was substantially reduced as a result of this improvement (Chapter 9, Table 9.10).

FIGURE 12.3 INITIAL AND FOLLOW-UP PROFILES FOR A PATIENT WITH CLINICAL DEPRESSION

SF-36 Health Status Profile

Patient ID: 865 Sex: Female Educ: 18
Site: 1 Age: 37 Race: White
Diagnosis: Clinical Depression -- Recovered

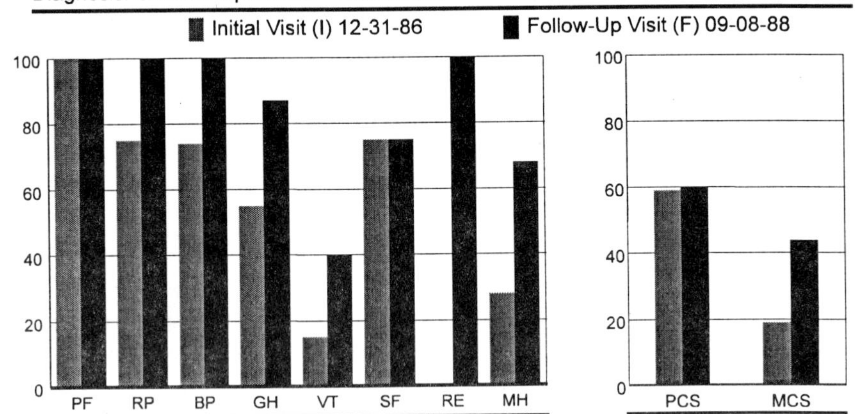

	PF	RP	BP	GH	VT	SF	RE	MH
I	100	75	74	55	15	75	0	28
F	100	100	100	87	40	75	100	68
△		▲	▲	▲	▲		▲	▲

	PCS	MCS
I	59	19
F	60	44
△		▲

Change in score (△) shows improvement (▲) or worsening (▼) beyond 95% CI for individual patient.

Data Quality	Initial	Follow-Up
Version used	Standard	Standard
Overall quality	Excellent	Excellent
Items complete %	100%	100%
Consistency of responses %	100%	100%

Figure 12.4 presents the last example of the longitudinal monitoring of PCS and MCS scores and the SF-36 profile for an individual patient. The patient is a 50-year old male who was diagnosed as having congestive heart failure (CHF) upon enrollment into the Medical Outcomes Study (MOS) (see criteria in Appendix B). The follow-up assessment was performed approximately eight months later. Comparison of his initial scores with the norms for patients with congestive heart failure indicate that this patient's PCS score was within two or three points of average for those patients with CHF in the MOS and scored well above average (at the 75th percentile) on the MCS (see norms in Appendix E25).

As was the case for the average MOS patient with CHF (see norms for change scores Appendix E39), the patient in Figure 12.4 declined nine points on the PCS scale (from 37 to 28) during the eight-month follow-up period. (It should be noted that norms for the PCS change scores reported in Appendix E cover a one-year period.) This amount of decline is more than four times the average for patients with CHF and is well below the 25th percentile of change scores for such patients. Underlying this change in PCS scores were significant declines (larger than the 95% confidence level) for the PF, RP, and VT scales. Scores for three other scales known to be most indicative of mental health status (MH, RE, and SF) did not decline more than would be expected by chance during the follow-up period. Consistent with these results, the MCS summary measure showed no significant change.

FIGURE 12.4 INITIAL AND FOLLOW-UP PROFILES FOR A PATIENT WITH CHF

SF-36 Health Status Profile

Patient ID: 1856	Sex: Male	Educ: 13
Site: 2	Age: 50	Race: Black
Diagnosis: Congestive Heart Failure		

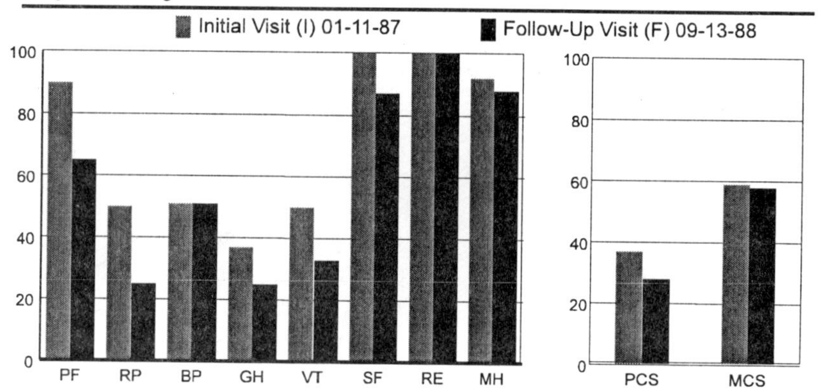

	PF	RP	BP	GH	VT	SF	RE	MH
I	90	50	51	37	50	100	100	92
F	55	25	51	25	33	87	100	88
Δ	▼	▼			▼			

	PCS	MCS
I	37	59
F	28	58
Δ	▼	

Change in score (Δ) shows improvement (▲) or worsening (▼) beyond 95% CI for individual patient.

Data Quality	Initial	Follow-Up
Version used	Standard	Standard
Overall quality	Excellent	Excellent
Items complete %	100%	100%
Consistency of responses %	100%	100%

Patient Screening

Another promising clinical application of the PCS and MCS summary scales is that of patient screening. Because more than half of the patients with depressive disorders go undetected in primary care practices (Berwick, Murphy, Goldman, et al., 1991; Wells, Hays, Burnam, et al., 1989), for example, there is much to be gained from using short-form surveys proven to be valid for purposes of patient screening. The SF-36 is an especially good candidate because it is very short — requiring only about five to ten minutes to complete — and because it is widely used for monitoring health status outcomes. Thus, the survey used in monitoring outcomes may serve the dual purpose of patient screening. In support of this application, the SF-36 MH scale, which is also often referred to as the MHI-5, has performed well in tests of sensitivity and specificity relative to other screening tools for depression and other mental disorders (Berwick, Murphy, Goldman, et al., 1991).

MCS And Clinical Depression

To evaluate the MCS scale as a screening tool for clinical depression, we used the same statistical methods as used elsewhere (Berwick, Murphy, Goldman, et al., 1991). SF-36 surveys were self-administered independently but in conjunction with a two-stage screening process that relied upon a short-form of the CESD and then the NIMH Diagnostic Interview Schedule (DIS) criteria for clinical depression, as described elsewhere (Burnam, Wells, Leake, et al., 1988; Wells, Hays, Burnam, et al., 1989). Using these methods, 503 of the 3,445 MOS patients (14.6%) were diagnosed with major depression and/or dysthymia.

Using receiver operating curve (ROC) analysis, we evaluated the sensitivity and specificity, as well as the ROC curve, which combines both, across the full range of MCS scores. The MH scale was also evaluated using the well-documented cut-off of 52 or below for detecting depression (Berwick, Murphy, Goldman, et al., 1991; Ware, Snow, Kosinski, et al., 1993). (Incidentally, the optimal MH cut-off of 52 was confirmed in these analyses.)

As summarized in Table 12.1, the best all-around cut-off for the MCS is at a score of 42 or below, which achieves an area under the ROC curve of 0.77 and a sensitivity and specificity of 73.7% and 80.6%, respectively. These results compare favorably with those for the MH scale in the same test. The area under the ROC curve for the MH scale was 0.76 with a sensitivity of 66.8% and a specificity of 86.2% (data not reported). For purposes of screening applications requiring larger or smaller rates of false positives or false negatives, other MCS scale cut-offs can be used as documented in Table 12.1.

The evaluation of the eight SF-36 scales and the MCS in screening patients for depression and other mental conditions is ongoing at NEMC and other sites. Both the SF-36 and SF-12 versions of the MCS (see Chapter 3) are being evaluated. Work in progress indicates that the three additional screening items shown in previous MOS studies to improve the performance of the CESD short-form (Burnam, Wells, Leake, et al., 1988) do not improve the performance of the SF-36. Thus, a 39-item questionnaire that adds three additional screening questions (about a two-week episode during the past year, depression over the past one- and two-year periods) does not appear to be worth the additional respondent burden for purposes of patient screening as described above.

TABLE 12.1 SUMMARY OF THE PERFORMANCE OF THE MCS (AT VARIOUS CUTPOINTS) IN SCREENING FOR CLINICAL DEPRESSION[1], MOS PATIENTS (N = 3,445)

	MCS SCALE CUTPOINTS					
	□ 23	□ 32	□ 37	□ 42	□ 47	□ 52
Sensitivity (%)	17.9	47.3	62.2	73.7	81.1	89.5
Specificity (%)	98.5	93.4	87.6	80.6	70.5	56.4
False Positive Rate (%)	1.5	6.6	12.4	19.4	29.5	43.6
False Negative Rate (%)	82.1	52.7	37.8	26.3	18.9	10.5
Area Under ROC Curve	0.58	0.70	0.75	0.77	0.76	0.73

[1] N = 503 (14.6%) patients from the MOS baseline sample were diagnosed with clinical depression; NIMH (DIS) criteria met for major depression and/or dysthymia (Wells, Hays, Burnam, et al., 1989).

PCS Scores And Physical Disease

Previous studies have shown that the probability of a diagnosable physical condition increases substantially with declines in general health status. For example, at the top levels of the General Health Rating Index (Davies & Ware, 1981; Ware, 1992), from which the SF-36 GH scale was constructed, only about five percent were diagnosed with a physical condition. That number increased to about 95% at the lower scale levels.

To evaluate the PCS scale as a screening tool for physical disease, ROC analyses (as described above) were performed across the full range of the PCS scores using data from a 1990 general population survey used to norm the SF-36 (see Chapter 8). Chronic physical conditions, as reported by patients, were based on definitions in Appendix B. A physical condition was counted if one or more of the following was reported: arthritis, angina, back pain/sciatica, chronic lung disease, CHF, diabetes, hypertension, limitation in use of arm(s)/leg(s), or myocardial infarction. In the general U.S. population (N = 2,474), 57.3% reported one or more of these conditions.

As summarized in Table 12.2, the best all around cut-off for the PCS is at a score of 50 or below, which achieves an area under the ROC curve of 0.72, a sensitivity of 60%, and a specificity of 84.8%. (Note that 50 is the average PCS score in the general U.S. population.) As shown in Table 10.2, the PCS cut-offs of 55 and 45 substantially increase sensitivity (to 83% and 98%) and decrease specificity (55% and 10%), respectively.

These results, which are consistent with estimates of the unique effects of each of these physical conditions on PCS scores (see Chapter 9, Table 9.14), suggest that there is a very high probability of physical disease underlying low PCS scores, and that the PCS may prove useful as a first-stage screener for such conditions.

TABLE 12.2 SUMMARY OF THE PERFORMANCE OF THE PCS (AT VARIOUS CUTPOINTS) IN SCREENING FOR A PHYSICAL CONDITION[1], GENERAL U.S. POPULATION (N = 2,474)

	PCS SCALE CUTPOINTS						
	< 30	< 35	< 40	< 45	< 50	< 55	< 60
Sensitivity (%)	12.7	21.0	31.3	42.4	60.0	83.4	97.7
Specificity (%)	99.4	98.6	96.3	92.7	84.8	55.3	9.5
False Positive (%)	0.6	1.5	3.7	40.07.3	15.3	44.7	90.5
False Negative (%)	87.3	79.0	68.7	57.6	39.9	16.6	2.3
ROC	0.56	0.60	0.64	0.68	0.72	0.69	0.54

1 Chronic conditions — presence of one or more of the following: arthritis, angina, back pain/sciatica, chronic lung disease, CHF, diabetes, hypertension, limitation in use of arm(s)/leg(s), or myocardial infarction.

Final Comment

There are many issues involved in using health status assessments in everyday clinical practice (Nelson, Wasson, Kirk, et al., 1987; Deyo & Carter, 1992; Ware, 1992). Practicality is essential. Measurement precision — a narrow confidence interval around each patient score — is a prerequisite for interpretation. Despite the "noise level" inherent in short-form scales, repeated assessments of the SF-36 yield interpretable estimates of changes in patient health status that would otherwise have been unknown to clinicians (Meyer, Espindle, DeGiacomo, et al., 1994).

The PCS and MCS scores increased measurement precision beyond that achieved by any of the eight SF-36 scales in psychometric evaluations documented in Chapter 7. As illustrated above, the PCS and MCS appear to yield reproducible and useful summaries of results in patient-level analyses. These examples also illustrate the gains in precision expected for both the PCS and MCS.

Another rate-limiting factor in clinical applications is the extent of understanding of what the scores mean and the availability of user-friendly documentation of that information. The PCS and MCS clearly have straightforward interpretations as measures of physical and mental health status, respectively. However, despite the fact that the PCS and MCS aggregate the most highly-related SF-36 scales, which are most likely to yield the same results, some information of value to clinicians may be lost in the "averaging" process. The display formats for presenting the PCS and MCS summary scales, in tandem with the richness of the SF-36 profile, should help to make the best of both apparent to clinicians. It is also hoped that interpretation guidelines documented in this manual will facilitate the use of the summary measures in everyday clinical practice.

References

Aaronson NK, Acquadro C, Alonso J, Apolone G, Bucquet D, Bullinger M, Bungay K, Fukuhara S, Gandek B, Keller S, Razavi D, Sanson-Fisher R, Sullivan M, Wood-Dauphinee S, Wagner AK, & Ware JE. International quality of life assessment (IQOLA) project. *Quality of Life Research* 1992; 1:349-351.

American College of Physicians. Comprehensive functional assessment for elderly patients. *Annals of Internal Medicine* 1988; 109:70-72.

American Psychological Association. *Standards for Educational and Psychological Testing*. Washington, D.C.: American Psychological Association, 1985.

Beaton DE, Bombardier C, & Hogg-Johnson S. Choose your tool: A comparison of the psychometric properties of five generic health status instruments in workers with soft tissue injuries. *Quality of Life Research* 1994; 3:50-56.

Bergner L, Bergner M, Hallstrom AP, Eisenberg M, & Cobb L. Health status of survivors of out-of-hospital cardiac arrest six months later. *American Journal of Public Health* 1984; 74(5):508-510.

Bergner M, Bobbitt RA, Carter WB, & Gilson BS. The Sickness Impact Profile: Development and final revision of a health status measure. *Medical Care* 1981; 19:787-805.

Bergner M & Rothman ML. Health status measures: An overview and guide for selection. *Annual Review of Public Health* 1987; 8:191-210.

Berwick DM, Murphy JM, Goldman PA, Ware JE, Barsky AJ, & Weinstein MC. Performance of a five-item mental health screening test. *Medical Care* 1991; 29:169-176.

Bonfils S. Les questionnaires de Qualité de View: Irremplaçables instruments d'approximation. *Impertinente Psychosomatique*. Montrouge: John Libbey Eurotext, 1993:293-300.

Bousquet J, Knani J, Dhivert H, Richard A, Chichoye A, Ware JE, & Michel FB. Quality-of-life in asthma: I. Internal consistency and validity of the SF-36® questionnaire. *American Journal of Respiratory and Critical Care Medicine* 1994; 149:371-375.

Brazier J. The SF-36® health survey questionnaire - a tool for economists. *Health Economics* 1993; 2.

Brazier J, Jones N, & Kind P. Testing the validity of the EuroQOL and comparing it with the SF-36® health survey questionnaire. *Quality of Life Research* 1993; 2:169-180.

Brazier JE, Harper R, Jones NMB, O'Cathain A, Thomas KJ, Usherwood T, & Westlake L. Validating the SF-36® health survey questionnaire: New outcome measure for primary care. *British Medical Journal* 1992; 305:160-164.

Brook RH, Ware JE, Rogers WH, *et al. The Effect of Coinsurance on the Health of Adults: Results from the RAND Health Insurance Experiment.* Santa Monica, CA: The RAND Corporation, 1984; R-3055-HHS.

Bullinger M. German translation and psychometric testing of the SF-36® Health Survey: Preliminary results from the IQOLA Project. *Social Science and Medicine* 1995.

Burnam MA, Wells KB, Leake B, & Landsverk J. Development of a brief screening instrument for detecting depressive disorders. *Medical Care* 1988; 26(8):775-789.

Cleary PD, Greenfield S, & McNeil BJ. Assessing quality of life after surgery. *Controlled Clinical Trials* 1991; 12:189S-203S.

Cohen J. *Statistical Power Analysis for the Behavioral Sciences -- Second Edition.* Hillsdale, NJ: Lawrence Erlbaum Associates, 1988.

Comrey AL. *A First Course in Factor Analysis.* New York: Academic Press, 1973.

Cook TD & Campbell DT. *Quasi-Experimentation: Design and Analysis Issues for Field Settings.* Chicago, IL: Rand McNally College Publishing Co., 1979.

Davies AR & Ware JE. *Measuring Health Perceptions in the Health Insurance Experiment.* Santa Monica, CA: Rand Corporation, 1981; R-2711-HHS. (Health Insurance Experiment Series).

Derogatis LR. The Psychosocial Adjustment to Illness Scale (PAIS). *Journal of Psychosomatic Research* 1986; 30(1):77-91.

Deyo RA & Carter WB. Strategies for improving and expanding the application of health status measure in clinical settings: A researcher-developer viewpoint. *Medical Care* May 1992; 30(5 Suppl.):MS176-MS186.

Dixon P, Heaton J, Long A, & Warburton A. Reviewing and applying the SF-36®. *Outcomes Briefing* August 1994; 4:3-25.

EuroQOL Group. EuroQOL - a new facility for the measurement of health-related quality of life. *Health Policy* 1990; 16:199-208.

Fowler FJ, Wennberg JE, Timothy RP, Barry MJ, Mulley AG, & Henley D. Symptom status and quality of life following prostatectomy. *Journal of the American Medical Association* 1988; 259:3018-3022.

Fryback DG, Dasbach EJ, Klein R, Klein BE, Dorn N, Peterson K, & Martin PA. The Beaver Dam health outcomes study: Initial catalog of health state quality factors. *Medical Decision Making* 1993; 13:89-102.

Garratt AM, MacDonald LM, Ruta DA, Russell IT, Buckingham JK, & Krukowski ZH. Towards measurement of outcome for patients with varicose veins. *Quality in Health Care* 1993; 2:5-10.

Garratt AM, Ruta DA, Abdalla MI, & Russell IT. The SF-36® Health Survey Questionnaire: II. Responsiveness to changes in health status for patients with four common conditions. *Quality in Health Care* 1995.

Garratt AM, Ruta DA, Abdalla MI, Buckingham JK, & Russell IT. The SF-36® Health survey questionnaire: An outcome measure suitable for routine use within the NHS? *British Medical Journal* 1993; 306:1440-1444.

Goldberg DP & Hillier V. A scaled version of the General Health Questionnaire. *Psychological Medicine* 1979; 9:139-145.

Greenfield S, Nelson EC, Zubkoff M, Manning WG, Rogers W, Kravitz RL, Keller A, Tarlov AR, & Ware JE. Variations in resource utilization among medical specialties and systems of care: Results from the Medical Outcomes Study. *Journal of the American Medical Association* 1992; 267:1624-1630.

Guilford JP. *Psychometric Methods.* New York: McGraw-Hill, 1954.

Guyatt G, Walter S, & Norman G. Measuring change over time: Assessing the usefulness of evaluative instruments. *Journal of Chronic Diseases* 1987; 40(2):171-178.

Haley SM, McHorney CA, & Ware JE. Evaluation of the MOS SF-36® Physical Functioning scale (PF-10): I. Unidimensionality and reproducibility of the Rasch item scale. *Journal of Clinical Epidemiology* 1994; 47:671-684.

Hall JA, Epstein AM, & McNeil BJ. Multidimensionality of health status in an elderly population: Construct validity of a measurement battery. *Medical Care* 1989; 27(3 Suppl..):S168-S177.

Hall JA, Epstein AM, DeCiantis ML, & McNeil BJ. Physicians' liking for their patients: More evidence for the role of affect in medical care. *Health Psychology* 1993; 12(2):140-146.

Harman HH. *Modern Factor Analysis*, 3rd edition, revised. Chicago: University of Chicago Press, 1976.

Harris ML & Harris CW. A factor analytic interpretation strategy. *Educational and Psychological Measurement* 1971; 31:589-606.

Hays RD, Sherbourne CD, & Mazel RM. The RAND 36-Item Health Survey 1.0. *Health Economics* 1993; 2:217-227.

Hays RD & Stewart AL. The structure of self-reported health in chronic disease patients. *Psychological Assessment: A Journal of Consulting and Clinical Psychology* 1990; 2:22-30.

Hill S & Harries U. Assessing the outcome of health care for the older person in community settings: Should we use the SF-36®. *Outcomes Briefing* 1994; 4:26-27.

Idler EL & Angel RJ. Age, chronic pain, and subjective assessments of health. *Advances in Medical Sociology* 1990; 1:131-152.

Jacobson AM, de Groot M, & Samson JA. The evaluation of two measures of quality of life in patients with Type I and Type II Diabetes Mellitus. *Diabetes Care* April 1994; 17(4):267-274.

Jenkinson C, Coulter A, & Wright L. Short form 36 (SF-36) Health Survey Questionnaire: Normative data for adults of working age. *British Medical Journal* 1993; 306:1437-1440.

Jenkinson C & Wright L. The SF-36® health survey questionnaire. *Auditorium* 1993; 2:7-12.

Jenkinson C, Wright L, & Coulter A. Criterion validity and reliability of the SF-36® in a population sample. *Quality of Life Research* 1994; 3:7-12.

Jenkinson C, Wright L, & Coulter A. *Quality of Life Measurement in Health Care: A Review of Measures and Population Norms for the UK SF-36.* Oxford, England: Health Services Research Unit, Department of Public Health and Primary Care, University of Oxford, June 1993.

Jette DU & Downing J. Health status of individuals entering a cardiac rehabilitation program as measured by the Medical Outcomes Study 36-Item Short-Form Survey (SF-36). *Physical Therapy,* 1994; 74(6):521-527.

Kantz ME, Harris WJ, Levitsky K, Ware JE, & Davies AR. Methods for assessing condition-specific and generic functional status outcomes after total knee replacement. *Medical Care* 1992; 30(Suppl.):MS240-MS252.

Kaplan RM & Anderson JP. The Quality of Well-Being Scale: Rational for a single quality of life index. in: Walker SR & Rosser RM. *Quality of Life: Assessment and Application.* Lancaster: MTP Press Limited, 1988:51-77.

Kappelle LJ, Adams HP, Heffner ML, Torner JC, Gomez F, & Biller J. Prognosis of young adults with ischemic stroke: A long-term follow-up study assessing recurent vascular events and functional outcome in the Iowa Registry of Stroke in Young Adults. *Stroke* 1994; 25(7):1360-1365.

Katz JN, Harris TM, Larson MG, Krushell RJ, Brown CH, Fossel AH, Liang MH. Predictors of functional outcomes after arthroscopic partial meniscectomy. *Journal of Rheumatology* 1992; 19(12):1938-1942.

Katz JN, Larson MG, Phillips CB, Fossel AH, & Liang MH. Comparative measurement sensitivity of short and longer health status instruments. *Medical Care* October 1992; 30(10):917-925.

Kazis LE, Anderson JJ, & Meenan RF. Effect sizes for interpreting changes in health status. *Medical Care* March 1989; 27(3 Suppl.):S178-S189.

Kerlinger FN. *Foundations of Behavioral Research.* New York: Holt, Rinehart and Winston, 1964.

Kravitz RL, Greenfield S, Rogers WH, Manning WG, Zubkoff M, Nelson E, Tarlov AR, & Ware JE. Differences in the mix of patients among medical specialties and systems of care: Results from the Medical Outcomes Study. *Journal of the American Medical Association* 1992; 267:1617-1623.

Krousel-Wood MA & Re RN. Health status assessment in a hypertension section of an internal medicine clinic. *American Journal of the Medical Sciences* 1994; 308(4):211-217.

Krousel-Wood MA, McCune TW, Abdoh A, & Re RN. Predicting work status for patients in an occupational medicine setting who report back pain. *Archives of Family Medicine* 1994; 3(4): 349-355.

Kurtin PS, Davies AR, Meyer KB, DeGiacomo JM, & Kantz ME. Patient-based health status measures in outpatient dialysis: Early experiences in developing an outcomes assessment program. *Medical Care* 1992; 30(Suppl.):MS136-MS149.

Kutner NG, Schechtman KB, Ory MG, & Baker DI. Older adult's perceptions of their health and functioning in relation to sleep disturbance, falling, and urinary incontinence. *Journal of the American Geriatrics Society* 1994; 42(7):757-62.

Lancaster TR, Singer DE, Sheehan MA, Oertel LB, Maraventano SW, Hughes RA, & Kistler JP. The impact of long-term warfarin therapy on quality of life: Evidence from a randomized trial. *Archives of Internal Medicine* 1991; 151:1944-1949.

Lansky D, Butler JBV, & Waller FT. Using health status measures in the hospital setting: From acute care to 'outcomes management'. *Medical Care* 199 2; 30(Suppl.):MS57-MS73.

Lembcke PA. Measuring the quality of medical care through vital statistics based on hospital service areas: 1. Comparative study of appendectomy rates. *American Journal of Public Health* 1952; 42:276-286.

Lerner DJ, Levine S, Malspeis S, & D'Agostino RB. Job strain and health-related quality of life in a national sample. *American Journal of Public Health* 1994; 84(10):1580-1585.

Levin NW, Lazarus JM, & Nissenson AR. National cooperative rHu erythropoietin study in patients with chronic renal failure -- an interim report. *American Journal of Kidney Disease* 1993; 22:3-12.

Liang J, Wu SC, Krause NM, Chiang TL, & Wu HY. The structure of the mental health inventory among Chinese in Taiwan. *Medical Care* 1992; 30(5):659-676.

Liang MH, Larson MG, Cullen KE, & Schwartz JA. Comparative measurement efficiency and sensitivity of five health status instruments for arthritis research. *Arthritis and Rheumatism* 1985; 28:542-547.

Lyons RA, Perry HM, & Littlepage BN. Evidence for the validity of the Short-Form 36 Questionnaire (SF-36) in an elderly population. *Age and Ageing* 1994; 23(3):182-184.

Mangione CM, Marcantonio ER, Goldman L, Cook EF, Donaldson MC, Sugarbaker DJ, Poss R, & Lee TH. Influence of age on measurement of health status in patients undergoing elective surgery. *Journal of the American Geriatrics Society* 1993; 41(4):377-383.

Martin C, Marquis P, & Bonfils S. A 'quality of life questionnaire' adapted to duodenal ulcer therapeutic trials. *Scandinavian Journal of Gastroenterology* 1994; 206(29 Suppl.):40-43.

Martin C, Marquis P, Ware JE, & Bonfils S. A Quality of life study of nizatidine in 581 DU patients: Maintenance treatment versus intermittent treatment. *Gasatroenterology* 1993; 104:A141.

Mason JH, Anderson JJ, & Meenan RF. A model of health status for rheumatoid arthritis: A factor analysis of the Arthritis Impact Measurement Scales. *Arthritis and Rheumatism* 1988; 31(6):714-720.

McCallum J. *The New "SF-36" Health Status Measure: Australian Validity Tests*. National Centre for Epidemiology and Population Health, The Australian National University, July 1994. (Record Linkage Pilot Study).

McHorney CA, Kosinski M, & Ware JE. Comparisons of the costs and quality of norms for the SF-36® Health Survey collected by mail versus telephone interview: Results from a national survey. *Medical Care* 1994; 32:551-567.

McHorney CA & Ware JE. Construction of an alternate form general mental health scale for the MOS SF-36® Health Survey. *Medical Care* 1995; 33:15-28.

McHorney CA, Ware JE, & Raczek AE. The MOS 36-Item Short-Form Health Survey (SF-36): II. Psychometric and clinical tests of validity in measuring physical and mental health constructs. *Medical Care* 1993; 31:247-263.

McHorney CA, Ware JE, Lu JFR, & Sherbourne CD. The MOS 36-Item Short-Form Health Survey (SF-36): III. Tests of data quality, scaling assumptions and reliability across diverse patient groups. *Medical Care* 1994; 32:40-66.

McHorney CA, Ware JE, Rogers WH, Raczek A, & Lu JFR. The validity and relative precision of MOS Short- and Long-Form Health Status Scales and Dartmouth COOP Charts: Results from the Medical Outcomes Study. *Medical Care* 1992; 30(Suppl.):MS253-MS265.

Medical Outcomes Trust. *How To Score the SF-36® Short-Form Health Survey.* Boston, MA: Medical Outcomes Trust, 1991.

Medical Outcomes Trust. *Scoring Exercise for the SF-36® Health Survey, 2nd edition.* Boston, MA: Medical Outcomes Trust, 1994.

Medical Outcomes Trust. *SF-36® Health Survey Scoring Manual for English Language Adaptations: Australia/New Zealand, Canada, United Kingdom.* Boston, MA: Medical Outcomes Trust, 1994.

Meyer KB, Espindle DM, DeGiacomo JM, Jenuleson CS, Kurtin PS, & Davies AR. Monitoring dialysis patients' health status. *American Journal of Kidney Diseases* 1994; 24(2):267-279.

Nelson EC, Wasson J, Kirk J, Keller A, Clark D, Dietrich A, Stewart A, & Zubkoff M. Assessment of function in routine clinical practice: Description of the COOP chart method and preliminary findings. *Journal of Chronic Disease* 1987; 40(Suppl. 1):55S-63S.

Nerenz DR, Repasky DP, Whitehouse FW, & Kahkonen DM. Ongoing assessment of health status in patients with diabetes mellitus. *Medical Care* 1992; 30(Suppl.):MS112-MS124.

Nunnally JC. *Psychometric Theory* 2nd edition. New York: McGraw-Hill, 1978.

Nunnally JC & Bernstein IH. *Psychometric Theory 3rd edition.* New York: McGraw-Hill, 1994.

Okun MA & Stock WA. Correlates and components of subjective well-being among the elderly. *Journal of Applied Gerontology* 1987; 6:95-112.

Orley J & Kuyken W (eds.). *Quality of Life Assessment: International Perspectives.* Berlin: Springer-Verlag, 1994.

Osterhaus JT, Townsend RJ, Gandek B, & Ware JE. Measuring the functional status and well-being of patients with migraine headaches. *Headache* June 1994; 34(6):337-343.

Park Nicollet Medical Foundation & The Johns Hopkins University. *A Comparison of Alternative Approaches to Risk Management.* Washington, D.C.: Physician Payment Review Commission, 1994. (Selected External Research Series).

Parkerson GR, Broadhead WE, Tse CKJ. The Duke health profile: A 17-item measure of health and disfunction. *Medical Care* 1990; 28:1056-1072.

Patrick DL & Erickson P. *Health Status and Health Policy: Allocating Resources to Health Care.* New York: Oxford University Press, 1993.

Phillips RC & Lansky DJ. Outcomes management in heart valve replacement surgery: Early experience. *Journal of Heart Valve Disease* 1992; 1:42-50.

Rampal P, Martin C, Marquis P, Ware JE, & Bonfils S. A quality of life study in five hundred and eighty-one duodenal ulcer patients: Maintenance versus intermittent treatment with nizatidine. *Scandinavian Journal of Gastroenterology* 1994; 206(29 Suppl.):44-51.

Rector TS, Ormaza SM, & Kubo SM. Health status of heart transplant recipients versus patients awaiting heart transplantation: A preliminary evaluation of the SF-36® Questionnaire. *Journal of Heart and Lung Transplantation* 1993; 12(6 Pt. 1): 983-986.

Rogers WH, Wells KB, Meredith LS, Sturm R, & Burnam A. Outcomes for adult outpatients with depression under prepaid or fee-for-service financing. *Archives of General Psychiatry* 1993; 50:517-525.

Rubenstein LV, McCoy JM, Cope DW, Barrett PA, Hirsch SH, Messer KS, & Young RT. Improving patient functional status: A randomized trial of computer-generate resource and management suggestions. Abstract presented at the American Federation of Clinical Research 1991.

Ruta DA, Abdalla MI, Garratt AM, Coutts A, & Russell IT. The SF-36® Health Survey Questionnaire: I. Reliability in two patient-based studies. *Quality in Health Care* 1995.

Ruta DA, Garratt AM, Wardlaw D, & Russell IT. Developing a valid and reliable measure of health outcome for patients with low back pain. *Spine* 1994; 19(17):1887-1896.

SAS Institute Inc. *SAS/STAT User's Guide, Version 6, Fourth Edition, Volume 1.* Cary, NC: SAS Institute Inc., 1989.

Schag CAC, Heinrich RL, Aadland RL, & Ganz PA. Assessing problems of cancer patients: Psychometric properties of the Cancer Inventory of Problem Situations. *Health Psychology* 1990; 9:83-102.

Schor EL, Lerner DJ, & Malspeis S. Physician's assessment of functional health status and well-being: The patient's perspective. *Archives of Internal Medicine* 1995.

Siu AL, Hays RD, Ouslander JG, Osterwell D, Valdez RB, Krynski M, & Gross A. Measuring functioning and health in the very old. *Journal of Gerontology* 1993; 48(1):M10-M14.

Snyder MK & Ware JE. *A Study of Twenty-two Hypothesized Dimensions of Patient Attitudes Regarding Medical Care.* Springfield, Virginia: National Technical Information Service, 1974; MHC 74-10, PB-239-518/AS 65.

Stevens J. *Applied Multivariate Statistics for the Social Sciences* 2nd edition. Hillsdale, NJ: Lawrence Erlbaum Associates, 1992.

Stewart AL, Greenfield S, Hays RD, Wells KB, Rogers WH, Berry SD, McGlynn EA, & Ware JE. Functional status and well-being of patients with chronic conditions: Results from the Medical Outcomes Study. *Journal of the American Medical Association* August 1989; 262(7):907-913.

Stewart AL, Hays RD, & Ware JE. Health perceptions, energy/fatigue, and health distress measures. In: Stewart AL & Ware JE. *Measuring Functioning and Well-Being: The Medical Outcomes Study Approach.* Durham, NC: Duke University Press, 1992:143-172.

Stewart AL & Ware JE. *Measuring Functioning and Well-Being: The Medical Outcomes Study Approach.* Durham, NC: Duke University Press, 1992.

Stoller EP. Self-assessments of health by the elderly: The impact of informal assistance. *Journal of Health and Social Behavior* September 1984; 25:260-270.

Street RL, Gold WR, & McDowell T. Using health status surveys in medical consultations. *Medical Care* 1994; 32(7):732-744.

Sullivan M. LIVSKVALITESMÄTNING. Nytt generellt och nytt tumörspecifikt formulär för utvärdering och planering. *Läkartidningen* 1994; 91:1340-1342.

Sullivan M, Karlsson J, & Ware JE. *SF-36 Hälsoenkät: Svensk Manual Och Tolkningsguide (Swedish Manual and Interpretation Guide).* Gothenburg: Sahlgrenska University Hospital, 1994.

Sullivan M, Karlsson J, & Ware JE. The Swedish SF-36® health survey: I. Evaluation of data quality, scaling assumptions, reliability, and construct validity across general populations in Sweden. *Social Science and Medicine* 1995.

Tarlov AR, Ware JE, Greenfield S, Nelson EC, Perrin E, & Zubkoff M. The Medical Outcomes Study: An application of methods for monitoring the results of medical care. *Journal of the American Medical Association* 1989; 262:925-930.

Thalji L, Haggerty CC, Rubin R, Berckmans TR, & Pardee BL. *1990 National Survey of Functional Health Status: Final Report.* Chicago, IL: NORC, 1991.

Usherwood T & Jones N. Self-perceived health status of hostel residents: use of the SF-36® Health Survey Questionnaire. *Journal of Public Health Medicine* 1994; 25(4):311-314.

van Tulder MW, Aaronson NK, & Bruning PF. The quality of life of long-term survivors of Hodgkin's disease. *Annals of Oncology* 1994; 5:153-158.

Veit CT & Ware JE. The structure of psychological distress and well-being in general populations. *Journal of Consulting and Clinical Psychology* 1983; 51:730-742.

Vickrey BG, Hays RD, Graber J, Rausch R, Engel J, & Brook RH. A health-related quality of life instrument for patients evaluated for epilepsy surgery. *Medical Care* 1992; 30:299-319.

Viramontes JL & O'Brien B. Relationship between symptoms and health-related quality of life in chronic lung disease. *Journal of General Internal Medicine* 1994; 9(1):46-48.

Wagner AK, Keller SD, Kosinski M, Baker GA, Jacoby A, Hsu M, Chadwick DW, & Ware JE. Advances in methods for assessing the impact of epilepsy and antiepileptic drug therapy on patients' health-related quality of life. *Quality of Life Research* 1995.

Ware JE. Captopril, enalapril, and quality of life (letter to the editor). *New England Journal of Medicine* 1993; 329(7):506-507.

Ware JE. Comments on the use of health status assessment in clinical settings. *Medical Care* 1992; 30:MS205-MS209.

Ware JE. Evaluating measures of general health concepts for use in clinical trials. in: Furberg CD & Schuttinga JA. *Quality of Life Assessment: Practice, Problems, and Promise.* U.S. Department of Health and Human Services, Public Health Service, National Institutes of Health, 1990: 51-63.

Ware JE. *How to Score the Revised MOS Short Form Health Scale (SF-36).* Boston, MA: The Health Institute, New England Medical Center Hospitals, 1988.

Ware JE. Measuring patients' views: The optimum outcome measure. *British Medical Journal* 1993; 306:1429-1430.

Ware JE. Methodological considerations in the selection of health status assessment procedures. in: Wenger NK, Mattson ME, Furberg CD, & Elinson J (eds.). *Assessment of Quality of Life in Clinical Trials of Cardiovascular Therapies.* New York: Le Jacq Publishing Co., 1984:87-111.

Ware JE. The MOS 36-Item Short-Form Health Survey (SF-36). in: Sederer LI & Dickey B. *Outcomes Assessment in Clinical Practice.* Baltimore, MD: Williams and Wilkins, 1995.

Ware JE. Scales for measuring general health perceptions. *Health Services Research* Winter 1976; 11(4):396-415.

Ware JE. The status of health assessment 1994. *Annual Review of Public Health* 1995; 16:327-354.

Ware JE, Brook RH, Rogers WH, Keeler EB, Davies AR, Sherbourne CD, Goldberg GA, Camp P, & Newhouse JP. Comparison of health outcomes at a health maintenance organization with those of fee-for-service care. *Lancet* 1986; 1017-1022.

Ware JE, Brook RH, Davies-Avery A, Williams KN, Stewart AL, Rogers WH, Donald CA, & Johnston SA. *Model of Health and Methodology.* Santa Monica, CA: Rand Corporation, May 1980; R-1987/1-HEW. 49. (Conceptualization and Measurement of Health for Adults in the Health Insurance Study; vol I).

Ware JE, Davies-Avery A, & Brook RH. *Analysis of Relationships Among Health Status Measures.* Santa Monica: Rand Corporation, 1980; R-1987/6-HEW. 61. (Conceptualization and Measurement of Health for Adults in the Health Insurance Study; vol VI).

Ware JE, Gandek B, & the IQOLA Project Group. The SF-36® Health Survey: Development and use in mental health research and the IQOLA Project. I*nternational Journal of Mental Health* 1994; 23(2):49-73.

Ware JE & Karmos AH. Scales for measuring general health perceptions. *Health Services Research* 1976; 11:396-415.

Ware JE, Keller SD, Gandek B, Brazier JE, Sullivan M, & the IQOLA Project team. Evaluating translations of health status questionnaires: Methods from the IQOLA Project. *International Journal of Technology Assessment in Health Care* 1995.

Ware JE, Kosinski M, Bayliss MS, McHorney CA, Rogers WH, & Raczek A. Comparison of methods for the scoring and statistical analysis of SF-36 health profile and summary measures: Summary of results from the Medical Outcomes Study. *Medical Care* 1995.

Ware JE, Manning WG, Duan N, Wells KB, & Newhouse JP. Health status and the use of outpatient mental health services. *American Psychologist* 1984; 39:1090-1100.

Ware JE, Miller WG, & Snyder MK. *Comparison of Factor Analytic Methods in the Development of Health Related Indexes from Questionnaire Data*. Rockville, MD: Health Services Research Methods Branch, 1973; PB-239 517. 58.

Ware JE & Sherbourne CD. The MOS 36-item short-form health survey (SF-36): I. Conceptual framework and item selection. *Medical Care* 1992; 30:473-483.

Ware JE, Snow KK, Kosinski M, & Gandek B. *SF-36® Health Survey Manual and Interpretation Guide*. Boston, MA: The Health Institute, New England Medical Center, 1993.

Ware JE & Snyder MK. Dimensions of patient attitudes regarding doctors and medical care services. *Medical Care* August 1975; 13(8):669-682.

Weinberger M, Kirkman MS, Samsa GP, et al. The relationship between glycemic control and health-related quality of life in patients with non-insulin-dependent diabetes mellitus. *Medical Care* 1994; 32(12):1173-1181.

Weinberger M, Samsa GP, Hanlon JT, Schmader KE, Doyle ME, Cowper PA, Utlech KM, Cohen HJ, & Feussner JR. An evaluation of a brief health status measure in elderly veterans. *Journal of the American Geriatrics Society* 1991; 39:691-694.

Wells KB, Burnam MA, Rogers W, et al. The course of depression in adult outpatients: Results from the Medical Outcomes Study. *Archives of General Psychiatry* 1992; 49:788-794.

Wells KB, Hays RD, Burnam MA, Rogers WH, Greenfield S, & Ware JE. Detection of depressive disorder for patients receiving prepaid or fee-for-service care: Results from the Medical Outcomes Study. *Journal of the American Medical Association* 1989; 262:3298-3302.

Wells KB, Stewart A, Hays RD, Burnam MA, Rogers W, Daniels M, Berry S, Greenfield S, & Ware JE. The functioning and well-being of depressed patients: Results from the Medical Outcomes Study. *Journal of the American Medical Association* 1989; 262(7):914-919.

Wiklund I, Lindvall K, Swedberg K, & Zupkis RV. Self-assessment of quality of life in severe heart failure: An instrument for clinical use. *Scandinavian Journal of Psychology* 1987; 28:220-225.

Winer BJ, Brown DR, & Michels KM. *Statistical Principles in Experimental Design* 3rd Edition. New York: McGraw-Hill, Inc., 1991.

Wood W, Rhodes N, & Whelan M. Sex differences in positive well-being: A consideration of emotional style and marital status. *Psychological Bulletin* 1989; 106:249.

SF-36® PCS and MCS Summary Measures References

This section is a comprehensive list of citations for 120 Studies where the SF-36® PCS and MCS Summary Measure was used or discussed extensively

Alemao Evo A, Larson Rodney A., Cady Paul S. Examining the Role of Health Status and Age in Patient Satisfaction with Prescription Services. American Association of Pharmacy- Projects and Abstracts [ ], 99. 1999 Jul 3.

Alter H J, Braun R, Zazzali J L. Health status disparities among public and private emergency department patients. Acad Emerg Med 6[7], 736-43. 1999 Jul.

Atroshi I et al. Symptoms, disability, and quality of life in patients with carpal tunnel syndrome. J Hand Surg [Am] 24[2], 398-404. 1999 Mar.

Baker J G et al. Predicting follow-up functional outcomes in outpatient rehabilitation [published erratum appears in Am J Phys Rehabit 1998 Sep-Oct,77(5):414]. Am J Phys Med Rehabil 77[3], 202-12. 1998 May-Jun.

Bauman Charles H, Arthur Heather M. Relationship between functional exercise capacity and general quality of life in nonsurgical patient with lower-extremity peripheral arterial disease. J Vasc Nurs 15[1], 21-8. 1997 Jan.

Benzo R et al. Effect of pulmonary rehabilitation on quality of life in patients with COPD: the use of SF-36® summary scores as outcomes measures [In Process Citation]. J Cardiopulm Rehabil 20[4], 231-4. 2000 Jul-Aug.

Beusterien K M, Steinwald B, Ware Jr J E. Usefulness of the SF-36® Health Survey in measuring health outcomes in the depressed elderly. J Geriatr Psychiatry Neurol 9[1], 13-21. 1996 Jan.

Binkley J M et al. The Lower Extremity Functional Scale (LEFS): scale development, measurement properties, and clinical application. North American Orthopaedic Rehabilitation Research Network. Phys Ther 79[4], 371-83. 1999 Apr.

Bobes J et al. Quality Of Life In Schizophrenia: Long-Term Follow-Up in 362 Chronic Spanish Schizophrenic Outpatients Undergoing Risperidone Maintenance Treatment. Eur Psychiatry 13[ ], 158-63. 1998.

Broeckel J A et al. Quality of life after adjuvant chemotherapy for breast cancer [In Process Citation]. Breast Cancer Res Treat 62[2], 141-50. 2000 Jul.

Brooks R. The reliability and validity of the Health of the Nation Outcome Scales: validation in relation to patient derived measures [In Process Citation]. Aust N Z J Psychiatry 34[3], 504-11, discussion 520-1. 2000 Jun.

Buchi S et al. PRISM (Pictorial Representation of Illness and Self Measure)- a novel visual method to assess the global burden of illness in patients with systemic lupus erythematosus. Lupus 9[5], 368-73. 2000.

Byles J E, Mishra G, Schofield M. Factors associated with hysterectomy among women in Australia. Health Place 6[4], 301-308. 2000 Dec 1.

Cass A R, Volk R J, Nease D E. Health-related quality of life in primary care patients with recognized and unrecognized mood and anxiety disorders. Int J Psychiatry Med 29[3], 293-309. 1999.

Chandola T, Jenkinson C. The new UK National Statistics Socio-Economic Classification (NS-SEC), investigating social class differences in self-reported health status [In Process Citation]. J Public Health Med 22[2], 182-90. 2000 Jun.

Clarke A E et al. An international perspective on the well being and health care costs for patients with systemic lupus erythematosus. Tri-Nation Study Group. J Rheumatol 26[7], 1500-11. 1999 Jul.

Coulehan J L et al. Treating depressed primary care patients improves their physical, mental, and social functioning. Arch Intern Med 157[10], 1113-20. 1997 May 26.

Da Costa D et al. Determinants of health status in fibromyalgia: a comparative study with systemic lupus erythematosus. J Rheumatol 27[2], 365-72. 2000 Feb.

Dagum A B et al. Salvage after severe lower-extremity trauma: are the outcomes worth the means? Plast Reconstr Surg 103[4], 1212-20. 1999 Apr.

DeOreo P B. Hemodialysis patient-assessed functional health status predicts continued survival, hospitalization, and dialysis-attendance compliance. Am J Kidney Dis 30[2], 204-12. 1997 Aug.

Diaz-Buxo J A et al. Quality-of-life evaluation using Short Form 36: comparison in hemodialysis and peritoneal dialysis patients. Am J Kidney Dis 35[2], 293-300. 2000 Feb.

Eisner M D et al. Environmental tobacco smoke and adult asthma. The impact of changing exposure status on health outcomes. Am J Respir Crit Care Med 158[1], 170-5. 1998 Jul.

Fanuele J C et al. The impact of spinal problems on the health status of patients: have we underestimated the effect? [see comments]. Spine 25[12], 1509-14. 2000 Jun 15.

Fazio V W, Wu J S, Lavery I C. Repeat ileal pouch-anal anastomosis to salvage septic complications of pelvic pouches: clinical outcome and quality of life assessment. Ann Surg 228[4], 588-97. 1998 Oct.

Friedman A W et al. Systemic lupus erythematosus in three ethnic groups. IV. Factors associated with self-reported functional outcome in a large cohort study. LUMINA Study Group. Lupus in Minority Populations, Nature versus Nurture. Arthritis Care Res 12[4], 256-66. 1999 Aug.

Funk G F et al. Baseline and post-treatment assessment of the general health status of head and neck cancer patients compared with United States population norms. Head Neck 19[8], 675-83. 1997 Dec.

Gandek B et al. Cross-validation of item selection and scoring for the SF-12 Health Survey in nine countries: results from the IQOLA Project. International Quality of Life Assessment. J Clin Epidemiol 51[11], 1171-8. 1998 Nov.

Garg N et al. Effect of gender, treatment site and psychiatric comorbidity on quality of life outcome in substance dependence. Am J Addict 8[1], 44-54. 1999 Winter.

Gartsman G M, Brinker M R, Khan M. Early effectiveness of arthroscopic repair for full-thickness tears of the rotator cuff: an outcome analysis. J Bone Joint Surg Am 80[1], 33-40. 1998 Jan.

Gartsman G M et al. Self-assessment of general health status in patients with five common shoulder conditions. J Shoulder Elbow Surg 7[3], 228-37. 1998 May-Jun.

Gartsman G M, Khan M, Hammerman S M. Arthroscopic repair of full-thickness tears of the rotator cuff. J Bone Joint Surg Am 80[6], 832-40. 1998 Jun.

Guldvog B. Can patient satisfaction improve health among patients with angina pectoris? Int J Qual Health Care 11[3], 233-40. 1999 Jun.

Hacker R J et al. A prospective randomized multicenter clinical evaluation of an anterior cervical fusion cage [In Process Citation]. Spine 25[20], 2646-55. 2000 Oct 15.

Hawk C et al. Chiropractic care for patients aged 55 years and older: report from a practice-based research program. J Am Geriatr Soc 48[5], 534-45. 2000 May.

Hays RD; Cunningham WE; Sherbourne CD et al., Health-related quality of life in patients with human immunodeficiency virus infection in the United States: results from the HIV Cost and Services Utilization Study, 2000 June 15; 108, (9): 714-722.

Jain R et al. Health Status Following Recessional Ulnar Osteotomy. Hand Surg 5[1], 11-17. 2000 Jul.

Jain R, Schemitsch E H, Waddell J P. Cementless acetabular revision arthroplasty [see comments]. Can J Surg 43[4], 269-75. 2000 Aug.

Jain R, Schemitsch E H, Waddell J P. Functional outcome after acetabular revision with roof reinforcement rings [see comments]. Can J Surg 43[4], 276-82. 2000 Aug.

Jenkinson C. The SF-36® physical and mental health summary measures: an example of how to interpret scores. J Health Serv Res Policy 3[2], 92-6. 1998 Apr.

Jenkinson C et al. Comparison of therapeutic and subtherapeutic nasal continuous positive airway pressure for obstructive sleep apnoea: a randomised prospective parallel trial [see comments]. Lancet 353[9170], 2100-5. 1999 Jun 19.

Jenkinson C et al. Evaluation of index and profile measures of health status in a randomized controlled trial. Comparison of the Medical Outcomes Study 36-Item Short Form Health Survey, EuroQol, and disease specific measures. Med Care 35[11], 1109-18. 1997 Nov.

Jenkinson C, Layte R. Development and testing of the UK SF-12 (short form health survey). J Health Serv Res Policy 2[1], 14-8. 1997 Jan.

Jenkinson C et al. A shorter form health survey: can the SF-12 replicate results from the SF-36® in longitudinal studies? J Public Health Med 19[2], 179-86. 1997 Jun.

Jenkinson C et al. Assessment of the SF-36 version 2 in the United Kingdom. J Epidemiol Community Health 53[1], 46-50. 1999 Jan.

Jenkinson C, Stradling J, Petersen S. Comparison of three measures of quality of life outcome in the evaluation of continuous positive airways pressure therapy for sleep apnoea. J Sleep Res 6[3], 199-204. 1997 Sep.

Jenkinson C, Stradling J, Petersen S. How should we evaluate health status? A comparison of three methods in patients presenting with obstructive sleep apnoea. Qual Life Res 7[2], 95-100. 1998 Feb.

Johnson J A, Coons S J. Comparison of the EQ-5D and SF-12 in an adult US sample. Qual Life Res 7[2], 155-66. 1998 Feb.

Johnson J A, Pickard A S. Comparison of the EQ-5D and SF-12 health surveys in a general population survey in Alberta, Canada. Med Care 38[1], 115-21. 2000 Jan.

Keller S D et al. The SF-36® Arthritis-Specific Health Index (ASHI): II. Tests of validity in four clinical trials. Med Care 37[5 Suppl], MS51-60. 1999 May.

Knoell D L et al. Measurement of outcomes in adults receiving pharmaceutical care in a comprehensive asthma outpatient clinic. Pharmacotherapy 18[6], 1365-74. 1998 Nov-Dec.

Ko C Y et al. Does better functional result equate with better quality of life? Implications for surgical treatment in familial adenomatous polyposis. Dis Colon Rectum 43[6], 829-35, discussion 835-7. 2000 Jun.

Kosinski M et al. The SF-36 Health Survey as a generic outcome measure in clinical trials of patients with osteoarthritis and rheumatoid arthritis: relative validity of scales in relation to clinical measures of arthritis severity. Med Care 37[5 Suppl], MS23-39. 1999 May.

Kressin N R, Spiro 3rd A, Skinner K M. Negative affectivity and health-related quality of life. Med Care 38[8], 858-67. 2000 Aug.

Lalonde L et al. Comparing the psychometric properties of preference-based and nonpreference-based health-related quality of life in coronary heart disease. Canadian Collaborative Cardiac Assessment Group. Qual Life Res 8[5], 399-409. 1999 Aug.

Leidy K N, Chan K S, Coughlin C. Is the asthma quality of life questionnaire a useful measure for low- income asthmatics? Am J Respir Crit Care Med 158[4], 1082-90. 1998 Oct.

Leidy N K et al. Seizure frequency and the health-related quality of life of adults with epilepsy. Neurology 53[1], 162-6. 1999 Jul 13.

Lieberman J R et al. Outcome after total hip arthroplasty. Comparison of a traditional disease-specific and a quality-of-life measurement of outcome. J Arthroplasty 12[6], 639-45. 1997 Sep.

Liu L et al. The impact of radiation therapy on quality of life in patients with cancer [In Process Citation]. Cancer Pract 6[4], 237-42. 1998 Jul-Aug.

Lofland J H et al. Changes in resource use and outcomes for patients with migraine treated with sumatriptan: a managed care perspective. Arch Intern Med 159[8], 857-63. 1999 Apr 26.

Louie B E et al. Treatment of osteonecrosis of the femoral head by free vascularized fibular grafting: an analysis of surgical outcome and patient health status. Can J Surg 42[4], 274-83. 1999 Aug.

Mahomed N N, Spellmann M, Goldberg M J. Functional health status of adults with achondroplasia. Am J Med Genet 78[1], 30-5. 1998 Jun 16.

Mancuso C A, Peterson M G, Charlson M E. Effects of depressive symptoms on health-related quality of life in asthma patients [In Process Citation]. J Gen Intern Med 15[5], 301-10. 2000 May.

Mancuso C A, Peterson M G, Charlson M E. Effects of depressive symptoms on health-related quality of life in asthma patients [see comments]. J Gen Intern Med 15[5], 301-10. 2000 May.

Mant J W et al. Use of the Short Form-36 to detect the influence of upper gastrointestinal disease on self-reported health status. Qual Life Res 7[3], 221-6. 1998 Apr.

Marrie T J et al. A controlled trial of a critical pathway for treatment of community-acquired pneumonia. CAPITAL Study Investigators. Community-Acquired Pneumonia Intervention Trial Assessing Levofloxacin

Martinez Martin P et al. The PDQ-39 Spanish version: reliability and correlation with the short-form health survey (SF-36). Neurologia 14[4], 159-63. 1999 Apr.

Maruish M E, Bershadsky B, Goldstein L. Reliability and validity of the SA-45: further evidence from a primary care setting. Assessment 5[4], 407-19. 1998 Dec.

McEwen S, Mayo N, Wood-Dauphinee S. Inferring quality of life from performance-based assessments [In Process Citation]. Disabil Rehabil 22[10], 456-63. 2000 Jul 10.

McGuire M S et al. The type of urinary diversion after radical cystectomy significantly impacts on the patient's quality of life [see comments]. Ann Surg Oncol 7[1], 4-8. 2000 Jan-Feb.

Merkus M P et al. Predictors of poor outcome in chronic dialysis patients: The Netherlands Cooperative Study on the Adequacy of Dialysis. The NECOSAD Study Group. Am J Kidney Dis 35[1], 69-79. 2000 Jan.

Miller D M et al. Clinical significance of the multiple sclerosis functional composite: relationship to patient-reported quality of life. Arch Neurol 57[9], 1319-24. 2000 Sep.

Miners A H et al. Assessing Health-Related Quality-of-Life In Patients With Severe Haemophilia A And B. Psychology, Health & Medicine 4[1], 5-15. 1999.

Money S R et al. Effect of cilostazol on walking distances in patients with intermittent claudication caused by peripheral vascular disease. J Vasc Surg 27[2], 267-74, discussion 274-5. 1998 Feb.

Morrin L, Black S, Reid R. Impact of duration in a cardiac rehabilitation program on coronary risk profile and health-related quality of life outcomes. J Cardiopulm Rehabil 20[2], 115-21. 2000 Mar-Apr.

Mortensen O S et al. Health related quality of life after conservative or invasive treatment of inducible postinfarction ischaemia [In Process Citation]. Heart 84[5], 535-40. 2000 Nov.

Mouton C P et al. The associations between health and domestic violence in older women: results of a pilot study. J Womens Health Gend Based Med 8[9], 1173-9. 1999 Nov.

Murray M, Lefort S, Ribeiro V. The SF-36®: Reliable And Valid For The Institutionalized Elderly? Aging & Mental Health 2[1], 24-7. 1998.

Nash I S, Curtis L H, Rubin H. Predictors of patient-reported physical and mental health 6 months after percutaneous coronary revascularization. Am Heart J 138[3 Pt 1], 422-9. 1999 Sep.

Nortvedt M W et al. Performance of the SF-36®, SF-12®, and RAND-36 summary scales in a multiple sclerosis population. Med Care 38[10], 1022-8. 2000 Oct.

O'Leary C J, Jones P W. The left ventricular dysfunction questionnaire (LVD-36): reliability, validity, and responsiveness. Heart 83[6], 634-40. 2000 Jun.

Painter P et al. Physical functioning and health-related quality-of-life changes with exercise training in hemodialysis patients. Am J Kidney Dis 35[3], 482-92. 2000 Mar.

Pearson S, Stewart S, Rubenach S. Is health-related quality of life among older, chronically ill patients associated with unplanned readmission to hospital? Aust N Z J Med 29[5], 701-6. 1999 Oct.

Philipp M, Kohnen R, Hiller K O. Hypericum extract versus imipramine or placebo in patients with moderate depression: randomised multicentre study of treatment for eight weeks [In Process Citation]. BMJ 319[7224], 1534-9. 1999 Dec 11.

Pickard A S et al. Replicability of SF-36® summary scores by the SF-12 in stroke patients. Stroke 30[6], 1213-7. 1999 Jun.

Pinson C W et al. Health-related quality of life after different types of solid organ transplantation [In Process Citation]. Ann Surg 232[4], 597-607. 2000 Oct.

Rai G S, Kiniorns M, Burns W. New Handicap Scale For Elderly In Hospital. Arch Gerontol Geriatr 28[ ], 99-104. 1999.

Ray Kim W et al. Reliability and validity of the NIDDK-QA instrument in the assessment of quality of life in ambulatory patients with cholestatic liver disease [In Process Citation]. Hepatology 32[5], 924-9. 2000 Nov.

Rebollo P et al. [Factors associated with health related quality of life in patients undergoing renal replacement therapy]. Nefrologia 20[2], 171-81. 2000 Mar-Apr.

Revicki D A et al. Complete resolution of heartburn symptoms and health-related quality of life in patients with gastro-oesophageal reflux disease. Aliment Pharmacol Ther 13[12], 1621-30. 1999 Dec.

Revicki D A et al. Depression, health-related quality of life, and medical cost outcomes of receiving recommended levels of antidepressant treatment. J Fam Pract 47[6], 446-52. 1998 Dec.

Revicki Dennis A et al. Olanzapine versus haloperidol in the treatment of schizophrenia and other psychotic disorders: Quality of life and clinical outcomes of a randomized clinical trial. Qual Life Res 8[5], 417-26. 1999 Aug.

Riddle D L, Stratford P W. Use of generic versus region-specific functional status measures on patients with cervical spine disorders. Phys Ther 78[9], 951-63. 1998 Sep.

Roberts Ron, Hemingway Harry, Marmot Michael. Psychometric and clinical validity of the SF-36® General Health Survey in the Whitehall II Study. British Journal of Health Psychology 2[ ], 285-300. 1997.

Rumsfeld J S et al. Health-related quality of life as a predictor of mortality following coronary artery bypass graft surgery. Participants of the Department of Veterans Affairs Cooperative Study Group on Processes, Structures, and Outcomes of Care in Cardiac Surgery. JAMA 281[14], 1298-303. 1999 Apr 14.

Ruta D A et al. Measuring health status in British patients with rheumatoid arthritis: reliability, validity and responsiveness of the short form 36-item health survey (SF-36). Br J Rheumatol 37[4], 425-36. 1998 Apr.

Salsberry P J et al. Self-reported health status of low-income mothers. Image J Nurs Sch 31[4], 375-80. 1999.

Schofield Margot J, Lattimore-Foot Glenda, Sanson-Fisher Rob. SF-36® Health Profiles of Recently Discharged Hospital Patients In Australia. Journal of Health Psychology 3[4], 551-63. 1998.

Schover L R et al. Having children after cancer. A pilot survey of survivors' attitudes and experiences. Cancer 86[4], 697-709. 1999 Aug 15.

Schumacher Gerald et al. Using Health Status Measures to Teach, Learn, and Obtain Data on Outcomes Assessment in the Classroom. American Association of Pharmacy [ ], 73. 1999 Jul 3.

Schwartz L M et al. Treatment and health outcomes of women and men in a cohort with coronary artery disease. Arch Intern Med 157[14], 1545-51. 1997 Jul 28.

Shmueli A. Subjective health status and health values in the general population. Med Decis Making 19[2], 122-7. 1999 Apr-Jun.

Silvers D et al. Domperidone in the management of symptoms of diabetic gastroparesis: efficacy, tolerability, and quality-of-life outcomes in a multicenter controlled trial. DOM-USA-5 Study Group. Clin Ther 20[3], 438-53. 1998 May-Jun.

Simon G E et al. SF-36® summary scores: are physical and mental health truly distinct? Med Care 36[4], 567-72. 1998 Apr.

Starz Terence, Irrgang James, Vogt Molly. Development of an osteoarthritis of the knee P-F-S severity index. Arthritis Rheum 40[9], S235. 1997.

Strand V et al. Function and health-related quality of life: results from a randomized controlled trial of leflunomide versus methotrexate or placebo in patients with active rheumatoid arthritis. Leflunomide Rheumatoid Arthritis Investigators Group. Arthritis Rheum 42[9], 1870-8. 1999 Sep.

Terrell J E et al. Health impact of head and neck cancer. Otolaryngol Head Neck Surg 120[6], 852-9. 1999 Jun.

Terrell J E et al. Head and neck cancer-specific quality of life: instrument validation. Arch Otolaryngol Head Neck Surg 123[10], 1125-32. 1997 Oct.

Tugwell P et al. Clinical improvement as reflected in measures of function and health-related quality of life following treatment with leflunomide compared with methotrexate in patients with rheumatoid arthritis: sensitivity and relative efficiency to detect a treatment e. Arthritis Rheum 43[3], 506-14. 2000 Mar.

von Steinbuchel N et al. Assessment of health-related quality-of-life in patients after heart transplantation under therapy with tacrolimus or cyclosporine [In Process Citation]. Transpl Int 13 Su[Suppl 1], S609-14. 2000.

Ware Jr J, Kosinski M, Keller S D. A 12-Item Short-Form Health Survey: construction of scales and preliminary tests of reliability and validity. Med Care 34[3], 220-33. 1996 Mar.

Ware Jr J E et al. The equivalence of SF-36® summary health scores estimated using standard and country-specific algorithms in 10 countries: results from the IQOLA Project. International Quality of Life Assessment. J Clin Epidemiol 51[11], 1167-70. 1998 Nov.

Ware Jr J E et al. The responsiveness of disease-specific and generic health measures to changes in the severity of asthma among adults. Qual Life Res 7[3], 235-44. 1998 Apr.

Ware Jr J E et al. Comparison of methods for the scoring and statistical analysis of SF-36® health profile and summary measures: summary of results from the Medical Outcomes Study. Med Care 33[4 Suppl], AS264-79. 1995 Apr.

Ware Jr J E et al. The factor structure of the SF-36® Health Survey in 10 countries: results from the IQOLA Project. International Quality of Life Assessment. J Clin Epidemiol 51[11], 1159-65. 1998 Nov.

Ware JE, Kosinski M. *SF-36® Physical and Mental Health Summary Scales: A Manual for Users of Version 1, 2nd Edition*. Lincoln, RI: QualityMetric Incorporated, 2001.

Ware JE, Kosinski M, Keller SK. *SF-36® Physical and Mental Health Summary Scales:* A User's Manual. Boston, MA: The Health Institute, 1994.

White P F et al. Percutaneous neuromodulation therapy: does the location of electrical stimulation effect the acute analgesic response? Anesth Analg 91[4], 949-54. 2000 Oct.

Williams Jr J W et al. Treatment of dysthymia and minor depression in primary care: A randomized controlled trial in older adults [see comments]. JAMA 284[12], 1519-26. 2000 Sep 27.

Younossi Z M et al. Cholestatic liver diseases and health-related quality of life. Am J Gastroenterol 95[2], 497-502. 2000 Feb.

Appendix A: Definitions Of Criterion Variables

TABLE A.1 DEFINITIONS OF CHRONIC CONDITIONS FROM THE GENERAL U.S. POPULATION SURVEY

CONDITION	DEFINITION
Hypertension	Has doctor ever told you that you have hypertension (sometimes called high blood pressure).
Congestive Heart Failure	Has doctor ever told you that you have congestive heart failure (heart failure or enlarged heart).
MI (Recent)	Has doctor ever told you that you had a heart attack in the last year (myocardial infarction).
Diabetes	Has doctor ever told you that you have diabetes (high blood sugar).
Angina	Has doctor ever told you that you have angina.
Cancer	Has doctor ever told you that you have cancer (except skin cancer).
Allergies	Do you now have chronic allergies or sinus trouble.
Arthritis	Do you now have arthritis of any kind or rheumatism.
Back Pain/Sciatica	Do you now have sciatica or chronic back problems.
Vision Impairment	Do you now have blindness or trouble seeing with one or both eyes, even when wearing glasses.
Chronic Lung Disease	Do you now have chronic lung disease (like chronic bronchitis, asthma, or emphysema).
Dermatitis	Do you now have dermatitis or other chronic skin rash.
Hearing Impairment	Do you now have deafness or other trouble hearing with one or both ears.
Limitations in use of arm(s)/leg(s)	Do you now have limitation in the use of an arm or leg (missing, paralyzed, or weakness).
Depression Screener	Two or more weeks in the past year feeling sad, blue, or depressed; or two years or more feeling depressed or sad most days; or feeling depressed or sad much of the time in the past year?
Stress	Quite a bit or a great deal of stress or pressure experienced in daily living in the past four weeks
Life Satisfaction	Extremely or very happy with personal life during the past four weeks

TABLE A.2 DEFINITIONS OF CRITERIA USED IN FIRST ROUND OF EMPIRICAL VALIDATION

CRITERION	DEFINITION
MOS Tracer Conditions (Table 8.1, column 1; Appendix B1)	
Hypertension	Physician report of current hypertension (or independently derived probability of hypertension if physician report missing or questionable).
Congestive Heart Failure	Physician report of current congestive heart failure (or independently derived probability of CHF if physician report missing or questionable).
MI (Recent)	Physician report of MI within the past year (or independently derived probability of MI if physician report of MI missing or questionable).
Diabetes, Type II	Physician report of diabetes with age at onset 30 years or older (or independently derived probability of diabetes and age at onset if actual information missing or questionable).
Severity of MOS Tracer Conditions (Table 8.1, column 2-4; Appendix B2)	
Hypertension	Severity defined by diastolic blood pressure above 100 mm Hg (2 levels)
Congestive Heart Failure	Severity defined by the presence of dyspnea on one-block exertion or while lying flat (2 levels)
MI (Recent)	Severity defined by the presence of premature ventricular contractions and/or angina (2 levels)
Diabetes, Type II	Severity defined by the presence of complications and duration of diabetes (4 levels: 1-free of complications and duration less than 10 years; 2-free of complications and duration 10 or more years; 3-complications of eye of foot only; 4-complications of diabetic heart and/or kidney disease)
MOS Comorbid Conditions (Table 8.1, column 5; Appendix B3)*	
Asthma	Had any asthma attacks in past six months
COPD	Now have lung disease ever diagnosed by physician as chronic obstructive pulmonary disease (like chronic bronchitis or emphysema) in past six months.
Angina - ever**	Ever told by physician have angina.
Angina, recent - no MI	Symptoms of angina in past six months in the absence of an MI within one year.
MI, past	Ever had a heart attack diagnosed by physician, more than one year ago.
Other lung disease	Any other lung disease such as tuberculosis or pneumonia in past six months.
Back pain/sciatica	Attacks of back pain or sciatica last six months.
Hip impairments	Ever told by physician have hip impairments
Rheumatoid arthritis	Now have active condition physician ever diagnosed as arthritis and physician labeled it rheumatoid arthritis and morning stiffness.

TABLE A.2 DEFINITIONS OF CRITERIA USED IN FIRST ROUND OF EMPIRICAL VALIDATION (CONTINUED)

CRITERION	DEFINITION
Osteoarthritis	Now have active condition physician ever diagnosed as arthritis and physician labeled it osteoarthritis or degenerative arthritis and patient is □ 55 years old.
Musculoskeletal complaints	Active condition physician ever diagnosed as arthritis but criteria for osteoarthritis or rheumatoid arthritis not met.
Other rheumatic disease**	Now have active rheumatic disease other than arthritis physician ever diagnosed (e.g., systemic lupus erythematosus, scleroderma, or gout).
Colitis**	Now have active disease physician ever diagnosed as Crohn's disease or ulcerative colitis (severe bowel irritation).
Diverticulitis**	Now have active disease physician ever diagnosed as diverticulitis.
Fistulas**	Now have active disease physician ever diagnosed as intestinal fistulas.
Gallbladder disease**	Now have active disease physician ever diagnosed as chronic gallbladder disease.
Irritable bowel disease	Ever told by physician have irritable bowel syndrome, functional bowel disease, or chronic bowel disease.
Liver disease**	Now have active disease physician ever diagnosed as chronic hepatitis or cirrhosis.
Diabetes, Type I**	Physician report of diabetes with age at onset younger than 30 years (or independently derived probability of diabetes and age at onset if actual information missing or questionable).
Ulcer	Now have active disease physician ever diagnosed as an ulcer (peptic, gastric, stomach, or duodenal).
Kidney disease**	Disease physician ever diagnosed as serious kidney disease in last six months.
Benign Prostatic Hypertrophy**	Male, age □ 50 years, history of nocturia in past six months, no serious kidney disease ever diagnosed, and no report of prostatic cancer.
UTI	Kidney or bladder infection diagnosed by physician in past six months.
Varicosities**	Now have condition physician ever diagnosed as varicose veins/deep varicosities.
Cancer**	Ever had cancer.
Dermatitis	Repeated episodes of dermatitis or skin rash in past six months.
Anemia	Told by doctor have anemia (past six months.)

(continued)

TABLE A.2 DEFINITIONS OF CRITERIA USED IN FIRST ROUND OF EMPIRICAL VALIDATION (CONTINUED)

CRITERION	DEFINITION
Symptom Clusters (Table 8.1, column 6-9; Appendix B4)	
Ear, nose & throat	Patient reported frequency of blurred vision, dry mouth or lump in throat in the past four weeks.
Central Nervous system	Patient report of fainting, drowsiness or dizziness, shortness of breath, chest pain heart palpitations, or frequent headaches in the past four weeks.
Musculoskeletal	Patient report of stiffness or soreness in the joints, backache, heavy feeling in arm or legs, or numbness in the feet in the past four weeks.
GI/GU	Patient report of acid indigestion, heartburn, nausea, or trouble passing urine in the past four weeks.
Clinical Depression Groups (Table 8.1, column 15-16; Appendix B8 & B9)	
Cross-sectional	NIMH (DIS) criteria met for major depression and/or dysthymia at baseline assessment.
Longitudinal	Major depression and/or dysthymia present at one-year follow-up but *not present* at two-year follow-up.
Age Groups (Table 8.1, column 10-11; Appendix B5 & B6)	
Age 18-44	Uncomplicated hypertensives (patients with hypertension and no other major medical conditions), age 18 - 44
Age 45-64	Uncomplicated hypertensives (patients with hypertension and no other major medical conditions), age 45 - 64
Age 65 or older	Uncomplicated hypertensives (patients with hypertension and no other major medical conditions), age >= 65
Self-Reported Transition Groups (Table 8.1, column 12-14; Appendix B7)	
Physical	Patient report at two-year follow-up of change in physical health over two years: (a lot more limited now, a little more limited now, about the same, somewhat less limited now or a lot less limited now.
General	Patient report at two-year follow-up of change in general health over two years: (a lot more limited now, a little more limited now, about the same, somewhat less limited now or a lot less limited now.
Mental	Patient report at two-year follow-up of change in mental health over two years: (a lot more limited now, a little more limited now, about the same, somewhat less limited now or a lot less limited now.

* Information regarding the comorbid medical conditions was obtained from the patient during a structured medical history interview conducted by a trained clinician. If information regarding a condition (or conditions) was missing, an independently derived probability of each diagnosis was substituted.

** Because of very low prevalence, the following conditions are incorporated into an index of eleven comorbid conditions: angina-ever, other rheumatic disease, colitis, diverticulitis, intestinal fistulas, gallbladder disease, liver disease, benign prostatic hypertrophy, varicosities, cancer, and type I diabetes.

Appendix B: Table Of Results

TABLE B.1 ADJUSTED MEAN SCORES FOR SF-36 SCALES AND COMPONENT SUMMARIES FOR FOUR CHRONIC CONDITIONS

	PF	RP	BP	GH	VT	SF	RE	MH	PCS	MCS
Hypertension	78.27 (0.8)	65.90 (1.4)	75.08 (1.0)	66.79 (0.7)	61.63 (0.8)	90.08 (0.6)	79.85 (1.3)	80.39 (0.6)	45.94 (0.3)	53.40 (0.3)
Congestive Heart Failure	59.47 (2.8)	46.33 (4.3)	69.57 (3.4)	50.18 (2.3)	47.15 (2.7)	78.59 (3.3)	69.02 (3.9)	78.54 (1.7)	38.29 (1.2)	51.43 (1.0)
Myocardial Infarction, Recent	72.40 (2.8)	50.60 (4.7)	76.15 (2.66)	61.59 (2.4)	56.10 (2.0)	87.68 (2.4)	73.04 (4.5)	76.33 (1.5)	43.51 (1.2)	51.69 (0.9)
Type II Diabetes	74.36 (2.1)	63.32 (3.7)	73.55 (2.2)	59.16 (1.9)	59.11 (1.7)	86.54 (1.9)	80.63 (2.8)	78.83 (1.4)	43.86 (1.0)	53.04 (0.8)
F for Four Conditions	21.76[a]	10.75[a]	3.05[c]	25.10[a]	11.48[a]	5.19[a]	2.99[c]	2.93[c]	17.85[a]	1.59
Adjusted R^2 (Four Conditions)	0.252	0.113	0.074	0.084	0.105	0.058	0.036	0.078	0.186	0.069
N	1413	1413	1413	1413	1413	1413	1413	1413	1413	1413

[a] p< 0.001, two-tailed test
[b] p< o.o1, two-tailed test
[c] p>0.05, two-tailed test
Note: Mean scores were estimated from linear regression models that controlled for demographics and MOS design variables.

TABLE B.2 ADJUSTED SF-36 AND COMPONENT SCALE SCORES FOR THE SEVERITY OF FOUR CHRONIC CONDITIONS

	PF	RP	BP	GH	VT	SF	RE	MH	PCS	MCS
Hypertension										
Severity 1	77.72 (0.8)	64.64 (1.6)	75.06 (1.1)	66.60 (0.8)	61.51 (0.9)	89.88 (0.7)	78.78 (1.6)	80.13 (0.7)	45.78 (0.4)	53.25 (0.4)
Severity 2	81.12 (2.9)	73.98 (5.2)	74.92 (3.6)	67.89 (3.0)	62.13 (2.0)	91.43 (1.9)	86.75 (3.4)	82.11 (2.1)	46.81 (1.4)	54.41 (0.9)
Congestive Heart Failure										
Severity 1	67.55 (3.5)	57.18 (5.4)	74.83 (3.9)	56.59 (3.0)	53.49 (3.2)	84.33 (3.9)	76.99 (4.3)	81.51 (1.7)	41.60 (1.7)	53.25 (1.2)
Severity 2	47.95 (2.7)	29.36 (4.8)	61.31 (4.8)	40.76 (2.8)	36.99 (3.6)	69.54 (4.9)	57.27 (5.0)	73.99 (2.9)	33.31 (1.2)	48.58 (1.7)
Type II Diabetes										
Severity 1	77.16 (2.7)	64.73 (4.8)	73.70 (2.6)	61.53 (2.3)	59.85 (1.9)	87.59 (2.5)	82.92 (3.7)	79.09 (1.9)	44.66 (1.3)	53.27 (1.0)
Severity 2	75.47 (2.8)	65.80 (4.9)	76.83 (2.9)	57.79 (3.1)	60.07 (3.1)	87.49 (2.5)	74.82 (4.6)	78.09 (2.4)	45.06 (1.3)	51.94 (1.3)
Severity 3	73.36 (5.0)	63.88 (8.1)	73.25 (5.0)	58.69 (5.8)	57.91 (3.2)	85.09 (3.9)	88.17 (5.8)	81.51 (2.9)	42.83 (2.3)	54.51 (1.2)
Severity 4	63.55 (3.8)	54.69 (7.3)	66.93 (5.2)	52.96 (2.8)	55.36 (3.2)	80.83 (4.3)	76.01 (5.2)	76.72 (2.1)	39.86 (1.7)	52.41 (1.2)
F for Severity of Hypertension	1.20	2.62	0.00	0.15	0.07	0.55	3.59	0.69	0.43	1.13
F for Severity of CHF	21.08[a]	17.31[a]	5.34[c]	17.25[a]	13.50[a]	5.65[c]	7.24[b]	5.32[c]	17.33[a]	5.01[c]
F for Severity of Diabetes	3.61[c]	0.89	1.42	2.61	0.70	0.94	1.44	1.02	2.94[c]	0.93
Adjusted R^2 (Severity)	0.270	0.126	0.080	0.098	0.113	0.069	0.047	0.081	0.202	0.074
N	1413	1413	1413	1413	1413	1413	1413	1413	1413	1413

[a] $p < 0.001$, two-tailed test
[b] $p < 0.01$, two-tailed test
[c] $p < 0.05$, two-tailed test
Note: Mean scores were estimated from linear regression models that controlled for demographics and MOS design variables.

TABLE B.3 ESTIMATES OF DIFFERENCES IN MEAN SCORES FOR SF-36 SCALES AND COMPONENT SUMMARIES FOR PATIENTS WITH COMORBIDITIES VS PATIENTS WITHOUT COMORBIDITIES

	PF	RP	BP	VT	GH	SF	RE	MH	PCS	MCS
Asthma	-10.72	-16.61[c]	-5.59	-4.50	-7.92	-2.98	-38.18[a]	-4.71	-2.21	-5.63[c]
	(6.2)	(8.2)	(5.8)	(5.4)	(4.8)	(5.3)	(11.0)	(4.2)	(2.8)	(2.8)
COPD	-5.86	-10.68[c]	-5.98	-9.01[b]	-4.57[c]	-4.80	-.82	-4.37	-3.65[c]	-1.06
	(3.4)	(5.4)	(3.1)	(2.8)	(2.2)	(3.6)	(4.1)	(2.2)	(1.5)	(1.2)
Angina (no MI)	-5.69[b]	-13.78[a]	-6.41[b]	-7.96[a]	-7.67[a]	-.89	-4.19	-2.06	-3.94[a]	-.72
	(2.1)	(3.4)	(2.2)	(1.7)	(2.0)	(1.9)	(3.2)	(1.5)	(.9)	(.9)
Past MI	-7.33[b]	-5.04	-3.59	-5.66[b]	-3.85	-4.32	-3.16	-1.61	-2.70[b]	-.71
	(2.5)	(3.9)	(2.7)	(2.1)	(2.1)	(2.5)	(4.7)	(2.2)	(1.0)	(1.3)
Other Lung Disease	.84	2.11	2.91	-2.02	9.25[c]	-4.15	-3.59	-6.00	1.68	-1.83
	(4.4)	(6.3)	(5.0)	(6.1)	(4.6)	(3.5)	(10.4)	(5.4)	(2.6)	(1.9)
Back Complaints	-4.92[b]	-11.71[a]	-13.39[a]	-3.04[c]	-4.86[b]	-5.50[a]	-2.46	-2.54[c]	-3.95[a]	-.71
	(1.7)	(3.1)	(1.9)	(1.2)	(1.7)	(1.6)	(3.0)	(1.2)	(.7)	(.7)
Hip Impairment	-15.41[a]	-6.29	-9.97[a]	-12.30[a]	-7.89[c]	-10.97[b]	-9.45	-4.07	-5.36[a]	-2.28
	(3.5)	(5.8)	(2.8)	(2.7)	(3.1)	(4.2)	(6.4)	(2.7)	(1.5)	(1.7)
Rheumatoid Arthritis	-7.90	-13.92[c]	-20.50[a]	-5.94	-.61	-2.99	4.56	-.33	-6.42[a]	2.20
	(5.8)	(6.9)	(4.6)	(3.7)	(3.5)	(3.8)	(7.0)	(4.1)	(1.9)	(2.0)
Osteoarthritis	-8.38[c]	-12.73[c]	-13.61[a]	-2.64	-5.36	-2.78	3.47	-1.33	-5.17[a]	1.05
	(3.3)	(5.1)	(3.1)	(2.2)	(3.0)	(2.7)	(5.0)	(2.0)	(1.3)	(1.1)
Musculoskeletal	-4.23[c]	-6.62[c]	-6.20[a]	-3.62[c]	-3.50	.36	-1.82	-3.48[b]	-2.29[b]	-.58
	(1.7)	(3.4)	(1.9)	(1.7)	(1.8)	(1.5)	(3.4)	(1.3)	(.8)	(.8)
Irritable Bowel	-6.08	-3.25	-5.04	-6.39	-6.16	-5.46	-3.40	-2.03	-2.57	-1.37
	(3.5)	(6.0)	(3.6)	(3.8)	(3.3)	(2.8)	(6.6)	(2.5)	(1.5)	(1.5)
Ulcers	-12.07[c]	-14.03[c]	-7.17	-9.29[c]	-6.01	-6.71	-7.42	-4.62	-4.87	-1.61
	(6.0)	(6.8)	(4.5)	(4.3)	(4.3)	(4.2)	(6.8)	(3.6)	(2.9)	(1.9)
Kidney Disease	-3.95	-13.78	-12.09†	-5.73	-7.24	-9.34	4.17	-7.35	-3.90	-1.93
	(5.7)	(12.2)	(7.2)	(5.9)	(4.2)	(7.5)	(13.9)	(6.7)	(3.0)	(4.1)
UTI	-.93	-1.77	-4.26	-1.83	-5.35	.07	-1.72	.42	-1.13	-.40
	2.1)	(4.7)	(2.5)	(2.4)	(2.8)	(3.4)	(5.4)	(1.9)	(1.0)	(1.3)
Dermatitis	3.22[c]	-6.50	-3.00	-2.04	-.88	-.76	-2.60	-1.37	-.40	-.86
	(1.6)	(3.9)	(2.6)	(1.6)	(1.9)	(1.9)	(3.5)	(1.9)	(.8)	(.9)
Anemia	-6.03	-4.66	-4.61	-9.51[b]	-5.62	-.62	5.25	-.69	-3.65[c]	.81
	(4.1)	(6.5)	(3.4)	(3.1)	(3.5)	(3.9)	(4.2)	(3.0)	(1.7)	(1.4)
Intercept	89.21[a]	6.22[a]	90.05[a]	72.92[a]	67.14[a]	95.66[a]	79.59[a]	83.02[a]	51.53[a]	53.27[a]
	(2.2)	(4.3)	(2.6)	(2.1)	(2.1)	(.21)	(3.5)	(1.8)	(1.1)	(1.0)
F for Significance of Comorbidities	8.48[a]	6.71[a]	14.50[a]	12.44[a]	6.98[a]	4.06[a]	1.72[c]	4.07[a]	12.63[a]	1.93[c]
Adjusted R^2	0.3436	0.1972	0.2451	0.1973	0.1852	0.1182	0.0670	0.1129	0.3310	0.0866
	n = 1413	n = 1413	n = 1413	n = 1413	n = 1413	n = 1413	n = 1413	n = 1413	n = 1413	n = 1413

[a] $p < 0.001$ [b] $p < 0.01$ [c] $p < 0.05$

Note: Each entry is the difference in score between having and not having the comorbid condition.

Note: These estimates are from a fully loaded model that controlled for demographics, diagnosis, and severity of diagnosis.

Note: Clinically depressed patients were excluded from the models.

TABLE B.4 CORRELATIONS[1] BETWEEN SYMPTOM FREQUENCY AND SF-36 SCALES AND COMPONENT SUMMARIES (N = 1,397)

			SF-36 Scales								Component Summaries	
Symptoms[2]	**Mean**	**SD**	**PF**	**RP**	**BP**	**GH**	**VT**	**SF**	**RE**	**MH**	**PCS[3]**	**MCS[4]**
Ears, Nose, and Throat												
Blurred Vision	1.55	1.01	-.31	-.32	-.29	-.30	-.30	-.29	-.20	-.21	-.32	-.18
Dry Mouth	2.13	1.27	-.38	-.37	-.34	-.35	-.37	-.31	-.22	-.29	-.37	-.22
Lump in throat	1.29	0.73	-.20	-.23	-.24	-.21	-.30	-.24	-.23	-.31	-.18	-.27
Under Central Nervous System Control												
Fainting or passing out	1.03	0.25	-.09	-.09	-.08	-.07	-.11	-.12	-.13	-.12	-.06	-.13
Shortness of breath (lying down)	1.38	0.89	-.43	-.37	.35	-.36	-.40	-.32	-.20	-.25	-.41	-.19
Feeling drowsy or sedated	1.88	1.09	-.33	-.41	-.36	-.38	-.52	-.40	-.34	-.40	-.34	-.38
Feeling dizzy when standing up	1.64	0.93	-.23	-.32	-.29	-.28	-.38	-.31	-.27	-.34	-.25	-.31
Chest pain relieved by nitroglycerin	1.31	0.79	-.36	-.31	-.25	-.33	-.28	-.23	-.17	-.12	-.35	-.10
Heart pounding or palpitations	1.50	0.88	-.31	-.32	-.32	-.31	-.36	-.30	-.28	-.33	-.29	-.28
Headaches more than usual	1.66	1.01	-.16	-.25	-.34	-.24	-.36	-.35	-.30	-.42	-.18	-.39
Musculoskeletal/Extremities												
Backaches or lower back pains	2.47	1.37	-.34	-.37	-.53	-.30	-.34	-.29	-.22	-.22	-.41	-.17
Pins and needles in your feet	1.75	1.17	-.35	-.34	.38	-.34	-.32	-.26	-.20	-.20	-.38	-.15
Heavy Feeling in arms and legs	1.51	0.97	-.40	-.42	-.45	-.36	-.42	-.39	-.31	-.29	-.42	-.26
Stiffness, pain in muscles	2.95	1.36	-.46	-.48	-.64	-.38	-.41	-.32	-.21	-.19	-.55	-.11
GI/GU												
Acid indigestion after meals	2.20	1.18	-.24	-.28	-.34	-.29	-.34	-.26	-.23	-.26	-.27	-.23
Trouble passing urine	1.23	0.69	-.12	-.19	-.16	-.18	-.19	-.16	-.15	-.18	-.15	-.16
Nausea (upset stomach)	1.57	0.92	-.21	-.31	-.34	-.29	-.33	-.35	-.29	-.37	-.24	-.33
Other												
Waking up early, not able to go back to sleep	2.21	1.22	-.35	-.39	-.34	-.33	-.38	-.31	-.28	-.31	-.34	-.26
Coughing producing sputum	1.81	1.19	-.22	-.28	-.25	-.29	-.27	-.23	-.16	-.20	-.26	-.16
F for All Symptoms			53.71[a]	53.93[a]	91.44[a]	38.83[a]	59.78[a]	34.94[a]	21.12[a]	36.11[a]	68.43[a]	29.33[a]
F for Significance of Ears, Nose & Throat			10.48[a]	3.36[c]	0.70	4.43[b]	2.44	1.63	0.96	9.53[a]	8.99[a]	5.36[a]
F for Significance of CNS Symptoms			25.76[a]	12.28[a]	7.77[a]	13.20[a]	34.37[a]	15.10[a]	13.02[a]	28.91[a]	20.98[a]	29.56[a]
F for Significance of GI/GU Symptoms			3.20[c]	1.05	2.89[c]	1.48	1.30	6.10[a]	2.72[c]	7.48[a]	0.38	6.94[a]
F for Significance of Musculoskeletal			56.55[a]	54.17[a]	199.61[a]	22.51[a]	25.54[a]	15.95[a]	6.45[a]	2.06	110.43[a]	5.93[a]
Adjusted R^2			0.418	0.418	0.552	0.340	0.444	0.316	0.215	0.323	0.479	0.278

1 The F-statistics summarized here and in the text are based on comparison of means for the symptom clusters. Those statistics are summarized as correlations coefficients so as to make the results presentable.

2 Reported frequency in the past four weeks scored as followed: 1=never, 2=once or twice, 3=a few times, 4=fairly often, 5=very often

3 Physical Component Summary Scale

4 Mental Component Summary Scale

Note: All correlations between symptom frequency and scales are significant at $p < .001$, except underlined correlations. Underlined correlations are not significant at $p < .05$.

TABLE B.5 CROSS SECTIONAL AGE RELATED DIFFERENCES IN HEALTH STATUS: UNCOMPLICATED HYPERTENSION[1]

	Age 18-44 (n=206)	Age 45-54 (n=193)	Age 55-64 (n=311)	Age 65+ (n=362)	(F)	RV
Physical Functioning (PF)	88.7 (1.3)	83.3 (1.5)	79.0 (1.3)	70.0 (1.3)	33.7[a]	1.00
Role-Physical (RP)	77.2 (2.4)	75.1 (2.5)	68.0 (2.2)	57.8 (2.2)	14.2[a]	0.42
Bodily Pain (BP)	78.4 (1.4)	75.3 (1.6)	75.1 (1.3)	70.9 (1.3)	4.8[b]	0.14
General Health (GH)	69.6 (1.3)	63.7 (2.7)	64.7 (1.1)	65.6 (1.0)	2.8[c]	0.08
Vitality (VT)	63.1 (1.4)	59.0 (1.6)	62.9 (1.1)	59.9 (1.2)	2.4	0.07
Social Functioning (SF)	90.6 (1.2)	90.6 (1.2)	91.5 (0.9)	90.1 (0.9)	0.4	0.01
Role Emotional (RE)	82.1 (2.4)	83.5 (2.3)	85.3 (1.8)	81.7 (1.8)	0.8	0.02
Mental Health (MH)	78.8 (1.1)	79.4 (1.1)	82.5 (0.8)	83.9 (0.8)	6.7[a]	0.19
Physical Component (PCS)	49.9 (0.6)	47.6 (0.7)	45.5 (0.6)	42.3 (0.6)	27.7[a]	0.82
Mental Component (MCS)	51.9 (0.6)	52.5 (0.6)	54.8 (0.4)	55.6 (0.4)	11.9[a]	0.35

a $p < .001$
b $p < .01$
c $p < .05$
1 Uncomplicated Hypertension is defined as patients with hypertension and classified as "Minor Medical" in previous sickgroup comparisons.

TABLE B.6 DETECTING TWO YEAR CHANGE IN HEALTH STATUS AMONG UNCOMPLICATED HYPERTENSIVE PATIENTS[1] (N = 591)

	Baseline	Exit[1]	Mean Difference	(F)	RV
Physical Functioning (PF)	78.8 (0.9)	75.3 (1.0)	-3.5 (0.7)	23.04[a]	0.62
Role Physical (RP)	66.4 (1.6)	67.4 (1.7)	1.0 (1.7)	0.36	0.01
Bodily Pain (BP)	74.0 (0.9)	75.5 (0.9)	1.5 (0.9)	2.89	0.08
General Health (GH)	67.0 (0.7)	62.7 (0.9)	-4.3 (0.7)	37.21[a]	1.00
Vitality (VT)	61.5 (0.8)	64.4 (0.8)	2.9 (0.7)	15.21[a]	0.41
Social Functioning (SF)	91.6 (0.6)	90.2 (0.7)	-1.4 (0.8)	3.24	0.09
Role Emotional (RE)	85.2 (1.3)	84.7 (1.3)	-0.5 (1.5)	0.09	0.00
Mental Health (MH)	81.8 (0.6)	82.1 (0.6)	0.3 (0.5)	0.49	0.01
Physical Component (PCS)	45.6 (0.4)	44.6 (0.4)	-1.0 (0.4)	7.29[b]	0.20
Mental Component (MCS)	54.4 (0.3)	54.9 (0.3)	0.5 (0.3)	2.56	0.07

a $p < .001$
b $p < .01$
c $p < .05$
1 Uncomplicated Hypertension is defined as patients with hypertension and classified as "Minor Medical" in previous sickgroup comparisons.

TABLE B.7 SF-36 AND COMPONENT ONE-YEAR DIFFERENCE SCORES BY SELF-REPORTED PHYSICAL, MENTAL, AND GENERAL HEALTH TRANSITIONS

	N	SF-36 Scales																Summary Scores			
		PF		RP		BP		GH		VT		SF		RE		MH		PCS		MCS	
		$\bar{x}$	SE	$\bar{x}$	SE	$\bar{x}$	SE	$\bar{x}$	SE	$\bar{x}$	SE	$\bar{x}$	SE	$\bar{x}$	SE	$\bar{x}$	SE	$\bar{x}$	SE	$\bar{x}$	SE
Physical																					
Lot more	97	-12.4	2.6	-12.4	3.8	-11.1	3.8	-13.9	2.1	-3.9	2.2	-14.7	3.0	-1.4	4.7	-2.9	1.7	-6.6	1.2	-0.9	1.1
Some more	200	-8.4	1.2	-9.0	3.0	-2.7	2.3	-11.3	1.1	-3.9	1.2	-7.6	1.8	-0.2	3.3	-2.2	1.0	-3.9	0.6	-0.7	0.7
Same	888	-0.3	0.5	5.1	1.2	1.6	0.9	-2.4	0.5	2.1	0.6	0.1	.7	5.5	1.2	1.5	0.5	-0.1	0.2	1.2	0.3
Some less	161	3.8	1.6	8.5	3.2	4.7	2.4	-1.8	1.4	3.9	1.6	2.0	1.9	0.8	3.3	2.6	1.2	1.4	0.7	0.7	0.8
Lot less	167	11.0	1.6	18.1	3.1	8.5	2.1	5.1	1.3	.6	1.6	11.7	1.9	16.4	3.4	7.5	1.3	3.8	0.7	4.4	0.8
F		44.7[a]		17.5[a]		9.0[a]		33.1[a]		13.5[a]		27.5[a]		5.1[a]		11.8[a]		35.5[a]		7.9[a]	
RV		1.00		0.39		0.20		0.74		0.30		0.61		0.11		0.26		0.79		0.18	
Mental																					
Lot more	51	-6.6	3.9	-12.2	5.9	-12.5	4.9	-15.9	3.1	-9.6	3.4	-18.1	4.1	-17.0	5.7	-13.0	3.1	-3.4	1.7	-7.3	1.6
Some more	146	-6.9	1.6	-5.8	3.3	-2.5	2.7	-9.5	1.5	-4.5	1.6	-11.5	2.1	-12.1	3.9	-6.2	1.2	-2.1	0.8	-4.0	0.8
Same	728	-0.8	0.6	4.2	1.3	1.1	1.0	-4.5	0.6	0.9	0.6	-1.0	0.7	1.7	1.3	0.1	0.4	-0.2	0.3	0.1	0.3
Some less	248	0.8	1.1	6.2	2.4	4.2	1.8	-0.1	1.0	4.5	1.1	0.6	1.4	11.7	2.6	3.0	1.0	0.2	0.5	2.5	0.6
Lot less	269	3.9	1.2	9.4	2.5	4.5	1.7	2.4	1.2	8.4	1.3	9.7	1.6	22.4	2.6	11.5	1.1	-0.1	0.6	7.2	0.7
F		11.2[a]		6.4[a]		5.2[a]		22.9[a]		20.1[a]		31.3[a]		27.2[a]		58.4[a]		3.3[b]		59.8[a]	
RV		0.19		0.11		0.09		0.39		0.34		0.53		0.46		1.00		0.05		1.02	
General																					
Lot more	24	-20.9	6.7	-28.1	8.0	-17.5	9.1	-28.0	5.2	-18.1	5.6	-29.7	7.0	-11.1	8.7	-8.8	3.8	-11.1	3.1	-5.3	2.4
Some more	188	-8.7	.3	-12.9	2.6	-8.8	2.4	-14.1	1.2	-5.2	1.2	-10.0	1.9	-3.7	3.3	-4.3	1.1	-5.3	0.6	-1.6	0.7
Same	827	-1.5	0.5	4.6	1.2	2.5	0.9	-3.4	0.5	1.5	0.6	-1.2	0.7	4.8	1.3	0.7	0.5	-0.2	0.2	0.7	0.3
Some less	251	3.4	1.1	7.5	2.5	3.0	1.8	0.6	1.1	4.8	1.1	3.8	1.4	8.4	2.8	5.0	1.0	0.6	0.5	2.7	0.7
Lot less	164	11.1	1.6	19.7	3.2	8.3	2.2	7.2	1.4	11.1	1.6	12.5	2.0	15.4	3.3	9.5	1.5	4.2	0.7	5.1	0.9
F		43.6[a]		22.2[a]		11.9[a]		55.3[a]		26.9[a]		36.0[a]		6.3[a]		25.7[a]		40.9[a]		16.3[a]	
RV		0.79		0.40		0.21		1.00		0.49		0.65		0.11		0.46		0.74		0.29	

The MANOVA F for the one year self-reported physical health transition was F = 9.35, p < .00001, df 32,1508.
The MANOVA F for the one year self-reported mental health transition was F = 10.97, p < .00001, df 32,1437.
The MANOVA F for the one year self-reported general health transition was F = 12.91, p < .00001, df 32,1449.

TABLE B.8 SUMMARY OF RESULTS FOR CROSS-SECTIONAL TESTS FOR DETECTING DIFFERENCES IN MENTAL HEALTH BETWEEN PATIENTS WITH CLINICAL DEPRESSION AND PATIENTS WITH MINOR MEDICAL CONDITIONS

Measures	Clinical Depression (N = 263)	Minor Medical (N = 999)	Mean Diff. (S.E.)	F	RV	ES[2]
Physical Functioning (PF)	79.2 (1.4)	79.5 (0.7)	-0.3 (1.6)	.03	--[e]	--[e]
Role Physical (RP)	48.7 (2.5)	68.4 (1.2)	-19.7 (2.7)	57.00[a]	.05	.58
Bodily Pain (BP)	62.9 (1.6)	75.3 (0.7)	-12.4 (1.7)	60.37[a]	.06	.52
General Health (GH)	55.2 (1.4)	66.5 (0.6)	-11.3 (1.5)	70.73[a]	.07	.55
Vitality (VT)	39.8 (1.3)	61.8 (0.6)	-22.0 (1.4)	251.85[a]	.24	1.05
Social Functioning (SF)	59.2 (1.6)	90.9 (0.5)	-31.7 (1.7)	603.19[a]	.58	1.39
Role Emotional (RE)	36.4 (2.4)	83.5 (1.0)	-47.1 (2.6)	430.15[a]	.41	1.42
Mental Health (MH)	46.0 (1.2)	81.7 (0.5)	-35.7 (1.3)	<u>1043.93[a]</u>	1.00[d]	1.98
Physical Component Summary (PCS)	47.8 (0.7)	46.0 (0.3)	1.8 (0.8)	5.95[c]	.01	.18
Mental Component Summary (MCS)	33.4 (0.7)	54.1 (0.3)	-20.7 (0.8)	1072.56[a]	1.03	2.07

[a] $p < .001$; [b] $p < .01$; [c] $p < .05$

1 Effect size determined by dividing the U.S. general population sd for each scale into each difference score.

d Best validity (highest F-ratio) among eight SF-36 scales is underlined

e Not statistically significant, RV and ES not estimated

RV = relative validity (see text)

ES = effect size (see text)

TABLE B.9 SUMMARY OF RESULTS FOR LONGITUDINAL TESTS FOR DIFFERENCES IN MENTAL HEALTH AFTER RECOVERY FROM CLINICAL DEPRESSION

Measures	Baseline	Follow-Up[1]	Average Change (SE)	F	RV	ES[2]
Physical Functioning (PF)	86.3 (1.6)	85.7 (1.8)	-0.5 (1.8)	.09	--[e]	--[e]
Role Physical (RP)	56.4 (4.1)	72.6 (3.9)	16.2 (4.7)	11.97[a]	.23	.48
Bodily Pain (BP)	69.7 (2.3)	69.9 (2.2)	0.2 (2.6)	.01	--[e]	--[e]
General Health (GH)	61.8 (2.1)	67.5 (2.4)	5.7 (2.0)	8.06[b]	.16	.28
Vitality (VT)	46.4 (1.9)	60.5 (1.9)	14.1 (1.9)	<u>51.84</u>[a]	<u>1.00</u>[d]	.67
Social Functioning (SF)	68.1 (2.4)	82.2 (1.9)	14.1 (2.7)	26.83[a]	.52	.62
Role Emotional (RE)	42.6 (4.2)	73.7 (3.7)	31.1 (4.7)	43.69[a]	.84	.93
Mental Health (MH)	51.9 (1.8)	67.3 (1.7)	15.4 (2.1)	50.98[a]	.98	.85
Physical Component Summary (PCS)	50.6 (1.0)	49.3 (1.1)	-1.3 (1.1)	1.34	--[e]	--[e]
Mental Component Summary (MCS)	36.3 (1.3)	47.2 (1.0)	10.9 (1.3)	74.99[a]	1.45	1.09

[a] $p < .001$; [b] $p < .01$; [c] $p < .05$

[1] Note: Follow-up scores were obtained two years after baseline (N = 94).

[2] Effect size determined by dividing the U.S. general population sd for each scale into each difference score.

[d] Best validity (highest F-ratio) among eight SF-36 scales is underlined

[e] Not statistically significant, RV and ES not estimated

RV = relative validity (see text)

ES = effect size (see text)

Appendix C: Scoring Algorithms: 1990 Norm-Based Scoring of PCS and MCS

This appendix reproduces Chapter 4 from the first edition of this manual (Ware et al., 1994) to document SF-36 (v1) PCS and MCS scoring based on 1990 norms.

Scoring of the Physical (PCS) and Mental (MCS) Component Summary measures involves three steps. First, the eight SF-36 scales are standardized using means and standard deviations from the general U.S. population. Second, they are aggregated using weights (factor score coefficients) from the general U.S. population. Finally aggregate PCS and MCS scores are standardized using a linear T-score transformation to have a mean of 50 and a standard deviation of 10, in the general U.S. population.

General U.S. population statistics used in the standardization and in the aggregation of SF-36 scale scores are presented in Table C.1. Detailed information including formulas for scale aggregation and transformation of scores are presented below. Formal checks can be performed to confirm the successful reproduction of PCS and MCS scales, as discussed later in the chapter. We strongly recommend these tests.

TABLE C.1 GENERAL U.S. POPULATION MEANS, STANDARD DEVIATIONS AND FACTOR SCORE COEFFICIENTS USED TO DERIVE PCS AND MCS SCALE SCORES

SF-36 SCALES	MEAN	SD	FACTOR SCORE COEFFICIENTS	
			PCS	MCS
Physical Functioning (PF)	84.52404	22.89490	0.42402	-0.22999
Role Physical (RP)	81.19907	33.79729	0.35119	-0.12329
Bodily Pain (BP)	75.49196	23.55879	0.31754	-0.09731
General Health (GH)	72.21316	20.16964	0.24954	-0.01571
Vitality (VT)	61.05453	20.86942	0.02877	0.23534
Social Functioning (SF)	83.59753	22.37642	-0.00753	0.26876
Role Emotional (RE)	81.29467	33.02717	-0.19206	0.43407
Mental Health (MH)	74.84212	18.01189	-0.22069	0.48581

Importance Of Standardization

As with the scoring of SF-36 items and scales, which are aggregated to score the summary measures, standardization of the scoring of the PCS and MCS scales is vital to their interpretation. Any changes in scoring of the SF-36 items, scales, or the algorithms for the summary scales may compromise their reliability and validity. Changes in scoring have also been shown to invalidate normative comparisons, and changes are likely to complicate or prevent meaningful comparisons of results across studies. (Ware, Snow, Kosinski, et al., 1993)

Norm-Based Scoring

The PCS and MCS scales are scored using norm-based methods. The means, standard deviations, and factor score coefficients used in scoring come from the general U.S. population. A linear T-score transformation method is used so that both the PCS and MCS have a mean of 50 and a standard deviation of 10 in the general U.S. population. This transformation is in contrast to the 0-100 scoring used to date for the eight SF-36 scales. The eight SF-36 scales have means ranging from 61 to

84 and standard deviations ranging from 18 to 34 in the general U.S. population (Ware, Snow, Kosinski, et al., 1993).

The advantage of the standardization and norm-based scoring of the PCS and MCS is that results for one can be meaningfully compared with the other and their scores have a direct interpretation in relation to the distribution of scores in the general U.S. population. Specifically, all scores above and below 50 are above and below the average, respectively, in the general U.S. population. Because the standard deviation is 10 for both PCS and MCS measures, each one point difference in scores also has a direct interpretation. A one point difference is one-tenth of a standard deviation. Advantages of norm-based scoring are illustrated in Appendix D.

Steps In Scoring

Following the scoring of the eight scales according to the standard SF-36 scoring algorithms (Medical Outcomes Trust, 1991, 1994; Ware, Snow, Kosinski, et al., 1993), PCS and MCS are scored in three steps as explained below.

Standardization Of Scales

First, each SF-36 *scale* is standardized using a z-score transformation and SF-36 scale means and standard deviations from the general U.S. population as given in Table 1. A z-score for each scale is computed by subtracting the general U.S. population mean from each SF-36 scale score and dividing the difference by the corresponding scale standard deviation from the general U.S. population. Formulas are listed below.

Step 1. Formulas for z-score standardizations of SF-36 scales.

PF_Z = (PF – 84.52404) / 22.89490
RP_Z = (RP – 81.19907) / 33.79729
BP_Z = (BP – 75.49196) / 23.55879
GH_Z = (GH – 72.21316) / 20.16964
VT_Z = (VT – 61.05453) / 20.86942
SF_Z = (SF – 83.59753) / 22.37642
RE_Z = (RE – 81.29467) / 33.02717
MH_Z = (MH – 74.84212) / 18.01189

Aggregation Of Scale Scores

After a z-score has been computed for each SF-36 scale, the second step involves computation of aggregate scores for the physical and mental components using the physical and mental factor score coefficients from the general U.S. population as given in Table C.1.

Computation of an aggregate physical component score consists of multiplying each SF-36 scale z-score by its respective physical factor score coefficient and summing the eight products, as shown below.

Similarly, an aggregate mental component score is obtained by multiplying each SF-36 scale z-score by its respective mental factor score coefficient and summing the eight products.

Step 2. Formulas for aggregating standardized scales in estimating aggregate physical and mental component scores:

AGG_PHYS = (PF_Z * .42402) + (RP_Z * .35119) + BP_Z * .31754+ (GH_Z * .24954) + (VT_Z * .02877) + (SF_Z * -.00753) + (RE_Z * -.19206) + (MH_Z * -.22069)

AGG_MENT = (PF_Z * -.22999) + (RP_Z * -.12329) + BP_Z * -.09731+ (GH_Z * -.01571) + (VT_Z * .23534) + (SF_Z * .26876) + (RE_Z * .43407) + (MH_Z * .48581)

Pending results from ongoing evaluations of other options, it is recommended that component scale scores be set to missing if the respondent is missing any one of the eight SF-36 scales. To minimize the number of component scores missing, we recommend estimating each of the eight scale scores if half or more of the items are complete, as documented elsewhere (Medical Outcomes Trust, 1991, 1994; Ware, Snow, Kosinski, et al., 1993)

Transformation Of Summary Scores

The third step involves transforming each component score to the norm-based (50, 10) scoring. This is accomplished by multiplying each aggregate component scale score by 10 and adding the resulting product to 50. Formulas are listed below.

Step 3. Formulas for T-score transformation of component scores.

Transformed Physical (PCS) = 50 + (AGG_PHYS * 10)
Transformed Mental (MCS) = 50 + (AGG_MENT * 10)

Features Of PCS And MCS Scores

The PCS and MCS were constructed and scored to achieve a number of advantages, in addition to reducing the SF-36 from an eight-scale profile to two summary measures without substantial loss of information. Features of the PCS and MCS scores, including their reliability, confidence intervals (CI), skewness (percent ceiling and floor), and number of levels observed in the general U.S. population, are summarized in Table C.2. These results confirm some of the theoretical advantages of the two summary measures as compared to the eight SF-36 scales, including a very large increase in the number of levels defined, smaller confidence intervals relative to each of the eight scales, as well as the elimination of both floor and ceiling effects. Reliability estimates and confidence intervals are discussed further in Chapter 7. Tradeoffs between the two summary measures versus the eight-scale profile are evaluated in Chapter 8.

TABLE C.2 COMPARISON OF FEATURES OF SF-36 SCALES AND SUMMARY MEASURES, GENERAL U.S. POPULATION

		SUMMARY MEASURES	
	SF-36 SCALES[b]	PCS	MCS
Reliability	.78 - .93	.93	.88
95% CI (±)	13 – 33	5.7	6.3
% Floor	1 – 24	0	0
% Ceiling	1 – 56	0	0
# of Levels[a]	4 – 26	567	493

[a] Scores rounded to first decimal place

[b] Statistics are presented as the range of results found across the eight SF-36 scales in the general U.S. population.

Scoring Checks

Because errors can lead to inaccurate scale scores, we strongly recommend formal scoring checks of SF-36 scales prior to computing the SF-36 component summary scales. These formal scoring checks are explained in full detail in the SF-36 Scoring Exercise available through the Medical Outcomes Trust (Medical Outcomes Trust, 1994).

The following scoring checks are also strongly recommended for the SF-36 component summary scales. Any discrepancies should be investigated for scoring errors:

1. Check correlations between the eight SF-36 scales and the PCS and MCS scales. The PF, RP, and BP scales should correlate highest with the PCS and lowest with the MCS. The MH, RE, and SF scales should correlate highest with the MCS and lowest with the PCS. The GH and VT scales should correlate moderately with both physical and mental component scales.

2. Check the correlation between the physical and mental component summary scales. The correlation should be very low.

Tables and text in Chapter 3 summarize results from these tests across numerous studies.

Scoring Exercise

The test dataset for this scoring exercise contains 100 administrations of the SF-36 Health Survey. The test dataset is called "RAWDATA." The SAS code for scoring the scales is called "SF36SUMM.SCR."

Table C.3 presents descriptive statistics for the eight SF-36 scales and the physical and mental component scales from the test dataset. After scoring the test data set, you should observe the same means, standard deviations, and minimum and maximum observed values as those presented in Table C.3.

Note that the missing data rate for each scale is artificially large as part of the scoring exercise. Consequently, the missing data rate for the two component summary scales is uncharacteristically high.

TABLE C.3 TEST DATASET DESCRIPTIVE STATISTICS SF-36 SCALES AND SUMMARY MEASURES (N = 100)

SF-36 SCALES	# OF CASES	MEAN	STANDARD DEVIATION	MINIMUM OBSERVED VALUE	MAXIMUM OBSERVED VALUE
Physical Functioning (PF)	99	75.8	25.1	5	100
Role Physical (RP)	93	58.0	40.5	0	100
Bodily Pain (BP)	98	69.5	25.1	0	100
General Health (GH)	96	59.6	22.9	5	100
Vitality (VT)	100	56.2	19.3	15	95
Social Functioning (SF)	100	83.5	24.7	12.5	100
Role Emotional (RE)	92	72.5	39.1	0	100
Mental Health (MH)	100	74.4	19.5	8	100
PCS	88	45.2	10.9	17.2	66.7
MCS	88	49.7	11.2	12.7	64.2

Appendix D: 1990 Norms for PCS and MCS

This appendix reproduces Chapter 10 from the first edition of this manual (Ware et al., 1994) to document the 1990 norms for the SF-36 Health Survey (v1).

Normative data makes it possible to interpret PCS and MCS scores for an individual respondent or the average for a group of respondents by comparing them with the distribution of scores for other individuals. Because the PCS and MCS scoring is "norm-based," they have the advantage of a direct interpretation in this regard (see Appendix C). For example, it is useful to know that all scores above and below 50 are above and below the mean, respectively, in the general U.S. population for both the PCS and MCS. However, because physical and mental health scores vary with age, gender, and with the presence of diseases and other conditions, specific norms for subgroups of the population will greatly facilitate the interpretation of PCS and MCS scores. (Some background information about the norming of the SF-36 and other health status surveys in the U.S. and other countries, is briefly summarized in the original *SF-36® User's Manual* (Ware, Snow, Kosinski, et al., 1993), which presents norms for the eight SF-36 scales.)

Organization Of This Chapter

This chapter presents norms for the PCS and MCS for both the general U.S. population and for specific groups of patients participating in the Medical Outcomes Study (MOS). In addition to 21 tables that mirror those previously published for the eight SF-36 scales, 29 additional tables of normative data are presented here, including:

1. Norms for "well" adults sampled from the general U.S. population and for those reporting each of 14 chronic physical conditions and for those in the general population who screened positive for possibility of clinical depression.
2. Norms for changes observed in PCS and MCS scores over a one-year period for MOS patients with various chronic conditions.

This chapter is divided into seven sections, beginning with background information about the use of norm-based interpretations and a summary of the methods used to collect normative data. Most of the chapter is devoted to tables of norms for the general U.S. population in total and by age and gender, norms for self-reported chronic conditions in the general U.S. population and for more rigorously determined "tracer" conditions and "comorbid" conditions, based on the MOS. The last section presents norms for one-year change scores for groups of patients with chronic conditions and comorbidities in the MOS.

To make it easier to find normative data among the 50 data tables presented at the end of this chapter, Figure D.1 lists all tables with their page numbers.

FIGURE D.1 GUIDE TO TABLES PRESENTING NORMATIVE DATA

General Population Database

Norms for the general U.S. population were estimated from responses to the 1990 National Survey of Functional Health Status (NSFHS), a survey that included the SF-36 conducted by the National Opinion Research Center (NORC) (Thalji, Haggerty, Rubin, et al., 1991). Respondents were drawn from the sample frame of the 1989 and 1990 General Social Survey (GSS), an annual interview survey of the noninstitutionalized adult U.S. population. The GSS consisted of a two-stage probability sample design. In the first stage, quota sampling was used based on age, gender, and employment status at the block level. The primary sampling units were Standard Metropolitan Statistical Areas or non-metropolitan counties. Primary sampling units were stratified according to region, age, and race before selection. The unit for selection at the second stage were blocked groups stratified by race and income. The sample frame was 1,537 households from the 1989 GSS and 1,372 households from the 1990 GSS, for a base sample of 2,909 households. Two categories of respondents were drawn from the 2,909 households. The first category of respondents drawn were single members (core sample) of each household who had been previously interviewed in the 1989 or 1990 GSS (N = 2,909). The second category of respondents was an oversample of elderly (age 65 years or older) members residing in the 2,909 GSS households (N = 342). The total designated sample was 3,251 persons residing in 2,909 households.

All core sample respondents were randomly assigned to a self-administered mail survey (80%) or to a telephone interview (20%), with oversampled respondents assigned to the same survey mode as their core household member. The mail survey was conducted in two waves, with a postcard prompt occurring in between each wave. A $2.00 incentive was provided to respondents assigned to the mail survey. Follow-up of nonresponders consisted of a telephone interview.

The telephone survey was a computer-assisted telephone interview. An advanced letter describing the purpose of the survey and how each respondent was selected was sent out prior to the interview. No incentive was provided to respondents assigned to the telephone survey. The first follow-up of nonresponders consisted of a personalized letter explaining the importance of the survey. Trained interviewers followed the letters five days later with a second attempt to administer the survey by telephone. On average, six calls were placed to each nonresponder. After all attempts to reach nonresponders by telephone failed, a self-administered mail survey was sent.

The data collection period was 10 weeks for the mail survey and eight weeks for the telephone survey between October 15, 1990 and December 22, 1990. At least 50% of the data collection period for both surveys overlapped. The locating protocol for both surveys followed three steps: (1) a call to directory assistance; (2) a check of returned envelopes for forwarding addresses; and (3) a review of the GSS case locator page and call record for possible locating leads. The unlocatable rate was 10% for respondents assigned to the mail survey and 12% for respondents assigned to the telephone survey. The overall response rate for the 1990 NSFHS was 77.1% using a combination of mail and telephone survey methods.

MOS Database

The MOS is an observational study of variations in functional status and well-being among adult patients sampled from various systems of care, as documented in detail elsewhere (Stewart, Greenfield, Hays, et al., 1989; Tarlov, Ware, Greenfield, et al., 1989; Greenfield, Nelson, Zubkoff, et al., 1992; Kravitz, Greenfield, Rogers, et al., 1992; Stewart & Ware, 1992).

Ages at baseline ranged from 18-98 with a mean of 58 years; 54% were female, 16% black, and 6% other minorities. One in five (22%) had household incomes below 200% of the poverty line and 42% were educated beyond the high school level. The characteristics of patients in each diagnostic group are documented in the lower panel of the table of norms for that group.

Effects Of Data Collection Method

A randomized trial of data collection methods conducted during the norming of the SF-36 confirmed the practical advantages of mail-out/mail-back (MO/MB) surveys and documented the lack of equivalence between responses to MO/MB surveys and those from telephone interviews (McHorney, Kosinski, & Ware, 1994). As shown in Figure D.2, average scores for the SF-36 Mental Component Summary (MCS) measure were 2.43 (±0.3, $p < 0.001$) points higher for those interviewed by telephone, in comparison with those who self-administered the SF-36 by MO/MB. This difference is nearly one-fourth of a standard deviation (SD = 10 for the MCS) and appears to be noteworthy in clinical terms. The effect of data collection method on MCS scores is approximately one-fourth the impact of depressive disorder. Underlying this difference in MCS scores were significant differences for seven of the eight SF-36 scales (all but General Health). There was no effect on the Physical Component Summary (PCS); a difference greater than half a point would have been significant. For this reason, data collection methods should be standardized for surveys of health status.

When results are compared across methods, the effect of methods should be taken into account and results should be interpreted with caution, as discussed elsewhere for the eight SF-36 scales (McHorney, Kosinski, & Ware, 1994). For the two summary measures, which take into account the correlations among the eight scales, the effect is apparent only in the MCS. When comparing results from telephone interviews with norms reported in this manual, it is important to consider the possibility that MCS scores from telephone interviews may be *inflated* by about two to three points, which is two to three tenths of an SD unit.

FIGURE D.2 EFFFECTS OF TELEPHONE INTERVIEWS ON THE PCS AND MCS SCORES IN THE GENERAL U.S. POPULATION

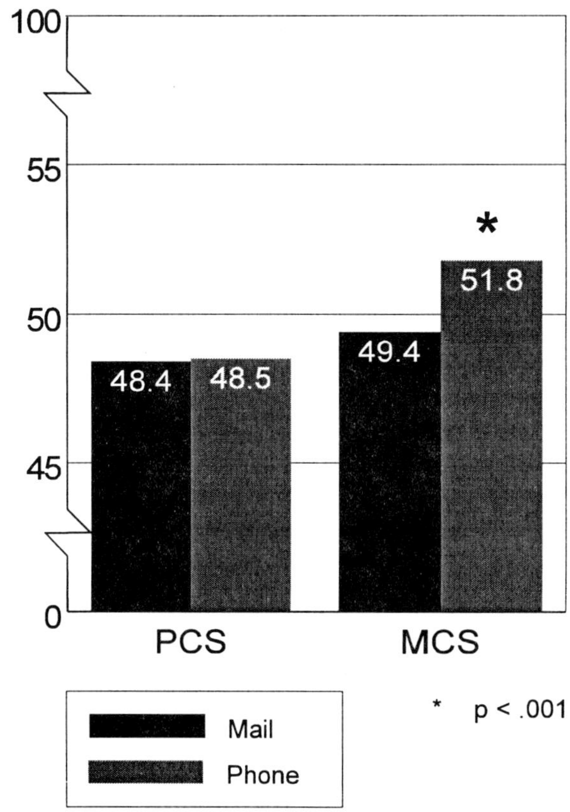

Note: Mean scores are adjusted for differences in demographics and chronic conditions between mail and telephone surveys

U.S. General Population Norms

Table D.1 presents descriptive statistics for PCS and MCS scores in the general U.S. population. Descriptive statistics include the mean, median (50th percentile), 25th and 75th percentiles, standard deviation, and the observed range of scores. The descriptive statistics presented in Table D.1 are for the total population (N = 2,474). Complete frequency distributions, including cumulative percentages (percentile ranks), for the PCS and MCS in the total population are presented in Table D.2. Note that among the advantages of the PCS and MCS, evidenced in Tables D.1 and D.2, are many more scale levels, standardized variances, and much less skewness of score distributions, relative to the eight SF-36 scales.

The mean and standard deviation are 50 and 10, respectively, for the PCS and MCS because of the scoring method used in their standardization (see Chapter 4). The medians for the PCS and MCS are higher than the means — 51.84 and 53.15, respectively. This reflects some skewness of the score distributions in the general U.S. population, with more respondents (about 60%) scoring above the mean. The frequency distributions in Table D.2 can be used to determine more precisely where in the distribution a score falls.

Norms For Males And Females

Table D.3 presents general U.S. population norms separately for males and females (all age groups combined). This table is useful in determining whether a score for males or females is above or below the average score for males and females in the general U.S. population. From Table D.3, it is evident that males score higher (more favorably) on average than females.

Norms For Age Groups

Table D.4 presents PCS and MCS general U.S. population norms for seven different age groups for males and females combined. These age groups were selected to: (1) be large enough to satisfy minimum standards for precision; and (2) correspond with standard practices for defining age-specific groups, which were also followed in norming the eight SF-36 scales. Consistent with the literature linking physical and mental health to age (Bergner, Bobbitt, Carter, et al., 1981; Stoller, 1984; Okun & Stock, 1987; Wood, Rhodes & Whelan, 1989; Idler & Angel, 1990; Idler, Kasl, & Lemke, 1990), the data in Table D.4 demonstrates a roughly linear decline in PCS scale scores for older age groups, while MCS scale scores do not.

Norms For Age Groups, Males And Females

Tables D.5 - D.6 present PCS and MCS norms by age group separately for males and females in the general U.S. population. These tables differ from the previous tables in that the oldest two age groups have been collapsed into one group (ages 65 and older) in order to have adequate sample sizes to maintain precision. Note that across all age groups, and consistent with previous literature linking gender to differences in health status, PCS and MCS scale scores are higher for males than for females (Bergner, Bergner, Hallstrom, et al., 1984; Wood, Rhodes, & Whelan, 1989; Liang, Wu, Krause, et al., 1992).

Norms For Chronic Conditions, General U.S. Population

Normative data for individuals with various chronic conditions were estimated using data from the general U.S. population (self-reported) and the MOS patient population (physician-reported).

The norms presented in these tables are not adjusted for differences in sociodemographic characteristics and comorbid conditions. Information about these variables is presented in the lower panel of each table to facilitate their consideration. It is important to keep these differences in mind when making comparisons. For example, in interpreting general population norms for those who report CHF (Table D.13), note that the majority also suffered from arthritis and that the average age was nearly 66 years. Analyses presented in Chapter 9, which used these data to estimate the unique effects of each condition on PCS and MCS scores, included statistical adjustments for differences in sociodemographic characteristics and comorbid conditions.

Norms For Chronic Conditions: General U.S. Population

The U.S. general population survey included a checklist of 14 chronic conditions. This checklist asked respondents if their doctor had ever told them they had any of the following conditions: hypertension, a heart attack in the last year, congestive heart failure (CHF), diabetes, angina, and cancer (except skin). In addition, respondents were asked if they now have any of the following conditions: chronic allergies or sinus troubles, arthritis of any kind or rheumatism, sciatica or chronic back problems, blindness or other trouble seeing with one or both eyes, chronic lung disease (like bronchitis, asthma, or emphysema), dermatitis or other chronic skin rash, deafness or other trouble hearing, and limitation in the use of an arm or leg (missing, paralyzed, or weakness). Definitions are repeated in footnotes to the data tables.

Tables D.7 - D.22 present PCS and MCS norms for the 14 chronic conditions and for a "well" group of respondents who did not report any of the 14 chronic conditions on the checklist and made no response to the "other" condition categories. At the bottom of each table is a sample description for each chronic condition, including the five most prevalent comorbidities. From comparing results for the chronic conditions to the "well" respondents in Tables D.7-D.22, it is clear that the "well" respondents have substantially better physical and mental health status than those respondents who reported chronic conditions. It is also evident that respondents with the more physically morbid conditions, such as CHF, MI, diabetes, and limitations in the use of an arm or leg, have lower PCS scale scores, on average, than those reporting other conditions. As expected, respondents who screened positive for possibility of depression have the lowest MCS scores on average.

Norms For Chronic Conditions: MOS

Norms for the PCS and MCS scales were estimated for patients with five "tracer" conditions selected for the longitudinal follow-up in the MOS: hypertension, CHF, recent MI, type II diabetes, and clinical depression (Tarlov, Ware, Greenfield, et al., 1989; Stewart & Ware, 1992). Diagnosis of the first four conditions (all but depression) was determined by standardized forms completed by the MOS physicians. The prevalence of these conditions among the 18,762 patients screened from doctor offices varied: 30.2% had hypertension, 3.2% had CHF, 1.5% had a recent MI, and 9.2% had diabetes, type II. An additional 4,335 patients were screened from offices of formally trained mental health providers. All patients were screened for clinical depression using a two-stage process with the CES-D and telephone administered diagnostic interview schedule (Wells, Hays, Burnam, et al., 1989).

Tables D.23 - D.28 present norms for the PCS and MCS for the total sample and for each of the five tracer groups. In addition, sample descriptions, including sociodemographic characteristics and the five most prevalent comorbid conditions, are presented for each tracer group.

Norms For Comorbid Conditions: MOS

To estimate the effects of comorbid conditions on PCS and MCS scores, we focused on the group of patients with hypertension because this represented the largest group of MOS patients and was the least morbid of the five MOS tracer conditions (Stewart, Greenfield, Hays, et al., 1989). Tables D.29 - D.36 present norms for MOS patients with hypertension and each of eight comorbid conditions including: angina (recent with no history of MI) (N = 256), back pain/sciatica (N = 481), benign prostatic hypertrophy symptoms (N = 184), chronic obstructive pulmonary disease (COPD) (N = 85), dermatitis (N = 231), musculoskeletal complaints (N = 341), osteoarthritis (N = 175), and varicosities (N = 222).

Norms for one-year change scores for the PCS and MCS were based on data from patients in the MOS with data at baseline and one-year follow-up assessments. These data are presented for five "tracer" conditions (hypertension, congestive heart failure, myocardial infarction, type II diabetes, and clinical depression) and for patients with conditions comorbid to hypertension. These norms can provide a basis for comparing the degree of change exhibited by a particular sample of patients. For example, one can assess whether there was more or less change in a sample of people, on average, than is typical of people with a condition such as hypertension. These norms can also be used for comparisons within a disease to see if the distribution of change scores exhibited in a particular sample is typical.

Computation Of Change Scores

One-year change scores were computed by subtracting baseline PCS and MCS scores from the PCS and MCS scores collected at the 12-month follow-up assessment. Change scores were categorized as "better," "stayed the same," or "worse" by comparing them with amounts equal to two standard errors of measurement (SEM) (see Chapter 7), which is approximately the 95% confidence interval for an individual score. Patients were classified as "worse" if their change score for the PCS/MCS indicated a decline greater than two SEMs. Patients were classified as "stayed the same" if their change score for the PCS/MCS was within two SEMs. Patients were classified as "better" if their change score for the PCS/MCS improved greater than two SEMs. The SEM for the PCS and MCS was computed by taking the square root of one minus the reliability for the PCS and MCS scales and multiplying the result by the standard deviation for the PCS/MCS in the general U.S. population (SD=10) (Nunnally, 1978). For the PCS, two SEM's equal ±5.42. For the MCS, two SEM's equal ±6.33. Thus, for example, patients with change scores showing improvement greater than 5.42 for the PCS and above 6.33 for the MCS were classified as "better." Patients with change scores below -5.42 for the PCS and below -6.33 for the MCS were classified as "worse." Patients with change scores between ±5.42 for the PCS and ±6.33 for the MCS were classified as "stayed the same."

The number of patients who died between baseline assessment and the one-year follow-up for each tracer group is noted at the bottom of each table. Those who died were not included in the analyses. They could be added to the "worse" category in the "better-same-worse" analysis.

Chronic Conditions: MOS

Tables D.37 - D.42 present norms for one-year change scores and the percent "better," "stayed the same," and "worse" for the total MOS sample and for the five MOS tracer conditions. Appendix A presents frequency distributions of one-year change scores for the total MOS sample and for the four most prevalent tracer conditions.

As shown in these tables, average one-year change scores ranged from -1.69 (for CHF) to .44 (for MI survivors) for the PCS and from .18 (for diabetes) to 3.86 (for depression) for the MCS for the five MOS tracer conditions. Underlying these average changes in physical and mental health status are noteworthy variations in the percentages who were classified as "better," "same," or "worse." Clinically depressed patients were more than twice as likely to improve (42.3%) than to decline (17.9%) in mental health. For patients with CHF, diabetes type II, and hypertension, a slightly greater percentage declined in physical health status than improved.

Tables D.43 - D.50 present one-year change score norms and the percent classified as "better," "stayed the same," or "worse" for the patients with hypertension and one of eight comorbid conditions. The results presented in each of these tables clearly demonstrates the added burden associated with a comorbidity on physical and mental health status for patients with hypertension.

TABLE D.1 NORMS FOR GENERAL U.S. POPULATION, TOTAL SAMPLE

Total Sample (N = 2,474)		PCS	MCS
	Mean	50.00	50.00
	25th Percentile	42.83	45.03
	50th Percentile (Median)	51.84	53.15
	75th Percentile	56.01	57.44
	Standard Deviation	10.00	10.00
	Range	8-73	10-74

TABLE D.2 FREQUENCY DISTRIBUTION FOR PCS AND MCS SCALE SCORES: GENERAL U.S. POPULATION (N =2,474)

PCS Scale				MCS Scale			
Score	f	%	Cum. %	Score	f	%	Cum. %
66-73	14	0.5	100.0	66-74	20	0.8	100.0
65	14	0.6	99.5	65	6	0.2	99.3
64	19	0.8	98.9	64	19	0.8	99.1
63	13	0.5	98.1	63	28	1.2	98.3
62	30	1.2	97.6	62	57	2.4	97.2
61	39	1.6	96.3	61	49	2.0	94.8
60	78	3.2	94.7	60	72	3.0	92.8
59	133	5.5	91.5	59	133	5.5	89.8
58	152	6.3	86.0	58	160	6.6	84.3
57	157	6.5	79.7	57	191	7.9	77.7
56	160	6.6	73.2	56	149	6.2	69.8
55	184	7.6	66.5	55	120	5.0	63.6
54	164	6.8	58.9	54	137	5.7	58.6
53	155	6.4	52.1	53	124	5.2	53.0
52	107	4.4	45.7	52	91	3.8	47.8
51	86	3.6	41.3	51	95	4.0	44.1
50	88	3.6	37.7	50	89	3.7	40.1
49	72	3.0	34.1	49	83	3.4	36.4
48	65	2.7	31.1	48	46	1.9	33.0
47	55	2.3	28.4	47	82	3.4	31.0
46	50	2.1	26.1	46	48	2.0	27.6
45	44	1.8	24.1	45	52	2.1	25.6
44	49	2.0	22.3	44	42	1.7	23.5
43	31	1.3	20.2	43	36	1.5	21.8
42	23	1.0	18.9	42	30	1.2	20.3
41	30	1.3	18.0	41	40	1.7	19.0
40	30	1.2	16.7	40	44	1.8	17.4
39	32	1.3	15.5	39	43	1.8	15.5
38	31	1.3	14.2	38	32	1.3	13.8
37	28	1.2	12.9	37	22	0.9	12.4
36	26	1.1	11.7	36	28	1.2	11.5
35	21	0.9	10.7	35	27	1.1	10.3
34	17	0.7	9.8	34	24	1.0	9.2
33	20	0.8	9.1	33	19	0.8	8.2
32	21	0.9	8.2	32	18	0.7	7.4
31	21	0.9	7.4	31	16	0.7	6.7
30	17	0.7	6.5	30	20	0.8	6.0
29	18	0.8	5.8	29	11	0.5	5.2
28	11	0.5	5.0	28	17	0.7	4.7
27	14	0.6	4.5	27	9	0.4	4.0
26	13	0.5	4.0	26	9	0.4	3.6
25	15	0.6	3.4	25	14	0.6	3.2
24	5	0.2	2.8	24	9	0.4	2.7
23	14	0.6	2.6	23	8	0.3	2.3
22	7	0.3	2.0	22	9	0.4	1.9
21	6	0.3	1.7	21	6	0.3	1.6
8-20	35	1.5	1.5	9-20	31	1.3	1.3
	2415				2415		

Frequency missing = 59

TABLE D.3 NORMS FOR MALES AND FEMALES: GENERAL U.S. POPULATION

Males (N = 1,055)		PCS	MCS
	Mean	51.05	50.73
	25th Percentile	44.95	46.89
	50th Percentile (Median)	52.91	53.81
	75th Percentile	56.38	57.78
	Standard Deviation	9.39	9.57
	Range	9-73	12-74
Females (N = 1,412)		**PCS**	**MCS**
	Mean	49.07	49.33
	25th Percentile	41.10	43.40
	50th Percentile (Median)	51.03	52.80
	75th Percentile	55.86	57.19
	Standard Deviation	10.42	10.32
	Range	8-69	10-71

TABLE D.4 NORMS FOR SEVEN AGE GROUPS, MALES AND FEMALES COMBINED: GENERAL U.S. POPULATION

Ages 18-24 (N = 173)		PCS	MCS
	Mean	53.44	49.11
	25th Percentile	51.36	44.82
	50th Percentile (Median)	55.03	51.13
	75th Percentile	58.32	56.48
	Standard Deviation	7.59	10.16
	Range	22-73	13-67

Ages 25-34 (N = 474)		PCS	MCS
	Mean	53.72	48.64
	25th Percentile	50.55	43.33
	50th Percentile (Median)	55.24	51.68
	75th Percentile	58.11	56.16
	Standard Deviation	7.13	10.22
	Range	18-69	13-64

Ages 35-44 (N = 503)		PCS	MCS
	Mean	52.15	49.91
	25th Percentile	49.22	45.13
	50th Percentile (Median)	53.98	52.32
	75th Percentile	57.21	56.64
	Standard Deviation	7.75	9.26
	Range	10-67	17-65

Ages 45-54 (N = 338)		PCS	MCS
	Mean	49.64	50.53
	25th Percentile	45.70	46.35
	50th Percentile (Median)	52.60	53.55
	75th Percentile	55.89	57.20
	Standard Deviation	9.67	10.02
	Range	14-67	10-68

TABLE D.4 NORMS FOR SEVEN AGE GROUPS, MALES AND FEMALES COMBINED: GENERAL U.S. POPULATION (CONTINUED)

Age 55-64 (N = 269)		PCS	MCS
	Mean	45.90	51.05
	25th Percentile	38.66	46.71
	50th Percentile (Median)	49.86	54.35
	75th Percentile	54.32	57.90
	Standard Deviation	11.25	9.69
	Range	13-62	13-65

Age 65-74 (N = 442)		PCS	MCS
	Mean	43.33	52.68
	25th Percentile	35.04	48.34
	50th Percentile (Median)	46.18	55.67
	75th Percentile	52.50	59.13
	Standard Deviation	11.16	9.29
	Range	8-59	21-74

Ages 75 & Over (N = 264)		PCS	MCS
	Mean	37.89	50.44
	25th Percentile	28.99	41.36
	50th Percentile (Median)	38.16	53.69
	75th Percentile	47.35	59.36
	Standard Deviation	11.16	11.66
	Range	13-59	18-71

TABLE D.5 NORMS FOR MALES BY AGE GROUP: GENERAL U.S. POPULATION

Ages 18-24 Males (N = 71)		PCS	MCS
	Mean	53.50	50.89
	25th Percentile	51.12	45.91
	50th Percentile (Median)	54.70	51.40
	75th Percentile	57.80	57.17
	Standard Deviation	6.22	8.66
	Range	35-73	13-62
Ages 25-34 Males (N = 199)		**PCS**	**MCS**
	Mean	54.98	48.93
	25th Percentile	52.74	45.12
	50th Percentile (Median)	55.82	51.87
	75th Percentile	58.64	56.67
	Standard Deviation	6.33	10.32
	Range	18-67	14-63
Ages 35-44 Males (N = 239)		**PCS**	**MCS**
	Mean	52.95	51.00
	25th Percentile	49.99	46.89
	50th Percentile (Median)	54.61	53.63
	75th Percentile	57.34	57.27
	Standard Deviation	7.03	8.90
	Range	22-67	21-65
Ages 45-54 Males (N = 145)		**PCS**	**MCS**
	Mean	50.40	51.03
	25th Percentile	48.14	48.10
	50th Percentile (Median)	53.36	53.94
	75th Percentile	56.13	57.51
	Standard Deviation	9.68	9.86
	Range	13-67	17-67

TABLE D.5 NORMS FOR MALES BY AGE GROUP: GENERAL U.S. POPULATION (CONTINUED)

Ages 55-64 Males (N = 105)		PCS	MCS
	Mean	46.90	51.60
	25th Percentile	40.57	48.46
	50th Percentile (Median)	49.80	54.63
	75th Percentile	54.99	57.58
	Standard Deviation	10.82	9.11
	Range	16-58	25-63

Ages 65 & Over Males (N = 293)		PCS	MCS
	Mean	41.95	52.51
	25th Percentile	33.48	47.95
	50th Percentile (Median)	43.84	54.83
	75th Percentile	51.64	59.44
	Standard Deviation	11.35	9.78
	Range	9-59	19-74

TABLE D.6 NORMS FOR FEMALES BY AGE GROUP: GENERAL U.S. POPULATION

Ages 18-24Females (N = 102)		PCS	MCS
	Mean	53.39	47.37
	25th Percentile	51.81	43.40
	50th Percentile (Median)	55.15	50.26
	75th Percentile	58.58	55.70
	Standard Deviation	8.74	11.18
	Range	22-68	15-67

Ages 25-34 Females (N = 275)		PCS	MCS
	Mean	52.46	48.34
	25th Percentile	49.32	41.90
	50th Percentile (Median)	54.43	51.31
	75th Percentile	57.67	55.22
	Standard Deviation	7.66	10.12
	Range	18-69	13-64

Ages 35-44 Females (N = 264)		PCS	MCS
	Mean	51.36	48.84
	25th Percentile	46.99	43.23
	50th Percentile (Median)	52.58	51.16
	75th Percentile	57.09	55.75
	Standard Deviation	8.34	9.49
	Range	10-65	17-64

Ages 45-54 Females (N = 193)		PCS	MCS
	Mean	48.95	50.07
	25th Percentile	43.40	45.55
	50th Percentile (Median)	51.61	53.48
	75th Percentile	55.79	56.99
	Standard Deviation	9.64	10.18
	Range	20-65	10-68

Ages 55-64 Females (N = 164)		PCS	MCS
	Mean	45.03	50.56
	25th Percentile	38.18	44.61
	50th Percentile (Median)	49.91	53.71
	75th Percentile	54.14	57.94
	Standard Deviation	11.57	10.16
	Range	13-62	13-65

TABLE D.6 NORMS FOR FEMALES BY AGE GROUP: GENERAL U.S. POPULATION (CONTINUED)

Ages 65 & Over Females (N = 413)		PCS	MCS
	Mean	41.02	51.44
	25th Percentile	32.00	43.43
	50th Percentile (Median)	42.93	55.08
	75th Percentile	49.83	58.96
	Standard Deviation	11.52	10.54
	Range	8-59	19-71

TABLE D.7 NORMS FOR "HEALTHY" GROUP WITH NO CHRONIC CONDITIONS: GENERAL U.S. POPULATION

	PCS	MCS
Mean	55.26	53.43
25th Percentile	53.69	50.33
50th Percentile (median)	55.85	54.74
75th Percentile	58.44	57.74
Standard Deviation	5.10	6.33
Range	23-67	23-67

Same Description

N	465	Five Most Prevalent Comorbidities
Mean Age	35.8	N/A[a]
Percent Over 65	3.9	N/A
Percent Female	45.2	N/A
Mean Education	13.7	N/A
Percent Nonwhite	18.1	N/A

[a] Not applicable, these respondents have no chronic conditions.

TABLE D.8 NORMS FOR ALLERGIES: GENERAL U.S. POPULATION

	PCS	MCS
Mean	47.44	48.23
25th Percentile	41.36	40.89
50th Percentile (median)	50.82	51.16
75th Percentile	55.36	56.67
Standard Deviation	10.81	10.74
Range	8-69	10-74

Same Description

N	**818**	**Five Most Prevalent Comorbidities**	
Mean Age	45.3	Depression Screener	46.2%
Percent Over 65	16.5	Arthritis	39.4%
Percent Female	59.2	Hypertension	30.8%
Mean Education	12.7	Back Pain/Sciatica	29.9%
Percent Nonwhite	15.5	Hearing Impairment	16.6%

Definition of allergies: Self-report of chronic allergies or sinus trouble

TABLE D.9 NORMS FOR ANGINA: GENERAL U.S. POPULATION

	PCS	MCS
Mean	36.36	48.04
25th Percentile	27.12	39.41
50th Percentile (median)	35.88	50.05
75th Percentile	46.95	58.33
Standard Deviation	12.38	12.42
Range	8-59	18-68

Sample Description

N	**107**	**Five Most Prevalent Comorbidities**	
Mean Age	62.6	Arthritis	75.1%
Percent Over 65	51.3	Hypertension	66.3%
Percent Female	58.6	Depression Screener	47.4%
Mean Education	11.7	Allergies	44.4%
Percent Nonwhite	12.6	Back Pain/Sciatica	39.1%

Definition of angina: Self-report of angina.

TABLE D.10 NORMS FOR ARTHRITIS: GENERAL U.S. POPULATION

	PCS	MCS
Mean	43.15	48.81
25th Percentile	34.71	41.40
50th Percentile (median)	45.83	51.74
75th Percentile	52.52	57.25
Standard Deviation	11.62	11.11
Range	8-65	13-74

Sample Description

N	**826**	**Five Most Prevalent Comorbidities**	
Mean Age	56.0	Allergies	45.9
Percent Over 65	34.5	Depression Screener	42.7
Percent Female	57.5	Hypertension	39.3
Mean Education	11.9	Back Pain/Sciatica	38.2
Percent Nonwhite	14.2	Hearing Impairment	25.0

Definition of arthritis: Self-report of arthritis or any kind of rheumatism.

TABLE D.11 NORMS FOR BACK PAIN/SCIATICA: GENERAL U.S. POPULATION

	PCS	MCS
Mean	43.14	46.88
25th Percentile	35.01	38.88
50th Percentile (median)	45.46	49.34
75th Percentile	52.41	56.67
Standard Deviation	11.56	11.73
Range	8-66	14-74

Sample Description

N	**519**	**Five Most Prevalent Comorbidities**	
Mean Age	49.1	Arthritis	55.7%
Percent Over 65	23.1	Allergies	50.8%
Percent Female	55.9	Depression Screener	49.1%
Mean Education	12.3	Hypertension	35.2%
Percent Nonwhite	13.8	Hearing Impairment	23.2%

Definition of back pain/sciatica: Self-report of sciatica or chronic back problems.

TABLE D.12 NORMS FOR CANCER: GENERAL U.S. POPULATION

	PCS	MCS
Mean	45.12	48.82
25th Percentile	36.61	43.40
50th Percentile (median)	47.39	53.03
75th Percentile	54.06	57.91
Standard Deviation	11.60	11.07
Range	16-64	13-65

Sample Description

N	**105**	**Five Most Prevalent Comorbidities**	
Mean Age	53.2	Depression Screener	45.7
Percent Over 65	40.4	Arthritis	43.6
Percent Female	57.3	Hypertension	36.3
Mean Education	12.2	Allergies	34.5
Percent Nonwhite	10.1	Back Pain/Sciatica	26.9

Definition of cancer: Self-report of cancer (except skin cancer).

TABLE D.13 NORMS FOR CONGESTIVE HEART FAILURE: GENERAL U.S. POPULATION

	PCS	MCS
Mean	31.02	45.65
25th Percentile	23.13	35.16
50th Percentile (median)	29.17	45.55
75th Percentile	35.79	56.03
Standard Deviation	10.64	12.49
Range	8-57	18-71

Sample Description

N	83	Five Most Prevalent Comorbidities	
Mean Age	65.6	Arthritis	64.8%
Percent Over 65	49.7	Hypertension	63.1%
Percent Female	59.1	Depression Screener	61.3%
Mean Education	10.5	Allergies	51.7%
Percent Nonwhite	28.3	Back Pain/Sciatica	39.8%

Definition of congestive heart failure: Self-report of congestive heart failure.

TABLE D.14 NORMS FOR DEPRESSION SCREENER: GENERAL U.S. POPULATION

	PCS	MCS
Mean	47.92	43.46
25th Percentile	39.78	35.41
50th Percentile (median)	51.37	45.24
75th Percentile	56.72	52.82
Standard Deviation	11.62	11.42
Range	13-73	13-67

Sample Description

N	881	Five Most Prevalent Comorbidities	
Mean Age	43.1	Allergies	41.3%
Percent Over 65	14.6	Arthritis	32.7%
Percent Female	57.7	Hypertension	28.8%
Mean Education	12.4	Back Pain/Sciatica	25.8%
Percent Nonwhite	21.1	Limited Use in Arm/Leg	16.3%

Definition of depression screener: Self-report of two weeks or more feeling sad, blue or depressed in the past year; or two years or more feeling sad or blue most days; or feeling depressed or sad much of the time in the past year.

TABLE D.15 NORMS FOR DERMATITIS: GENERAL U.S. POPULATION

	PCS	MCS
Mean	46.88	46.16
25th Percentile	38.99	38.48
50th Percentile (median)	50.96	50.16
75th Percentile	55.87	56.63
Standard Deviation	11.49	12.06
Range	13-65	18-64

Sample Description

N	214	Five Most Prevalent Comorbidities	
Mean Age	46.4	Allergies	52.5
Percent Over 65	19.2	Depression Screener	48.3
Percent Female	53.7	Arthritis	42.0
Mean Education	13.0	Back Pain/Sciatica	29.1
Percent Nonwhite	13.9	Hypertension	25.4

Definition of dermatitis: Self-report of dermatitis or other chronic skin rash.

TABLE D.16 NORMS FOR DIABETES: GENERAL U.S. POPULATION

	PCS	MCS
Mean	39.30	47.90
25th Percentile	29.97	39.52
50th Percentile (median)	38.22	49.92
75th Percentile	49.35	56.66
Standard Deviation	11.32	11.37
Range	13-60	18-67

Sample Description

N	145	Five Most Prevalent Comorbidities	
Mean Age	56.2	Hypertension	57.6
Percent Over 65	38.0	Depression Screener	53.1
Percent Female	59.2	Arthritis	51.9
Mean Education	11.2	Allergies	38.2
Percent Nonwhite	34.7	Back Pain/Sciatica	33.4

Definition of diabetes: Self-report of diabetes.

TABLE D.17 NORMS FOR HEARING IMPAIRMENT: GENERAL U.S. POPULATION

	PCS	MCS
Mean	43.70	48.74
25th Percentile	34.61	42.72
50th Percentile (median)	46.74	51.09
75th Percentile	53.31	56.80
Standard Deviation	12.18	10.62
Range	8-67	13-74

Sample Description

N	387	Five Most Prevalent Comorbidities	
Mean Age	57.6	Arthritis	55.7%
Percent Over 65	43.8	Allergies	43.3%
Percent Female	37.1	Depression Screener	39.8%
Mean Education	11.8	Hypertension	39.2%
Percent Nonwhite	11.3	Back Pain/Sciatica	35.6%

Definition of hearing impairment: Self-report of deafness or other trouble hearing with one or both ears.

TABLE D.18 NORMS FOR HYPERTENSION: GENERAL U.S. POPULATION

	PCS	MCS
Mean	44.57	49.24
25th Percentile	37.29	42.15
50th Percentile (median)	47.39	52.07
75th Percentile	53.51	57.15
Standard Deviation	11.29	10.55
Range	9-67	14-74

Sample Description

N	670	Five Most Prevalent Comorbidities	
Mean Age	54.0	Arthritis	46.7%
Percent Over 65	32.4	Depression Screener	44.7%
Percent Female	51.4	Allergies	42.6%
Mean Education	12.1	Back Pain/Sciatica	28.7%
Percent Nonwhite	25.7	Hearing Impairment	20.8%

Definition of hypertension: Self-report of current hypertension.

TABLE D.19 NORMS FOR LIMITATION IN THE USE OF AN ARM(S) OR LEG(S): GENERAL U.S. POPULATION

	PCS	MCS
Mean	37.74	45.89
25th Percentile	26.61	38.42
50th Percentile (median)	37.36	46.50
75th Percentile	49.37	56.03
Standard Deviation	12.99	11.57
Range	8-60	18-71

Sample Description

N	263	Five Most Prevalent Comorbidities	
Mean Age	51.5	Arthritis	64.2
Percent Over 65	28.2	Depression Screener	63.3
Percent Female	54.1	Allergies	48.2
Mean Education	11.8	Back Pain/Sciatica	43.6
Percent Nonwhite	18.9	Hypertension	39.4

Definition of limitations in use of arm(s)/leg(s): Self-report of limitations in the use of an arm or leg (missing, paralyzed or weakness).

TABLE D.20 NORMS FOR CHRONIC LUNG DISEASE: GENERAL U.S. POPULATION

	PCS	MCS
Mean	42.31	44.47
25th Percentile	30.09	35.30
50th Percentile (median)	45.71	46.59
75th Percentile	53.74	55.06
Standard Deviation	14.08	12.28
Range	8-69	10-68

Sample Description

N	182	Five Most Prevalent Comorbidities	
Mean Age	48.9	Allergies	63.3%
Percent Over 65	24.1	Depression Screener	55.4%
Percent Female	59.4	Arthritis	52.1%
Mean Education	11.7	Back Pain/Sciatica	33.8%
Percent Nonwhite	14.6	Hypertension	32.7%

Definition of chronic lung disease: Self-report of chronic lung disease (like chronic bronchitis, asthma, or emphysema).

TABLE D.21 NORMS FOR MYOCARDIAL INFARCTION: GENERAL U.S. POPULATION

	PCS	MCS
Mean	35.97	45.73
25th Percentile	25.17	35.65
50th Percentile (median)	34.51	47.34
75th Percentile	46.95	56.28
Standard Deviation	12.10	12.41
Range	13-59	18-68

Sample Description

N	**62**	**Five Most Prevalent Comorbidities**	
Mean Age	60.6	Hypertension	67.9
Percent Over 65	42.8	Arthritis	63.1
Percent Female	46.5	Depression Screener	56.1
Mean Education	11.0	Allergies	54.0
Percent Nonwhite	21.2	Angina	39.7

Definition of myocardial infarction: Self-report of myocardial infarction in the past year.

TABLE D.22 NORMS FOR VISION IMPAIRMENT: GENERAL U.S. POPULATION

	PCS	MCS
Mean	41.86	45.21
25th Percentile	31.50	35.65
50th Percentile (median)	44.22	47.06
75th Percentile	53.26	56.86
Standard Deviation	12.52	12.81
Range	8-62	16-68

Sample Description

N	259	Five Most Prevalent Comorbidities	
Mean Age	54.6	Arthritis	54.3
Percent Over 65	34.2	Depression Screener	53.2
Percent Female	59.0	Allergies	51.2
Mean Education	11.6	Hypertension	48.7
Percent Nonwhite	20.0	Back Pain/Sciatica	38.0

Definition of vision impairment: Self-report of blindness or other trouble seeing with one or both eyes, even when wearing glasses.

TABLE D.23 NORMS FOR ALL CONDITIONS COMBINED, MOS PARTICIPANTS

	PCS	MCS
Mean	44.92	48.44
25th Percentile	38.01	41.08
50th Percentile (Median)	47.18	52.01
75th Percentile	53.42	57.35
Standard Deviation	10.94	11.77
Range	8-71	3-71

Sample Description

N	**3445**	**Prevalence of Five MOS Conditions**	
Mean Age	54.3	Hypertension	60.6%
Percent Over 65	28.6	Myocardial Infarction	3.1%
Percent Female	61.7	Congestive Heart Failure	6.3%
Mean Education	13.3	Diabetes Type II	15.7%
Percent Poverty	19.8	Clinical Depression	14.6%

TABLE D.24 NORMS FOR CLINICAL DEPRESSION, MOS PARTICIPANTS

	PCS	MCS
Mean	44.96	34.84
25th Percentile	36.57	25.60
50th Percentile (median)	45.63	33.30
75th Percentile	54.29	43.63
Standard Deviation	12.05	12.17
Range	14-71	3-64

Sample Description

N	502	Five Most Prevalent Comorbidities	
Mean Age	41.6	Back Pain/Sciatica	45.9%
Percent Over 65	6.0	Angina-Recent	25.0%
Percent Female	75.8	Hypertension	20.9%
Mean Education	13.4	Musculoskeletal Complaints	17.6%
Percent Poverty	23.3	Dermatitis	17.5%

Definition of clinical depression: NIMH (DIS) criteria met for major depression and/or dysthymia.

TABLE D.25 NORMS FOR CONGESTIVE HEART FAILURE, MOS PARTICIPANTS

	PCS	MCS
Mean	34.50	50.43
25th Percentile	25.44	45.03
50th Percentile (median)	34.03	52.88
75th Percentile	43.54	58.37
Standard Deviation	12.08	11.13
Range	12-64	15-69

Sample Description

N	**216**	**Five Most Prevalent Comorbidities**	
Mean Age	67.4	Hypertension	52.8%
Percent Over 65	59.7	Back Pain/Sciatica	47.4%
Percent Female	52.3	Past MI	45.7%
Mean Education	12.2	Angina-Recent	40.2%
Percent Poverty	27.3	Musculoskeletal Complaints	32.7%

Definition of congestive heart failure: Physician report of current congestive heart failure.

TABLE D.26 NORMS FOR DIABETES TYPE II, MOS PARTICIPANTS

	PCS	MCS
Mean	41.52	51.90
25th Percentile	33.38	48.07
50th Percentile (median)	43.72	54.56
75th Percentile	50.41	58.43
Standard Deviation	11.27	9.55
Range	8-64	19-71

Sample Description

N	541	Five Most Prevalent Comorbidities	
Mean Age	60.2	Hypertension	64.3%
Percent Over 65	37.7	Back Pain/Sciatica	31.0%
Percent Female	55.6	Musculoskeletal Complaints	25.6%
Mean Education	12.5	Angina-Recent	18.6%
Percent Poverty	22.7	Dermatitis	17.0%

Definition of diabetes type II: Physician report of diabetes with age of onset 30 years or older.

TABLE D.27 NORMS FOR HYPERTENSION, MOS PARTICIPANTS

	PCS	MCS
Mean	44.31	52.22
25th Percentile	37.75	47.20
50th Percentile (Median)	47.00	54.95
75th Percentile	52.77	58.81
Standard Deviation	10.76	9.28
Range	8-67	19-71

Sample Description

N	2089	Five Most Prevalent Comorbidities	
Mean Age	59.1	Back Pain/Sciatica	34.0%
Percent Over 65	35.7	Musculoskeletal Complaints	24.6%
Percent Female	58.5	Recent Angina	16.3%
Mean Education	12.5	Diabetes Type II	16.2%
Percent Poverty	19.2	Varicosities	15.1%

Definition of hypertension: Physician report of current hypertension.

TABLE D.28 NORMS FOR MYOCARDIAL INFARCTION, MOS PARTICIPANTS

	PCS	MCS
Mean	42.64	51.67
25th Percentile	36.32	47.39
50th Percentile (median)	43.57	53.14
75th Percentile	49.81	57.51
Standard Deviation	10.02	8.19
Range	17-58	23-65

Sample Description

N	**107**	**Five Most Prevalent Comorbidities**	
Mean Age	59.2	Angina-Ever	55.8%
Percent Over 65	29.0	Angina-Recent	50.7%
Percent Female	30.8	Hypertension	42.5%
Mean Education	12.8	Back Pain/Sciatica	28.7%
Percent Poverty	14.0	Diabetes Type II	24.3%

Definition of myocardial infarction: Physician report of myocardial infarction within the past year.

TABLE D.29 NORMS FOR COMORBID RECENT ANGINA WITHOUT MYOCARDIAL INFARCTION, WITH HYPERTENSION, MOS PARTICIPANTS

	PCS	MCS
Mean	38.63	50.43
25th Percentile	29.57	44.89
50th Percentile (median)	40.64	52.82
75th Percentile	48.00	57.96
Standard Deviation	11.04	9.68
Range	14-58	19-68

Sample Description

N	256	Five Most Prevalent Comorbidities	
Mean Age	59.7	Back Pain/Sciatica	50.0%
Percent Over 65	39.4	Musculoskeletal Complaints	29.0%
Percent Female	55.1	Past MI	24.0%
Mean Education	12.7	Dermatitis	21.0%
Percent Poverty	23.0	Osteoarthritis	18.0%

Definition of angina: Symptoms of angina in past six months in the absence of an MI within one year.

TABLE D.30 NORMS FOR COMORBID BACK PAIN/SCIATICA WITH HYPERTENSION, MOS PARTICIPANTS

	PCS	MCS
Mean	39.67	51.37
25th Percentile	29.57	45.01
50th Percentile (median)	41.22	54.39
75th Percentile	49.54	59.11
Standard Deviation	11.71	10.32
Range	12-71	21-71

Sample Description

N	**481**	**Five Most Prevalent Comorbidities**	
Mean Age	60.4	Musculoskeletal Complaints	30.0%
Percent Over 65	35.8	Angina-Recent	28.0%
Percent Female	64.2	Angina-No MI	27.0%
Mean Education	12.2	Varicosities	21.0%
Percent Poverty	20.6	Osteoarthritis	21.0%

Definition of back pain/sciatica: Attacks of back pain or sciatica in last six months.

TABLE D.31 NORMS FOR COMORBID BENIGN PROSTATIC HYPERTROPHY (BPH) SYMPTOMS WITH HYPERTENSION, MOS PARTICIPANTS

	PCS	MCS
Mean	43.84	54.13
25th Percentile	38.28	49.95
50th Percentile (median)	46.44	57.04
75th Percentile	51.63	59.67
Standard Deviation	10.28	8.72
Range	13-59	26-70

Sample Description

N	184	Five Most Prevalent Comorbidities	
Mean Age	67.1	Back Pain/Sciatica	32.0%
Percent Over 65	53.8	Musculoskeletal Complaints	27.0%
Percent Female	0.0	Past MI	22.0%
Mean Education	12.5	Angina-Recent	22.0%
Percent Poverty	17.6	Angina-No MI	21.0%

Definition of BPH symptoms: Male, age 50 years or older, history of nocturia in past six months, no serious kidney disease ever diagnosed, and no report of prostatic cancer.

TABLE D.32 NORMS FOR COMORBID CHRONIC OBSTRUCTIVE PULMONARY DISEASE (COPD) WITH HYPERTENSION, MOS PARTICIPANTS

	PCS	MCS
Mean	35.90	47.73
25th Percentile	25.71	39.97
50th Percentile (median)	36.51	50.93
75th Percentile	43.52	57.79
Standard Deviation	10.38	11.44
Range	17-55	19-68

Sample Description

N	85	Five Most Prevalent Comorbidities	
Mean Age	62.4	Back Pain/Sciatica	55.0%
Percent Over 65	42.4	Angina-Recent	38.0%
Percent Female	63.5	Angina-No MI	36.0%
Mean Education	11.6	Varicosities	31.0%
Percent Poverty	34.7	Musculoskeletal Complaints	27.0%

Definition of COPD: Lung disease diagnosed by physician as COPD in past six months.

TABLE D.33 NORMS FOR COMORBID DERMATITIS WITH HYPERTENSION, MOS PARTICIPANTS

	PCS	MCS
Mean	43.06	51.94
25th Percentile	35.43	46.72
50th Percentile (median)	46.19	54.00
75th Percentile	52.22	58.64
Standard Deviation	10.89	8.93
Range	10-63	24-68

Sample Description

N	231	Five Most Prevalent Comorbidities	
Mean Age	57.6	Back Pain/Sciatica	55.0%
Percent Over 65	35.5	Musculoskeletal Complaints	38.0%
Percent Female	48.5	Angina-Recent	36.0%
Mean Education	13.2	Angina-No MI	31.0%
Percent Poverty	16.3	Varicosities	27.0%

Definition of dermatitis: Now have condition that physician ever diagnosed chronic skin rash.

TABLE D.34 NORMS FOR COMORBID MUSCULOSKELETAL COMPLAINTS WITH HYPERTENSION, MOS PARTICIPANTS

	PCS	MCS
Mean	41.60	52.79
25th Percentile	33.43	46.17
50th Percentile (median)	43.15	55.80
75th Percentile	50.26	59.71
Standard Deviation	10.42	9.76
Range	13-59	21-70

Sample Description

N	**341**	**Five Most Prevalent Comorbidities**	
Mean Age	61.4	Back Pain/Sciatica	43.0%
Percent Over 65	41.6	Angina-Recent	23.0%
Percent Female	63.0	Varicosities	22.0%
Mean Education	12.0	Angina-No MI	21.0%
Percent Poverty	22.7	Dermatitis	18.0%

Definition of musculoskeletal complaints: Now have active condition physician ever diagnosed arthritis, but criteria for osteoarthritis or rheumatoid arthritis not met.

TABLE D.35 NORMS FOR COMORBID OSTEOARTHRITIS WITH HYPERTENSION, MOS PARTICIPANTS

	PCS	MCS
Mean	36.10	53.43
25th Percentile	25.71	48.68
50th Percentile (median)	37.00	56.30
75th Percentile	46.83	60.50
Standard Deviation	12.00	10.20
Range	12-57	24-71

Sample Description

N	175	Five Most Prevalent Comorbidities	
Mean Age	67.8	Back Pain/Sciatica	57.0%
Percent Over 65	58.9	Varicosities	27.0%
Percent Female	74.3	Angina-No MI	26.0%
Mean Education	11.9	Angina-Recent	26.0%
Percent Poverty	23.8	Musculoskeletal Complaints	19.0%

Definition of osteoarthritis: Now have active condition physician ever diagnosed as arthritis, and physician ever labeled it osteoarthritis or degenerative arthritis, and patient is 55 years or older.

TABLE D.36 NORMS FOR COMORBID VARICOSITIES WITH HYPERTENSION, MOS PARTICIPANTS

	PCS	MCS
Mean	41.91	51.66
25th Percentile	34.47	46.15
50th Percentile (median)	43.54	54.60
75th Percentile	49.97	58.85
Standard Deviation	10.64	10.01
Range	10-64	20-70

Sample Description

N	222	Five Most Prevalent Comorbidities	
Mean Age	61.8	Back Pain/Sciatica	45.0%
Percent Over 65	39.2	Musculoskeletal Complaints	34.0%
Percent Female	72.1	Angina-Recent	25.0%
Mean Education	12.2	Angina-No MI	25.0%
Percent Poverty	20.1	Osteoarthritis	21.0%

Definition of varicosities: Now have condition that physician ever diagnosed as varicose veins/deep varicosities.

TABLE D.37 NORMS FOR ONE-YEAR CHANGE SCORES, TOTAL MOS SAMPLE (N = 1539)

	PCS	MCS
Mean	-0.53	1.10
25th Percentile	-4.96	-3.76
50th Percentile (Median)	-0.39	0.36
75th Percentile	4.15	5.46
Standard Deviation	8.91	9.53
Range	-43 to 34	-37 to 45

Percent Classified as Better, Stayed the Same, or Worse:[1] Total

PCS	f	%	MCS	f	%
Worse	358	23.3	Worse	238	15.5
Stayed the Same	874	56.8	Stayed the Same	960	62.4
Better	307	19.9	Better	341	22.1

Note: 39 patients who died between baseline and one-year follow-up are excluded.

TABLE D.38 NORMS FOR ONE YEAR CHANGE SCORES, CLINICAL DEPRESSION (N = 279)

	PCS	MCS
Mean	-0.64	3.86
25th Percentile	-6.04	-4.33
50th Percentile (median)	-0.25	2.78
75th Percentile	4.70	11.30
Standard Deviation	9.31	13.18
Range	-36 to 34	-35 to 45

Percent Classified as Better, Stayed the Same, or Worse:[1] Depression

PCS	f	%	MCS	f	%
Worse	81	29.0	Worse	50	17.9
Stayed the Same	139	49.8	Stayed the Same	111	39.8
Better	59	21.2	Better	118	42.3

Note: 5 patients who died between baseline and one-year follow-up are excluded.

[1] Patients classified as "better" or "worse" have one year difference scores greater than ±2 SEMs. Patients with one year difference scores within ±2 SEMs are classified as "stayed the same" (2 SEMs: PCS = ±5.42; MCS = ±6.33).

TABLE D.39 NORMS FOR ONE YEAR CHANGE SCORES, CONGESTIVE HEART FAILURE (N = 131)

	PCS	MCS
Mean	-1.69	0.91
25th Percentile	-5.50	-2.83
50th Percentile (median)	-0.80	0.64
75th Percentile	2.55	4.53
Standard Deviation	8.82	9.44
Range	-34 to 20	-27 to 33

Percent Classified as Better, Stayed the Same, or Worse:[1] CHF

PCS	f	%	MCS	f	%
Worse	35	26.7	Worse	23	17.6
Stayed the Same	66	50.4	Stayed the Same	80	61.1
Better	30	22.9	Better	28	21.3

Note: 15 patients who died between baseline and one-year follow-up are excluded.

TABLE D.40 NORMS FOR ONE YEAR CHANGE SCORES, DIABETES TYPE II (N = 291)

	PCS	MCS
Mean	0.22	0.18
25th Percentile	-4.52	-3.87
50th Percentile (median)	0.11	-0.29
75th Percentile	5.39	4.32
Standard Deviation	8.83	8.60
Range	-28 to 27	-22 to 24

Percent Classified as Better, Stayed the Same, or Worse:[1] Diabetes

PCS	f	%	MCS	f	%
% Worse	71	24.4	% Worse	48	16.5
% Stayed the Same	159	54.6	% Stayed the Same	191	65.6
% Better	61	21.0	% Better	52	17.9

Note: 11 patients who died between baseline and one-year follow-up are excluded.

1 Patients classified as "better" or "worse" have one year differences scores greater than ±2 SEMs of the mean. Patients with one year difference scores within ±2 SEM's are classified as "stayed the same" (2 SEM's: PCS = ±5.42; MCS = ±6.33).

TABLE D.41 NORMS FOR ONE YEAR CHANGE SCORES, HYPERTENSION (N = 895)

	PCS	MCS
Mean	-0.40	0.20
25th Percentile	-4.86	-3.73
50th Percentile (Median)	-0.40	-0.02
75th Percentile	4.16	4.08
Standard Deviation	9.09	8.07
Range	-43 to 33	-37 to 33

Percent Classified as Better, Stayed the Same, or Worse:[1] Hypertension

PCS	%	MCS	%
Worse	21.6	Worse	14.3
Stayed the Same	58.5	Stayed the Same	69.5
Better	19.9	Better	16.2

Note: 25 patients who died between baseline and one-year follow-up are excluded.

TABLE D.42 NORMS FOR ONE YEAR CHANGE SCORES, MYOCARDIAL INFARCTION (N = 67)

	PCS	MCS
Mean	0.44	1.57
25th Percentile	-1.92	-2.54
50th Percentile (median)	0.98	1.94
75th Percentile	3.64	5.34
Standard Deviation	6.05	7.79
Range	-17 to 19	-20 to 26

Percent Classified as Better, Stayed the Same, or Worse:[1] MI

PCS	f	%	MCS	f	%
Worse	10	14.9	Worse	7	10.5
Stayed the Same	44	65.7	Stayed the Same	50	74.6
Better	13	19.4	Better	10	14.9

Note: 4 patients who died between baseline and one-year follow-up are excluded.

1 Patients classified as "better" or "worse have one year difference greater than ±2 SEMs. Patients with one year difference scores within ±2 SEM's are classified as "stayed the same" (2 SEMs for PCS = ±5.42, MCS = ±6.33).

TABLE D.43 NORMS FOR ONE YEAR CHANGE SCORES, RECENT ANGINA WITHOUT MYOCARDIAL INFARCTION, WITH HYPERTENSION (N = 133)

	PCS	MCS
Mean	-1.24	0.10
25th Percentile	-4.91	-5.03
50th Percentile (median)	-1.04	-0.05
75th Percentile	3.44	6.11
Standard Deviation	8.82	9.65
Range	-23 to 21	-36 to 26

Percent Classified as Better, Stayed the Same, or Worse:[1] Angina

PCS	f	%	MCS	f	%
Worse	33	24.9	Worse	25	18.8
Stayed the Same	80	60.1	Stayed the Same	77	57.9
Better	20	15.0	Better	31	23.3

Note: 6 patients who died between baseline and one-year follow-up are excluded.

TABLE D.44 NORMS FOR ONE YEAR CHANGE SCORES, BACK PAINS / SCIATICA WITH HYPERTENSION (N = 241)

	PCS	MCS
Mean	-0.33	-0.56
25th Percentile	-5.65	-5.04
50th Percentile (median)	-0.62	-0.34
75th Percentile	5.13	4.40
Standard Deviation	10.15	9.42
Range	-33 to 29	-36 to 29

Percent Classified as Better, Stayed the Same, or Worse:[1] Back Pain/Sciatica

PCS	f	%	MCS	f	%
Worse	61	25.3	Worse	47	19.5
Stayed the Same	129	53.5	Stayed the Same	150	62.2
Better	51	21.2	Better	44	18.3

Note: 6 patients who died between baseline and one-year follow-up are excluded.

1 Patients classifies as "better" or "worse" have one year difference scores greater than ±2 SEMs. Patients with one year difference scores within ±2 SEMs are classified as "stayed the same" (2 SEM: PCS = ±5.42; MCS = ±6.33).

TABLE D.45 NORMS FOR ONE YEAR CHANGE SCORES, BENIGN PROSTATIC HYPERTROPHY SYMPTOMS (BPH) WITH HYPERTENSION (N = 101)

	PCS	MCS
Mean	-0.70	-0.13
25th Percentile	-4.34	-4.21
50th Percentile (median)	-1.67	0.35
75th Percentile	3.44	3.99
Standard Deviation	7.83	6.95
Range	-23 to 25	-21 to 26

Percent Classified as Better, Stayed the Same, or Worse[1] BPH

PCS	f	%	MCS	f	%
Worse	25	24.8	Worse	16	15.8
Stayed the Same	56	55.4	Stayed the Same	70	69.3
Better	20	19.8	Better	15	14.9

Note: 5 patients who died between baseline and one-year follow-up are excluded.

TABLE D.46 NORMS FOR ONE YEAR CHANGE SCORES, CHRONIC OBSTRUCTIVE PULMONARY DISEASE (COPD) WITH HYPERTENSION (N = 46)

	PCS	MCS
Mean	-3.30	4.78
25th Percentile	-7.78	-2.81
50th Percentile (median)	-3.23	3.49
75th Percentile	0.44	9.40
Standard Deviation	6.84	11.48
Range	-18 to 19	-20 to 33

Percent Classified as Better, Stayed the Same, or Worse:[1] COPD

PCS	f	%	MCS	f	%
Worse	14	30.5	Worse	7	15.2
Stayed the Same	26	56.5	Stayed the Same	26	56.5
Better	6	13.0	Better	13	28.3

Note: 1 patient who died between baseline and one-year follow-up is excluded.

1 Patients classifies as "better" or "worse" have one year difference scores greater then ±2 SEMs. Patients with one year difference scores within ±2 SEMs are classified as "stayed the same" (2 SEMs: PCS = ±5.42; MCS = ±6.33).

TABLE D.47 NORMS FOR ONE YEAR CHANGE SCORES, DERMATITIS WITH HYPERTENSION (N = 125)

	PCS	MCS
Mean	-0.20	-0.17
25th Percentile	-5.49	-4.60
50th Percentile (median)	-1.54	0.21
75th Percentile	3.86	4.68
Standard Deviation	8.90	7.73
Range	-20 to 31	-29 to 17

Percent Classified as Better, Stayed the Same, or Worse:[1] Dermatitis

PCS	f	%	MCS	f	%
Worse	29	23.2	Worse	21	16.8
Stayed the Same	71	56.8	Stayed the Same	85	68.0
Better	25	20.0	Better	19	15.2

Note: 4 patients who died between baseline and one-year follow-up are excluded.

TABLE D.48 NORMS FOR ONE YEAR CHANGE SCORES, MUSCULOSKELETAL COMPLAINTS WITH HYPERTENSION (N = 168)

	PCS	MCS
Mean	-1.96	-1.24
25th Percentile	-5.87	-5.11
50th Percentile (median)	-1.22	-0.29
75th Percentile	4.15	3.16
Standard Deviation	10.89	9.09
Range	-38 to 32	-36 to 33

Percent Classified as Better, Stayed the Same, or Worse:[1] Musculoskeletal Comp.

PCS	f	%	MCS	f	%
Worse	38	22.6	Worse	27	16.1
Stayed the Same	93	55.4	Stayed the Same	116	69.0
Better	37	22.0	Better	25	14.9

Note: 7 patients who died between baseline and one-year follow-up are excluded.

1 Patients classified as "better" or "worse" have one year difference scores greater than ±2 SEMs. Patients with one year difference scores within ±2 SEMs are classified as "stayed the same" (2 SEMs: PCS = ±5.42; MCS = ±6.33).

TABLE D.49 NORMS FOR ONE YEAR CHANGE SCORES, OSTEOARTHRITIS WITH HYPERTENSION (N = 102)

	PCS	MCS
Mean	-2.09	-0.21
25th Percentile	-8.98	-4.82
50th Percentile (median)	-3.34	-0.20
75th Percentile	3.20	3.81
Standard Deviation	8.13	8.53
Range	-23 - 19	-20 - 26

Percent Classified as Better, Stayed the Same, or Worse:[1] Osteoarthritis

PCS	f	%	MCS	f	%
Worse	31	30.4	Worse	23	22.6
Stayed the Same	52	51.0	Stayed the Same	65	63.7
Better	19	18.6	Better	14	13.7

Note: 2 patients who died between baseline and one-year follow-up are excluded.

TABLE D.50 NORMS FOR ONE YEAR CHANGE SCORES, VARICOSITIES WITH HYPERTENSION (N = 130)

	PCS	MCS
Mean	-0.70	-1.00
25th Percentile	-4.89	-6.38
50th Percentile (median)	-0.40	0.76
75th Percentile	3.75	3.63
Standard Deviation	8.31	8.02
Range	-28 to 32	-26 to 19

Percent Classified as Better, Stayed the Same, or Worse:[1] Varicosities

PCS	f	%	MCS	f	%
Worse	30	23.1	Worse	30	23.1
Stayed the Same	73	56.1	Stayed the Same	83	63.8
Better	27	20.8	Better	17	13.1

1 Patients classified as "better" or "worse" have one year difference scores greater than ±2 SEMs. Patients with one year difference scores within ±2 SEMs are classified as "stayed the same" (2 SEMs: PCS = ±5.42; MCS = ±6.33).

Index

V